This book is dedicated to my wife
HILDA
AND to a female Vizsla of *hers* named
TRIXIE
and to her daughter CSECSE,
her granddaughter FLEETA
and her great granddaughter CARLA

The VIZSLA
by B. C. Boggs

1982
Glenbrier Publishing Company
P. O. Box 546
Jackson, Ohio 45640

Library of Congress Card Number 82-82337
ISBN Number 0-9608838-0-0

Printed in USA.

Foreword

The initial acceptance of **The Vizsla** was most gratifying for both author and publisher. It was awarded "Best Breed Book" by the Dog Writers Association of America. It has been enthusiastically complimented by all who have read it.

The "heart" of the book regarding care, training, history and the various activities pursued with the breed did not need much change, but after the passage of almost ten years, it was time to revise, rather than just reprint the text.

Statistical matter needed updating. There are some rule changes. Certainly "new history" has happened. New dogs are being actively campaigned and used in breeding programs.

Certain sections have been greatly expanded. The Vizsla standard is given broader treatment. Examined separately is the application of the standard to the dog. A section on breeding has been added. Discussion of diseases and health hazards has been expanded.

The original book was prepared for distribution in the United States. Acceptance of the text in other countries has prompted the addition of a chapter on Vizslas in other countries.

It was the objective of the original book to inform, educate and stimulate Vizsla owners to get the most from their dog, and to support the breed generally. Truly, every time a new Vizsla owner has success with his dog, it helps all Vizslas. Whether as a winning competitor in the field, or just on the street, a Vizsla seen by other people doing what he is supposed to do **correctly** is an endorsement for the quality of all Vizslas. If this revised text improves achieving that objective in any way, then it has been worth the effort.

Contents

The author has generated considerable good will for the Vizsla through demonstrations at public events. Here Dual Ch. Behi's Csinos Csiny, C.D. demonstrates an uncommon ability to climb ladders.

CHAPTER 1

Introduction

The Vizsla originated in Hungary and was called the Magyar Vizsla when it was first introduced to the United States. But when the American Kennel Club admitted this breed to its registry, the descriptive "Magyar" was not allowed and was dropped from use.

The correct sound in English for *Vizsla* is pronounced VIZHLA.

Although it was not generally available to the ordinary man., the Vizsla held a place with noble families down through the centuries. He was preserved pure for centuries by the land-owning aristocracy, held in high esteem, and guarded jealously by the early warlords and barons.

The Hungarians have always loved and expertly bred a number of different animals, but in their culture they did not have very many dog breeds-only four. They developed the Vizsla as an all-round hunting dog, family companion and discriminating protector. This development became one with class, style, and aristocratic bearing. The Vizsla may be the oldest sporting dog—and certainly one which easily meets the requirements for working both as a pointer and retriever.

The Vizsla is one of the most expressive breeds. One can quickly read his face to know how he feels or what he wants.

The Vizsla breed first appeared in the United States to stay in the early 1950's, and in 1960 it became the 115th breed officially recognized at the time by the American Kennel Club. This was accomplished by devotees of the Vizsla who formed what is now the Vizsla Club of America, Inc.

The Vizsla is a distinctively different dog. To own one is to know the truth of this statement. He fills the need of the family interested in a friend, companion and hunting dog.

From constant association with his master in the home, the Vizsla has improved in intelligence. He readily accepts the role of protector, friend and hunter, but in turn expects the degree of respect and rank not ordinarily shown to a dog.

In the home he is a loyal, lovable clown and a gentleman too. He combines the finest in beauty, character, brains and hunting ability and has a *strong* desire to please. He is content to be entertained by the family members or will invent his own games, but he is not one that you can take for granted.

To say that a Vizsla hates confinement is an understatement. Dogs of this breed do not care for being placed in a kennel or staked out. While some do adjust, others do not and will most always cause the owner problems.

A Vizsla serves best, and is a better dog, when properly supervised and is allowed the relative freedom of the home. Those who want a Vizsla someday will do well to keep this in mind. It can save money, time, labor and even heartbreak.

The Vizsla is versatile. He has guarded great and valuable treasures in his native Hungary, has guarded world leaders, has served in the Hungarian Army as a guard dog, has worked for police in tracking down people, has acted in movies and has worked as a guide dog for the blind.

He has a happy attitude (although many people say that he looks sad), a gentle disposition, is loyal and devoted. He is a kindly dog that reacts best to kindness. Timid he is not. He establishes rapport so easily with those he knows, trusts and loves that it might seem that he is everyone's dog.

Whenever the Vizsla moves in with a family he takes over the house and everyone in it, and is happiest when he lies between husband and wife in their bed. Yet, a Vizsla will spend a full day afield without anyone suspecting that he is a pampered member of a household.

The degree of specialization for the Vizsla to hunt any one bird or animal will depend mostly on the type and degree of training given. The more varied the owner's interest and activities, the more training will be needed for his dog. And each additional kind of hunting desired will require more and more training which will reduce the dog's ability to specialize or achieve a high level of perfection in everything.

11

Usually no dog will be as good at two different kinds of hunting as he will be with one. This is true for any breed, but you may find it easier to achieve a higher degree of success in several areas with the Vizsla.

The Vizsla is in good hands and is becoming a better dog. He is proving to be a strong competitor in Continental pointing breed trials, which takes exposure, for it is not easy for the field trial patrons to acclimate themselves to a new breed. While Vizslas have won many placements in Pointer and Setter trials, it is not likely that anyone would seriously consider the breed for that kind of competition.

A true evaluation of the Vizsla in the field is in the future yet for the general public. Vizsla owners for the most part, started as novice handlers who ran their first Vizsla in their very first field trial, but this is perhaps normal for any new breed. It will take some time yet to develop the professional handlers who will come mostly from these ranks.

In Hungary, the Vizsla was nearly impossible to beat in any form of competition, and claims made there for the breed's good qualities are now being demonstrated and proven in competition in the United States. The breed is now winning the respect and admiration of many other dog fanciers and sportsmen.

The beauty and eye appeal of the Vizsla will make it increasingly popular with all dog lovers. It has had a remarkable past and its future now seems secure.

In conformation and hunting ability there are both good and bad Vizslas. This will always be so. But from the best to the worst they are distinctively Vizslas.

A hunter can start and stop hunting according to his desires and his Vizsla will do likewise without being commanded to do so. A family member can take a Vizsla for a walk into a busy city with very little training and keep it under perfect control. Shown the property boundaries just a few times and given the command to stay inside, the dog will quickly learn to respect the imaginary line. In this area the Vizsla will be as protective as the occasion demands.

The Vizsla is the next to smallest of the pointing breeds and is unique in that he is of the same basic color shade—rust-gold all over, including the nose, eyes and the inside of his mouth.

The Vizsla is a medium size dog. It is lighter in bone and body structure than the Weimaraner or German Shorthaired Pointer. A very striking difference also is the tail dock where only one third of the tail is removed. Sometimes it appears that the tail has not been docked at all. Some breeders read the standard incorrectly, or do not know it, and leave only one third. The Vizsla has better style and overall balance with the longer tail and he looks better. A high tail carriage seems to improve his looks even more.

Males should be 22 to 24 inches at the withers and weigh 55 to 65 pounds; females should be 21 to 23 inches at the withers and weigh 45 to 55 pounds. As expected, some breeders either by accident or design, breed and sell Vizslas as small as 18 inches and as large as 27 inches. The standard allows one inch over and under the stated heights before disqualification. The enforcement of this disqualification has been limited to shows.

The golden rust-colored Vizsla coat is short and rich looking in texture and is without an undercoat which keeps them very clean looking. Vizslas normally clean themselves. Only in between the pads of their feet do Vizslas carry dirt into the house. Care and grooming of the coat is negligible. A Vizsla can be fully field trained in less time than is required to keep a long haired dog properly groomed for shows.

CHAPTER 2

History

Although the origin of the Vizsla is unknown, it is believed that the yellow dog was already established as long ago as 1500 years in Asia. This is approximately the time (375-455) that the Huns were in Central Europe and they are a distant relative of the Magyars. The word Magyar developed from Mansieri or Magyeri, a Finnish word, and from Oguri (Ugrian root) came the later European forms of hungarus, Ungar and Hungarian. Magyar and Hungarian are interchangeable.

In this movement of the different tribes from the steppes of Asia, the Moravian-Slovak tribes came into the Carpathian Basin in 830 under chieftain Svatopluk. It was in 895-896 that the Hungarians crossed the Carpathian Mountains at the Pass of Verecke under chieftain Árpád.

These two tribes engaged in battle at a later time and the Hungarians won. This insured these pagan and nomadic people a place to live from that time on. It is a known fact that falconry was a favorite pastime before this tribe came into Hungary. They rode horseback and used dogs to find birds ahead of them.

The proof of lineage or descent of the Vizsla depends on three prime

14

contributors, Count Béla Hadik of Seregélyes, Hungary and now the United States (d. 1971) Mike (Mihalyi) Kende of Hungary (d. 1969), Colonel Jëno Dús (d. 1963) director and breeder of the Vizsla Club of Hungary. Their knowledge, experiences, personal records and individual research into recorded history establishes the basis of the presumed origin and subsequent history of the Vizsla breed until its arrival in the United States.

It is claimed by some that the Vizsla descended from the hound. Béla Hadik believed that the Magyars divided their hound-type dogs into two categories before coming into Hungary. The ones that search for and chased birds were used for falconry and the others for big game with the hares being hunted by the greyhound. According to him, there were four types of dogs: the hound which had excellent tracking ability and characteristically sounded voice on fur-bearing animals; the greyhound, which never makes sound, follows game by sight at fast speeds over open country and has no nose for game; the ancient shepherd dogs (Komondor & Kuvasz) also hunting dogs, which were used to protect the flocks and herds from wolves, bears and lynxes; and, the bird dog which was an agile dog used to hunt with its nose only and never gave sound while hunting. This dog is the Hungarian Vizsla, which resembles the wild dogs of the steppes in color (the lighter ones) and quality of coat even today. It is this dog that was bred and used for bird hunting ever since the migration of the tribes from Asia.

After the year 900 there are specific references made to Pannon and Transylvania Kopo, white bird hounds, yellow colored dogs (hounds), Transylvania Beagles and Buckhounds. It is unknown what bearing, if any, these dogs had on the further development of the Vizsla but claims are made that they were used in their development.

Game was then killed by javelin, spear, sword or caught using the falcon or nets. One type of dog tracked big game and drove it in front of hunters as do bear hounds today. Another type was used for following the blood spoor and was kept on leash during the initial chase and baying. And still another dog is shown with the falcon and hunters. Primitive stone etchings show this particular scene according to Jenö Dús that are claimed to have survived down through the centuries, and in spite of rudimentary handling shows the characteristic curved lines of the Vizsla anatomy.

Under István the first King of Hungary (997) later crowned King Stephen I (1001) under Pope Sylvester II who had the crown delivered by papal envoy, Hungary adopted Christianity and accepted Latin as their written language. They changed then from a tribal and nomadic people and quit ravaging Central Europe. This confirmed the Apostolic Kingdom of Hungary. The crown is important to the history of the Vizsla and Hungarian nationalism. King Stephen was made a saint after his death.

15

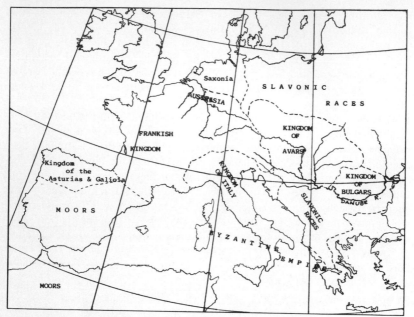

maps of Hungary, above 800 A.D. below 1190 A.D.

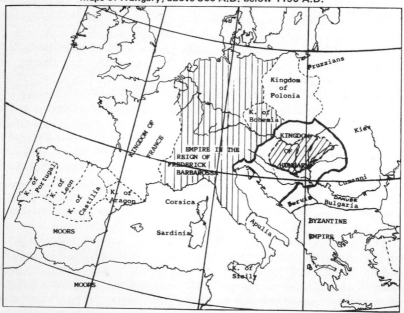

///// Hungary 1920 A.D.

16

Between wars and during their leisure hours, the nobility concentrated on horses, dogs and hunting. Fighting was their basic vocation. Hunting was an exciting demonstration and helped in the training of skillful warriors and leaders. Their bird dog was apparently bred and perfected to hunt partridge and hare after the early splitting off and specialization. It is logical to assume that this dog's versatility was later improved and it was further developed for use in the heat and dryness of the plains for hunting rabbit, quail, partridge, pheasant, waterfowl and for retrieving these; for forest driven shoots; for tracking wounded game; for pointing; for baying or leading to wounded or dead game; and, hunting in cooperation with the hunting hawk.

A hamlet called "Vizsla" in the Danube Valley bore this name in the 12th century based on the collection of papers provided to Jenö Dùs by Colonel Vértessy, chairman of the Hungarian Vizsla Club.

The first known documentation of Hungarian culture other than the stone etchings showing falconry is in the "Illustrated Vienna Chronicle" prepared on order of King Lajos the Great (Louis) by the Carmelite Frairs in 1357. This written manuscript is the oldest known illustrated record of their history. The Chronicle has five paintings or drawings of the 12th and 13th century depicting hunting scenes. One shows a hunting dog locating and flushing a bird. The dog drawn is represented as a fast stepping bird dog which was used in the rich river valleys that abounded in partridge and hare. Also the Chronicle mentions the Vizsla by name.

A later history of Hungary was written by Italian Marco Antonio Bonfini (1434-1502) at the time the earliest press was established at Buda (1471), now Budapest. None of the three referenced primary history contributors mention this publication.

Also, some letters written in 1515 and 1563 mentioning dogs used for quail and retrieving and used with falcons are reported to be in the Hungarian National Record Office in Budapest. The Vizsla name is also mentioned in this time period in letters written between the Danubian provinces and the High Porta (Court of the Sultan of Istanbul). At the same time correspondence from Transylvania only mentions the Kopo or drive hound. Jenö Dùs wrote of correspondence June 11, 1569 to the wife of the Hungarian Lord Chancellor which read: ". . . besides the falconer of Milady Batthyanyi says that his mistress has two Vizslas and three falcons, and would give me one of each if I asked for them."

Other private and public documents, drawings, paintings, tapestry and sculptures which existed prior to 1526 are said to have been destroyed by the Turks during their occupation of Hungary (1526-1686). The Turks were part of the Asian people and were non-Christian which influenced Hungarian culture and history for more than 160 years. The Turks did not hunt to eat the meat of the killed game and it is likely that the Vizsla dog

17

was not used for hunting except as a form of sport with them. Nothing in history indicates that they were a bird hunting people. The Turks could only eat meat that was killed according to their customs and religious rituals. It is claimed that the Vizsla was crossed with the eastern yellow and sand colored Turkish hunting dogs which further improved it.

After the Vizsla was once established it was very much a part of the sport-seeking nobility and the warlords who were his only owners for centuries. Whether the control was maintained through law, by decree, or high taxes, their numbers were always small.

The Vizsla, Tigris (or Tiger), was owned by Bethlen Gabor a Transylvanian sovereign, and it was one of the yellow colored dogs. This was in the early 1700's and it was in this time period that falconry and netting finally gave way to the new method of hunting with firearms. The search for the development of the Vizsla breed, for the purpose we use it, must begin with this kind of hunting. Then, with the introduction of the shotgun, came the classic Vizsla selection and training for outstanding pointing and retrieving ability.

The Zay family bred Vizslas from 1712, and by the end of the eighteenth century their strain was the most sought after. During this period, the Vizsla achieved heights of performance in hunting that many owners like to think is a **true** representation of the Vizsla. This was the era of the gentleman sportsman and a time when the Vizsla and falcon were used less and less as a team. By the end of the eighteenth century the most commonly found Vizslas in the Carpathian Valley were of the yellow strain.

Once the Vizsla breed was firmly established, it is believed that his blood was kept pure for a number of centuries, perhaps even as late as the nineteenth century. Their owners guarded them jealously and it is evident that they had a purpose behind the breeding of dogs with the same rust-gold coloration over its entire body. They were perfectly camouflaged in the ripe grain fields.

There has been much controversy over what "yellow" means relative to the early Vizsla. Whether it was light yellow, fawn, dark golden brown, mahogany, sedge-yellow, sarga (color of the crust of bread) or rust-gold it is impossible to say, but there seems to have been a distinction between the light yellow Vizslas and other yellow shades. They still have a range of color in the yellow band with a distinctive darker color along the topline and two symmetrical lighter spots just behind the shoulders. Rust-gold is generally agreed as being the most descriptive, but there is no argument that the color is nearly the same from the tip of their noses, including the iris of their eyes, to the tip of their tails (now docked). These specific breed markings and characteristics do not occur in other pointer breeds or varieties.

18

The State of Upper Hungary
"Preparation of a Contest"

The drawing is dated 1017 and looking closely at the hunting party one can see a falconer. It is believed that the early Vizsla was used for falconry which could make this an early illustration of Vizslas or their forerunners.

19

One story is told by a previous Weimaraner owner who took an interest in the history of that breed. He said that the Hungarian nobility or warlords gave the German warlords (their counterparts in Germany) male Vizslas only, a few at a time, for use on their hunting estates. This was supposedly done to prevent the breeding of Vizslas outside Hungary. It is told that on some hunts with Russian dignitaries, who brought and used their own wolf-like dogs, that the Germans used their Vizslas and hunted them with the Russians and their dogs.

Descriptions of the hunt indicate that both breeds were bold and fearless. The fields in Germany were broken up and divided by thorn hedges — a new experience for the Vizsla which in his native country had vast wide open grain fields to hunt upon. In pursuing game, both dog breeds went through the thorny bushes in their zeal. The Russian breed of dog came out intact, but the Vizsla's skin, which was protected by only a single coat of thin hair, was shredded. Then when the game was killed, the Russian's dog promptly ate it and the German's Vizsla delivered the small game to hand. The Russians wanted some dogs of this breed badly, but learned that they could not be obtained outside of Hungary as there was no breeding stock.

There was no way to prevent the use of the male Vizsla in breeding to other female dogs however. It was then that the Germans hit upon the idea of developing a new breed, and it is believed that the Weimaraner was thus born — or at least a start toward this breed was made. The Germans may have crossed the Vizsla with the Russian dog and others which resulted in the Weimaraner.

This is a story, for what it is worth, but nobody can deny that there is a striking resemblance in the build and profiles of these two dogs. This could also help explain the American public's confusion when the Vizsla was first seen in the United States, for they immediately recognized the Vizsla as a red-haired Weimaraner.

The hey-days of the Hungarian Vizsla ended around 1880 when English pointers and later German pointers were introduced. It was in 1882 that the first Vizsla field trials were held on a Danube Island near Budapest where the English pure-breds and the common Vizslas (presumably included English Vizslas and German Vizslas) competed in separate trials. In 1883 the Vizsla field trial had very few competing Vizslas, and the field trials lost favor because they did not represent hunting conditions well enough to build and maintain interest.

Shortly after this a few Vizsla owners began to fear for the breed. There had been much indiscriminate breeding carried on with the Vizsla using foreign retrievers, pointers, setters and bloodhounds. It is also believed that the Vizsla was used to improve the pointing instinct of the German pointers. A careful search revealed the existence of only a dozen true

20

"Hunting Scene of the Early XIV Century"
"Spoor Trailing Hounds"

The above is after the Bicserdy copy of the Illustrated Vienna Chronicle. 1358. (Illustrated by J.L. Tuvell).

Vizslas. It was at this time that expert dog breeders, perhaps some of the very ones guilty for much of this cross breeding, took these Vizslas and, using new foundation stock, re-established the breed. Whatever other breeds were used in conjunction with these dogs is unknown, but there is little doubt that these breeders did truly regain the original form of the **yellow** Vizsla.

According to Bill Kemenes-Kettner, a Hungarian repatriated to Canada and active with the Vizsla there, the most powerful argument of the ancient origin of the Vizsla is his color. He uses the scientific research by Dr. Anghi Csaba Geyza, professor of the Veterinary College of Budapest, which proved the original European ancient large mammals were all one color as evidence.

There has been much interest and conjecture as to what dogs were used to re-establish the Vizsla late in the nineteenth century. Some fanciers

21

believe that the Transylvanian type of pointer (Rumania and Bulgaria) and the Weimaraner, and one or more other pointers were used. According to Mrs. Jane Tallman the Transylvanian pointer was used every ten generations to bolster the breed as a general practice. It is also believed that the Vizsla breed re-establishment brought white into it and efforts are being made to minimize it. Where the white originated nobody really knows, nor do they know what breeds or methods were used to bring back the true Vizsla in numbers. One fact which must be remembered is that the Hungarians always were expert breeders of both horses and dogs and ranked high in educational facilities for this purpose. Jenö Dùs, as an example, was one official who approved Vizsla breedings and then decided which six (if more than that occured in a litter) puppies would be allowed to live.

Then to further aggravate the breed's chance to survive, there was a further decline in their numbers prior to 1916. Aside from the problem of finding Vizslas of pure strain and collecting enough dedicated breed lovers to carry on, there was very stiff competition from the English and German pointers. Their owners were quite active in selling their breeds.

Just before World War I, in November 1916 in the hunting magazine *Nimrod (Nimrod Vadaszujsag),* the chief natural registrar Tibor Thuroczy made a plea to save the yellow Vizslas from extinction. It was also in this same year that this hunting magazine *(Nimrod)* was placed at the disposal of the Vizsla breed to help create interest in this dog in direct competition with *Hunter-Journal* which was being used to promote the English and German pointing dogs. *Nimrod* was owned by Coloman Kittenberger, a Vizsla owner and African hunter, and was published by Dr. Tibor Thuroczy. This magazine also influenced the formation of the organization "Hubertus" Hungarian Hunters Association. In November 1917, the magazine's hunting dogs department laid down word by word the yellow Hungarian Vizsla temporary rule book.

Dr. Gyula Popovich wrote in *Nimrod* that his stud "Witti" was obtained at six years of age in raw form (reference to being untrained) and within three months was trained as an outstanding dog. He was used to resuscitate the breed. His picture shows all toes are white, but this could be the effect of aging where the color change starts on the muzzle and toes first. The name of this dog appears in every pedigree dated 1918. For 16 years his puppies were inbred and those with white were culled and no adverse effects were noted. An outstanding offspring was Ch. Szikra.

The rejuvenation of the Vizsla breed was perhaps hurt by the Treaty of Trianon (1920) which separated Hungary by ethnic groups which gave 71.4 percent of her territory to Czechoslovakia, Rumania, Yugoslavia and Austria. The Carpathian Mountain ranges which formed the country's natural frontiers for a thousand years were also lost. This left Vizslas that

22

were once in Hungary outside of it, but a wave of nationalism then sprung up and was manifested in dog breeding, among other things.

The Hungarian Vizsla Breeding Association in Kaposvar was formed in May 1920. The heads of this organization were Karoly Baba, Balazs Otvos, Dr. Kålmån Polgår and André Felix. In 1920 they set up their first field trial and it was this time that the breed really began to win over converts.

Such landowners as Dr. Kålmån Polgår of Czechslovakia, Elemer Petocz and Count Låzslo Esterhåzy of Sårosd, Hungary, Dr. Ferenc Korbas and the Mihalyi's of eastern Hungary were responsible for re-establishing the breed after World War I.

The show and field kept separate stud books and Count Låzslo Esterhåzy, a friend and neighbor of Béla Hadik in Hungary, Dr. Kålmån Polgår and Elémer Petöcz organized the first Vizsla show and field trial on the property of Count Vilmos Festetics in the fall of 1922. A further boost for the breed was achieved in 1924 when Kåroly Båba with his Vizsla, Ch. Vegvari Betyar, won first place over several prize winning English and German pointers. This dog could beat the corn patches from morning until night on the hottest day in August while at the age of thirteen.

Ch. Vegvari Betyar's record was surpassed by the National Ch. "Kati" which at 13 years of age was edged out of first place by one point in a trial partly due to a mistake on the part of the handler. Mike Kende said that she had earned the greatest number of awards and was the best working Vizsla. She gave birth to some 73 puppies.

To further produce evidence that the Vizsla can stand hot weather and get better the longer he hunts, Ferenc Graf's "Borcsa" weighed 84 pounds and hunted from morning to night without showing any fatigue.

The Orszågos Vizsla Club was founded in 1924 with Dr. Kålmån Polgår president, Count Låzslo Esterhåzy honorary president, Elemér Petöcz treasurer and József Stifft registrar.

André Felix wrote books on and trained Vizslas with emphasis on persuasive training methods.

Dr. Kålmån Polgår wrote the history of saving the Vizsla which appeared in the May and June 1934 *Nimrod* hunting magazine. He named all the dogs used as foundation stock in 1918.

It was in 1935 that the Vizsla characteristics were finalized and the Federation Cynologique Internationale (F.C.I.) recognized the Vizsla as a separate breed.

Mike Kende sold the first Vizsla into the United States in January 1938. He sold his Zsoka of Sashegy to a Mr. Pulitzer who apparently won or placed against pointers with this bitch as well as a daughter of her's later on.

Prior to World War II, large estates were characteristic of the Hungarian

23

countryside and great emphasis had been put on livestock and horse breeding. In April 1941, German pressures forced Hungary into a partial participation in the Axis invasion of Yugoslavia.

In 1943, Derek Peters, a British Intelligence Agent, was reported to have parachuted into Hungary to steal the Crown of St. Stephen (Hungary's first King, (997-1038) which represents the symbol of Hungary's sovereignty. He was attacked by two Vizslas in the crown room and they held him until the guards arrived. From that time on, all Derek Peters could think of was those two dogs and how he would get one for himself. He later escaped prison and returned to England.

At this time there were 5,000 registered Vizslas in Hungary.

On March 19, 1944 the regent was forcefully detained by Hitler and German armies occupied the country with a resulting terroristic Nazi government in power. By January 1945, after a siege, the Russian armies occupied Budapest. The occupation was completed in April 1945 and remains a primary factor in Hungary's history since. The Russians ravaged the country and reduced the livestock population to less than one third and left only 10 to 20 percent of the Vizslas.

As the Austrian and German soldiers and Hungarians fled the occupation, a forester in charge of Count Esterhàzy's kennels gave F. Hofbauer a male puppy which he took to Vienna, Austria. Many Hungarians killed their own horses and dogs to prevent their falling into Russian hands or to prevent abandoning them to an uncertain future. Stud Master, Colonel Jenö Dùs (d. 1963) upon leaving, concealed the three Vizsla Stud Books near the Austrian border.

Mrs. Elizabeth Mihalyi made good her escape into Austria in 1945. (She is now repatriated to the United States and lives in California.) There she did portrait painting for British soldiers to earn her living and to feed Panni. She later inquired through the Austrian Kennel Club if any other Vizslas were in Austria. She was contacted by F. Hofbauer of Vienna. This Vizsla was named *Betyar* and was registered UngK. 1 in the Austrian foundation stock for the breed and Panni was registered as the first bitch UngK. 2.

Wars always change the lives of men, horses and dogs. The Vizsla's history is tied somewhat to the spoils of war from the time of the Turkish occupation to World War II, and the subsequent Russian occupation. Each period in history and each war has its own individual stories of intrigue and bravery for the Vizsla and its owners, but certainly none like after World War II.

In 1948, Derek Peters went back to Hungary, but failed to get a dog. A year later he succeeded and was found with a male Vizsla at the border. Both had been shot to death by Russian border guards.

24

"Hunting Scene of the Early XIV Century"
"Baying Hounds"

The above is after the Bicserdy copy of the Illustrated Vienna Chronicle. 1358.
(Illustrated by J.L. Tuvell).

The barbarous acts of the Russians caused the entry of the British and American Commissions into the Vizsla business, and the smuggling began in earnest. It was during this period that the Hungarians were torn between two fears — the loss of their prized Vizslas and of being caught in illegal dog traffic across the border. Some dogs and people lost their lives in trying to get Vizslas across the border, but many got through.

At the end of World War II, two Vizsla clubs in Hungary, one field and one show, compiled available records and started their respective Vizsla stud books.

During the period of and following the Russian Occupation, there were many refugees who came out of Hungary to Rome. Emmett Scanlan of the United States State Department worked with them and heard stories of the Vizsla and became interested in it. His first contact with one came from his work with repatriations where a refugee left her dog back in Hungary desparately ill, probably from malnutrition since her dog at that time was fed only on the liquid left from the potatoes which she fed herself with — which was the only food available to her and many others. Later on an Army Sergeant brought out her dog in a duffel bag and returned it to her in Rome. While in Rome this beautiful woman met, fell in love with, and married a Jewish cab driver. He was scheduled for repatriation to Israel. In Rome her dog, *Sari* (pronounced Chari), was bred to a Vizsla named Bobbi and he was killed by a car before the puppies were born. On learning that she would have to put Sari in quarantine for a year before being permitted to immigrate into Israel she decided not to subject Sari to this treatment. Sari was given to Steve Shuttack. Emmett Scanlan then obtained the dog and sent her and her two puppies (one male and one female, born while waiting to clear the red tape) to his friend, Frank J. Tallman in Kansas City. Sari and her two puppies arrived October 7, 1950.

Frank Tallman liked Sari and the breed so well that the next year he worked through Scanlan to get a two year old male Vizsla, *Rex* (Rex Del Gelsimino, born 8-1-49, bred by Enrico Galeazzia, Rome, Italy), and he arrived in July 1951. Mrs. Jane Tallman said that Rex was a very large and gentle dog that brought all solid color to their breedings.

Sari, Shasta and Tito (her two puppies) were first *exhibited* at the Heart of America Kennel Club, Kansas City in February 1951 and a few months later at the Chicago International Kennel Club on special permission from the American Kennel Club. It required 18 months for Tallman to get approval for showing Vizslas in the miscellaneous classes.

Two men from Minnesota, Jack A. Hatfield and William A. Olsen (d. 1961) were at the Chicago International Kennel Club show in 1951 and were very much interested in the Vizslas. Jack Baird of Connecticut introduced these two men to the Tallmans. Maxwell Riddle was there

26

"Hunting Scene of the Early XIV Century"
"A Vizsla"

The above is after the Bicserdy copy of the Illustrated Vienna Chronicle. 1358.
(Illustrated by J.L. Tuvell).

and he too was very much interested in the new breed and took pictures at the time.

Jack Hatfield and William Olsen were able to get their first Vizslas imported from Germany and then from those other countries bordering Hungary. According to advertisements in the *Field & Stream*, Mr. Olsen got his first Vizsla in 1951 and in May 1952 at the Chicago International Kennel Club show they had dogs entered in the miscellaneous classes along with Frank Tallman. Frank Tallman showed Tito, Jack Hatfield and William Olsen showed Gemme V Schloss Loosdorf and William Olsen showed Gelse V Schloss Loosdorf.

Mr. Olsen was later able to get dogs from the litter bred by Mrs. Elizabeth Mihalyi in Austria. From the Betyar ex Panni XV litter there were several puppies and they were named such names as Csilla, Csitri, Csatt, Csitt, etc., and he got some of these. (Panni XV is the name used for this breeding when registered in the American Field Stud Book, but this dog is referred to as Panni IV in the November 1954 *Field & Stream* and the *Complete Dog Book* by the American Kennel Club.)

From their five Vizslas Rex and Sari, (whose first litter of two males and four females were whelped April 1952) Tik, Shasta and Tito, there were about 63 descendents that helped establish the Vizsla in the mid-western United States. Tik was approximately 10-12 years old when brought over for the Tallmans by a Marine Captain. Tik was later given to Jenö Dùs who had repatriated to the United States and was then living in Hamburg, New York. Tallmans never bred for profit and usually gave their puppies to friends who had to promise to train and hunt them. When money was taken in exchange it was only that amount to cover the cost of veterinarian expenses. Their dogs were taken to Tennessee and trained by Tom Lunsford for hunting.

The Tallmans only registered their dogs in the American Field Stud Book.

The early Vizsla importers and breeders in the United States had difficulty in obtaining pedigress, or dogs certified of pure breeding. Hungarian family papers were lost during the war and Russian occupation, and Colonel Jenö Dùs refused to reveal the hiding place of the stud books which could have helped solve this problem. He did work with the people here and was very helpful.

The Hatfields were the first to import a Vizsla with complete papers. Eventually under the Magyar Vizsla Club of America, Incorporated in Missouri June 25, 1953 the breed owners organized formally with Frank Tallman as president, Emmett Scanlan, vice-president, Jenö Dùs, vice-president, William Olsen, vice-president and treasurer and Jack Baird secretary and executive director.

Nikki of Bayview, by Brok Olca out of Iskra Kubis, was bred by Dr. I. S. Osborn and owned by George Yamamoto.

Ch. Nikki's Arco, by Pepe Z Selle out of Nikki of Bayview, was bred by George Yamamoto and owned by Robert S. Foster.

Ch. Hunor, by Nikki's Arco out of Shirbob's Folly, was bred by Robert S. Foster and owned by Bela Hadik.

DUAL CH. FUTAKI DAROCZ
by Ch. Hunor out of Piri
Breeder/Owner: Bela Hadik
First Vizsla Dual Champion
VCA Hall of Fame, 1978

The *American Field* opened its stud book to the Vizsla on Thanksgiving 1953 with the registration of 17 Vizslas.

Advertisements in the *Field & Stream* and *Outdoor Life* in November 1954 and later read: "America's new golden gun-dog. Gift of Kings with 1000 years recorded history. Chokebore nose shorthaired natural pointer & retriever." (Chokebore means having a keen accurate nose.) "VIZSLA European Import America's Newest and Finest Bird Dog! Keen Intelligence - Superior Stamina - Natural Pointer - Soft Mouthed Retriever. Vizsla . . . The new aristocrat, rust golden, shorthaired bird dog of American Hunting Circles. A versatile hunter and very affectionate."

These and other advertisements were made and with the publicity afforded this dog by the national sporting magazines, Dr. I. S. Osborn (veterinarian), William A. Olsen, Roy W. Hawkinson and Charles Hunt started selling Vizslas to the American public as a business undertaking. Jack Hatfield apparently did not participate in the national advertising at that date. At this time there were 51 known adult Vizslas in the United States.

It is interesting to note that imported Gelse V Schloss Lossdorf became the first Vizsla Companion Dog title winner in the United States with an average score in 196 in three straight shows just after the Vizsla publicity came out.

From 1945 to 1956 there was no breeder's association in Hungary. Then the Communists organized and compiled stud records and they were lost or misplaced again in the uprising of 1956. Then it was set up again under the direction of Mike Kende.

The first national field trial of the Magyar Vizsla Club of America was held at Fort Snelling, Minnesota, September 23, 1956 with three puppy entries, four derby entries, and 11 shooting dog entries, and the shooting dog stake was won by Osborn's male, Brok Olca. Fred Shultze handled dogs for Dr. Osborn at this trial and he and Paul Sabo, Jr. handled dogs at other Vizsla trials for several years. Paul Sabo handled dogs for R. W. Hawkinson and others at the second trial in Kansas City on May 12, 1956. These two men became the first professional handlers in the breed and often entertained the gallery and other handlers with their bantering at one another while handling their dogs when braced together.

In 1958 the Canadian Kennel Club recognized the Vizsla breed.

In 1959, Mike Kende was in a Hungarian Dog show where the Hungarian participants were dressed in the old costumes of the times and hunting during the time of King Matyas (1457-1489). Of the 517 dogs entered, 72 were Vizslas. Mike Kende led the grand march in the colors of King Matyas followed by a falconer with his falcon on his left arm and a Vizsla by his side. It showed the Hungarian pride in the Vizsla as their National Dog and reflected a symbol of Hungarian sovereignty in a small way.

The Magyar Vizsla Club of America was required by the American Kennel Club to submit approximately 500 Vizslas as a prerequisite to recognition and registration of the breed. A three generation pedigree was required although it did accept for registration some with incomplete pedigrees. This requirement was met through the efforts of Charles Hunt and on November 25, 1960 the Vizsla was officially recognized as the 115th breed at the time by the American Kennel Club.

In 1961, Dr. I. S. Osborn advised owners of the possible existence of hip dysplasia in the breed and talked on his monograph "Congenital Hip Dysplasia and Its Ramifications" at an annual meeting of the Vizsla Club of America. At this meeting a resolution was approved to x-ray all breeding stock.

The first show champion title was earned in California by Harvey Warholm with Miklos Schloss Loosdorf in 1961. The next day Csisckas of Goncoltanya, owned by Joan Hunt the wife of Charles Hunt, completed his championship in Tennessee. Ch. Paton's Zsomi Selle was the first dog

31

FLD. CH. BROK SELLE
by Brok Olca out of Baba Selle

Breeder: Dr. I. S. Osborn

Owner: Don Anderson

First Vizsla Field Champion

to place in the Group with a third at the Central Ohio Kennel Club April 21, 1961.

The Vizsla club's field trials moved around and were held as far west as Oregon until November 3-4, 1962 when the American Kennel Club granted a license for the club's first field trial which awarded points toward the champion title and it was held at New Sharon, Iowa. It was open to breeds other than the Vizsla and with the five stakes it had 44 entries. It was not until 1964 that the first field champion title was earned by Don Anderson of Colorado with Brok Selle. The next year Bêla Hadik's Futaki Darocz earned the first dual champion title.

The first best in show title in America was won by Ch. Piros of Mile High in 1964 in Mexico City under procedures of its kennel club. Owned by Mrs. Ann DeBarr of Mexico City, Piros was bred by Mile High Kennels owned by Robert Holcomb of Colorado.

Ch. Gypsy's Bronze Bomber, owned by Mrs. Harriet Anderson, won the first group first placement at the Kokomo Kennel Club in 1965, shortly after winning the first Vizsla specialty show held in conjunction with the Chagrin Valley Kennel Club in Ohio.

Spring 1965 the Vizsla Club of America first restricted to Vizslas the spring national field trial at Greenup, Illinois. Efforts directed toward opening it again in the fall to other breeds were defeated because many owners did not want to travel such long distances only to face dogs of other breeds which they had to do locally if they entered trials. This finally enabled breeders to make direct comparisons to other Vizslas throughout the United States and assured them that the Vizsla Club of America had passed the long ardurous test of making the Vizsla a viable hunting dog in America. This was further reinforced in 1969 with the first breed futurity with 26 entries held the day following the national field trial in Wisconsin at the Bong Recreation Area.

32

In 1970 the first Vizsla bitch dual champion title was earned by Ch. Szekeres' Kis Szereto owned by Mrs. Carole Smith wife of Chauncey M. Smith, Jr. who finished Dual Champion Futaki Darocz in the field. This bitch was sired by Dual Champion Futaki Darocz.

While the Vizsla is a natural water dog, the Vizsla Club of America has not yet held events of this type, although some of the local specialty clubs have.

The first sanctioned water trial was held in Ohio in 1970 for the Vizsla breed, and this was also the year that left the Vizsla out of the water tests for the field champion title when the American Kennel Club revised its rules for the Continental pointing breeds. Local specialty clubs held water fun trials for several years preceding this sanctioned trial.

The first best in show title in the United States was won by American, Canadian & Mexican Champion Napkelte Vadasz Dalos at the Terry-All Kennel Club in Colorado May 24, 1970. He is owned by Mr. & Mrs. William Totton of California. The first dual champion having an

DUAL & AMTR. FLD. CH. AMBER'S WINDY AUTUMN
by Amtr. Fld. Ch. & Fld. Ch. Jodi of Czuki Barat
out of Dual Ch. Brook's Amber Mist
Breeder: Anthony J. Lucas   Owner: Phil Rosenberg
First Amateur Field Champion and Field Champion

obedience title was achieved by the author's Dual Champion Behi's Csinos Csiny, C.D. in 1971. The first field champion and amateur field champion titles were earned by Amber's Windy Autumn, owned by Phil Rosenberg of Illinois in 1971.

The American Kennel Club set up rules and provisions for the title of obedience trials champion in 1980. The first dog of any breed to win the show champion, field champion and obedience trials champion title was Cariad's Kutya Kai Costa in 1980. He is owned by Robert and Marianne Costa, Staten Island, New York. This completes all the firsts for the Vizsla in American Kennel Club titles in the United States.

The Vizsla Club of America, Inc. met one of its charter objectives by becoming a member of the American Kennel Club in the fall of 1971.

CHAPTER 3

Vizsla

Standards

DIFFERENCES IN VIZSLA STANDARDS

All Vizslas in the world today can be traced to a common ancestry. There are actual variations in size, shape and color in the Vizsla breed that are not a result of the different standards in use. These same variations occur in every country.

This breed was exclusively Hungarian and the question is so often asked, "why was not the Hungarian standard adopted word for word?" It cannot be answered. It might not have been readily available to our first Vizsla owners. The Hungarian language is difficult to translate into any other language which could have caused some of the early problems. But there has been sufficient time to correct that.

All members of the Federation Cynologique Internationale use standards established and approved by that organization. The United States is not a member. We can assume that any country not using those standards is not a member and has developed its own.

The Federation Cynologique Internationale Vizsla standards include the differences between shorthaired and wirehaired Vizslas as translated from the German language, but only for the shorthaired Vizslas as translated from the Hungarian language. You will note that the only differences in these two breeds relate to origin and the color and texture of their coats. Nothing else. The wirehaired Vizsla organization in the United States call this breed the "Versatile Uplander" or "Uplander." It cannot be registered as a wirecoat Vizsla in the American Kennel Club, but can in the Canadian Kennel Club. The organization for this breed is struggling and was trying to set up its own registry. The demand for this variation in the Vizsla is not growing well enough at this time to ever expect registration with the American Kennel Club.

THE BLUEPRINT

The Vizsla standard describes what a Vizsla is, and what the breed looks like. It is also an attempt to guide the breeder in striving for the distinct features and abilities of the Vizsla. It helps judges to make decisions among the breed entries at shows and, to a certain extent, in field events.

The standard is not as precise as a blueprint of a machine or machine part. Interpretations of any dog breed's standard vary from person to person depending on individual personalities, beliefs, experiences and understandings of word meaning.

The first time you read the Vizsla standard, you may not understand it. And, until you gain familiarity with the breed, all Vizslas may look alike.

The standard attempts to give in words the Vizsla's size, movement, temperament (disposition), intelligence, appearance, stamina, courage, endurance and natural abilities.

The owner and breeder can learn the purpose for which the Vizsla is bred and used by reading the standard. A new buyer may attempt to use it in selecting a puppy which is not possible. He might use it to try and compare with the dam but will lack the necessary experience.

Some breeds recognized by the American Kennel Club tend to develop into two distinct divisions, one of show dogs and another one for which they were developed such as: hunting, guarding, chasing, tracking and retrieving. The seriousness and degree of this division is directly related to the breed's popularity with the general public and the breeder's practices that deviate from the standard to meet the increased demand. When a breed is difficult to sell there are less variations in type because of fewer dogs and breeders. Such splits are rarely designed, but occur as a number of factors "force" a "double standard."

36

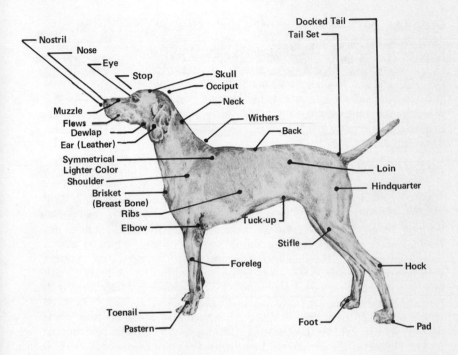

Nostril
Nose
Eye
Stop
Muzzle
Flews
Dewlap
Ear (Leather)
Symmetrical
Lighter Color
Shoulder
Brisket
(Breast Bone)
Ribs
Elbow
Toenail
Pastern

Skull
Occiput
Neck
Withers
Back

Docked Tail
Tail Set

Loin
Hindquarter

Tuck-up
Stifle

Foreleg

Hock

Foot
Pad

PARTS OF THE VIZSLA

FIGURE 3-1

37

VIZSLA STANDARD APPROVED IN 1982 BY THE AMERICAN KENNEL CLUB

GENERAL APPEARANCE – That of a medium sized short coated hunting dog of distinguished appearance and bearing. Robust but rather lightly built; the coat is an attractive solid golden rust. This is a dog of power and drive in the field yet a tractable and affectionate companion in the home. It is strongly emphasized that field conditioned coats, as well as brawny or sinewy muscular condition and honorable scars indicating a working and hunting dog are never to be penalized in this dog. The qualities that make a "dual dog" are always to be appreciated not depreciated.

HEAD – LEAN AND MUSCULAR. Skull moderately wide between the ears with a median line down the forehead. Stop between skull and foreface is moderate, not deep. Foreface or muzzle is of equal length or slightly shorter than skull when viewed in profile, should taper gradually from stop to tip of nose. Muzzle square and deep. It must not turn up as in a "dish" face nor should it turn down. Whiskers serve a functional purpose; their removal is permitted but not preferred. Nostrils slightly open. Brown nose. Any other color is faulty. **A totally black nose is a disqualification**. Ears, thin, silky and proportionately long, with rounded-leather ends, set fairly low and hanging close to cheeks. Jaws are strong with well developed white teeth meeting in a scissors bite. Eyes medium in size and depth of setting, their surrounding tissue covering the whites. Color of the iris should blend with the color of the coat. Yellow or any other color is faulty. Prominent pop-eyes are faulty. Lower eyelids should neither turn in nor out since both conditions allow seeds and dust to irritate the eye. Lips cover the jaws completely but are neither loose nor pendulous.

NECK AND BODY – Neck strong, smooth and muscular, moderately long, arched and devoid of dewlap, broadening nicely into shoulders which are moderately laid back. This is mandatory to maintain balance with the moderately angulated hind quarters. Body is strong and well proportioned. Back short. Withers high and the topline slightly rounded over the loin to the set on of the tail. Chest moderately broad and deep reaching down to the elbows. Ribs well-sprung; underline exhibiting a slight tuck-up beneath the loin. Tail set just below the level of the croup, thicker at the root and docked one-third off. Ideally, it should reach to the back of the stifle joint and be carried at or near the horizontal. An undocked tail is faulty.

FOREQUARTERS — Shoulder blades proportionately long and wide sloping moderately back and fairly close at the top. Forelegs straight and muscular with elbows close. Feet cat-like round and compact with toes close. Nails brown and short. Pads thick and tough. Dewclaws, if any, to be removed on front and rear feet. Hare feet are faulty.

HINDQUARTERS — Hind legs have well developed thighs with moderately angulated stifles and hocks in balance with the moderately laid back shoulders. They must be straight as viewed from behind. Too much angulation at the hocks is as faulty as too little. The hocks are let down and parallel to each other.

COAT — Short, smooth, dense and close-lying without woolly undercoat.

COLOR — Solid golden rust in different shadings. Solid dark Mahogany red and pale yellow are faulty. Small white spots on chest are not faulted but massive areas of white on chest or white anywhere else on the body is a disqualification. Occasional white hairs on toes are acceptable but solid white extending above the toes is a disqualification. White due to aging shall not be faulted. Any noticeable area of black in the coat is a serious fault.

GAIT — Far reaching, light footed, graceful and smooth. When moving at a fast trot, a properly built dog single tracks.

SIZE — The ideal male is 22 to 24 inches at the highest point over the shoulder blades. The ideal female is 21 to 23 inches. Because the Vizsla is meant to be a medium-sized hunter, any dog measuring more than 1½ inches over or under these limits must be disqualified.

TEMPERAMENT — A natural hunter endowed with a good nose and above-average ability to take training. Lively, gentle-mannered, demonstrably affectionate and sensitive though fearless with a well developed protective instinct. Shyness, timidity or nervousness should be penalized.

DISQUALIFICATIONS — Completely black nose, massive areas of white on chest; white anywhere else on the body; solid white extending above the toes; any male over 25½ inches, or under 20½ inches and any female over 24½ inches or under 19½ inches at the highest point over the shoulder blades.

FEDERATION CYNOLOGIQUE INTERNATIONALE (F.C.I.)
Hungarian Translation
VIZSLA STANDARD (1966)
Name: VIZSLA SHORT-HAIRED (Short-haired Hungarian Pointer).

I. General characteristics, features, its uses.

It is a middle-statured greyhound species: facile, of noble appearance, lean muscled, with a fine bony frame, steely sinews, dry limbs. It shows liveliness and great intelligence. Its hair is short, dark and sandy-coloured. It was bred in the XVIIIth century from the ancient Hungarian Foxhound and the Turkish yellow coloured Greyhound. It got its present fashionable figure in the XIXth century when it got improved by breeding with more foreign Greyhounds.

It is intelligent, docile, quiet, but a type of vivacious temper. It has an excellent good nose. It is quiet as it stops the game at bay. It works readily even on moist ground. It is affectionate. It bears very well any guiding. It is obedient but susceptible of bad treatment. It is a mansided Greyhound.

II. Head

The head is gaunt and noble. The nape-bone is moderately protruding. The skull is broad and forms a slight hump, it is vigorously sinewy, along the middle-line somewhat ditched; in state of rest the forehead smooth. The eye-arches are medium developed. The stop-line shows a moderate curvature.

The frontal part of the muzzle ends bluntly in every direction and it does not get pointed. The nasal backbone is straight and forms an angle of 30-35° with the crown of the head.

The "nasal mirror" is well developed, broad, the nostrils wide. The jaw bone and the mandible are vigorously developed. The incisors of the standard set of teeth close like scissors.

The lips and the dewlaps of the jowl are moderate, dry and do not hang down and shut the slit of the mouth. The eyes are not deeply set, neither protruding. The look is lively, sensible. The eyelid's edge fits tight to the apple of the eye so that nothing can be seen either from the white of the eye or the conjunctiva. The colour of the eye is always a hue darker. The windhover, fish-like or black eye is not allowed.

The ears are set in middle height. They are covered with a thin skin, are not fleshy. They are hanging down and show a V-like, rounded off shape, longer than the medium.

The neck is of medium length, of moderate curve and sinewy. It has no dewlaps on the neck.

Tail
Should be of moderate thickness, rather low set, with one-third docked off. While moving should be held horizontally.

Size
Optimum weight 48½-66 lbs. (22-30 Kg) Height at withers 22½-25 in. (57-63.5 cm) Bitches 21-23½ (53-60 cm).

Faults
Any departure from the foregoing points should be considered a fault and the seriousness of the fault should be in exact proportion to its degree.

Note
Male animals should have two apparently normal testicles fully descended into the scrotum.

III. Forequarters.
The shoulder-blade is fixed to the trunk quite firmly. This shoulder is richly muscled. It is slanting. The elbow keeps to the longitudinal axis of the trunk and does not protrude either inward or outward. The forearm is long. The foot-root is large, the shank is short. The paws are round, closed, the sole-pad full and resilient. The claws are short, developed and darker than the hair's ground-colour. Bastard fingers are regarded as a fault.

IV. Body
The withers is distinct, long; the back straight, short, well muscled. The groin is medium long, tightly closed, broad and sinewy. It does not form a flank, the hindquarters are straight, but not horizontal. It is well muscled. The breast is bulging onward, medium broad and very muscled. The chest is deep and long, not too staved; the ribs are moderately arched.

The belly is slightly lifted. The loin is somewhat caved in.

The tail is attached a bit low and is of moderate thickness. It is cut off, only the two thirds of its whole length is left. So it reaches the popliteal space. While moving, it keeps it horizontally.

V. Hindquarters.
The hind limbs are a bit open-angled and of stretched standing. The bones and the thighs are long. The knee articulation shows an angle of 110-120°. The hocks are low situated. The paws are well closed. The solepad is tight and resilient.

VI.   Hide and Hair.

The hide is tight and without wrinkles. The edges of the mouth and those of the eyelid are pigmented and dark brown coloured.

The hair is short and straight running down, of strong thread, thick, fitting to the body and shiny. It resists very well to the adversities of the weather.

The colour is dark sandy, without marks.

VII.   Size and Weight.

The heights of the withers, measured with a stick is: with males: 57-64 cm; with bitches: 53-60 cm.

The relative measurement of the single parts of the body is in % of that of the withers:

Length of the trunk	100%
Depth of the chest	44%
Broadness of the breast	33%
Measurement of the girdle	117%
Length of the head	42%

The length of the muzzle (nose) equals the 46% of the head.
The length of the ear comes up to the 76% of that of the head.
Weight of the body: 22-30 kgs.

VIII. Motion.

It is brisk and of graceful, elegant gait. Its classic gait accentuates very well the perfect form of the type.

IX.   Typefaults, defects.

Refined organism, loose organism. Too small or too big figure. Weak bone-frame. Rough head that reminds that of a Bloodhound. Slack eyelid. Hanging lips. Deficient set of teeth. Thin hair. Badly cut or frizzing tail.

Motives of exclusion.

It does not come up to the type. The height of the withers is less than 56 cm with the male and 52 with the bitch, or more than 65 cm with the male and 62 with the bitch. Medley of colours, spottiness, mark on the breast exceeding the extent of 5 cm, white paws. Spotty or black "mirror of the muzzle." Hanging, open eyelid. Pendent slobbering lips. Down-bite or overbite greater than 2 mm. Cream or brown coloured.

This standard covers both the Vizsla (shorthaired) as we know him in the United States and the wirehaired version. We have attempted to assist in understanding which provisions apply to which breed by setting the type differently.

The boldface used in this line indicates provision of the standard that applies to both breeds.

This light type face that is in the same "style" as the bold, is used when the standard refers to the "shorthaired Vizsla."

This plain type face (no serifs) is used when the standard is referring to the requirements for the "wirehaired Vizsla."

FEDERATION CYNOLOGIQUE INTERNATIONALE (F.C.I.)
VIZSLA STANDARD
(Translated from German)

Name: VIZSLA SHORTHAIR (Shorthaired Hungarian Pointer).
Name: VIZSLA WIREHAIR (Wire-haired Hungarian Pointer).

General Features, Use:

Medium sized hunting dog, wiry, noble, with a fine bone structure, tendons like steel, lean legs. Cheerful, very intelligent. The colour of the coat is a vivid reddish yellow (in Hungarian it is called: "roll"-yellow).

The coat is wire-haired and its colour is dark yellow.

The breed was bred in Hungary from the native hungarian hound and the yellow turkish hunting dog. He got his present, modern shape in the 19th century by inbreeding of other, foreign hunting dogs. **He is intelligent, docile, quiet, but with a lively temper, excellent nose. He points steady, loves water, is affectionate, easy to lead, tractable - an allround hunting dog, sensitive to a rough treatment.**

From a spontaneous mutation of the shorthaired hungarian pointer and by crossbreeding with wire-haired German Pointers, this breed was developed in the Thirties of the 20th century. . .

Head:

Lean, noble. Occiput moderate prominent. Broad skull, slightly domed, with a moderate median line down the forehead, in repose no wrinkles on the forehead. Eyebrow-bone medium developed, moderate stop.

43

The muzzle is blunt (viewed from either side). The top of the muzzle is straight, forms with the skull a 30-35° angle. Nose well developed, broad, with wide nostrils. Strongly developed jaws, even scissors bite. Flews moderate, contiguous to the teeth, do not hang over.

The eyes have an attentive, intelligent look, eyelids closing tightly, the white does not show. The colour of the eyes should be a shade darker than the coat. Blue or black eyes are not allowed.

The ears are set medium high, covered with a thin skin, not fleshy. Hanging down, longer than medium long, their shape is like a rounded "V".

Neck medium long, moderately arched, muscular, without dewlap.

Forehand:

The shoulder blades are strong connected with the trunk heavily muscled, sloping. Close elbows, forearm long, carpal bone strong, metacarpal bone short. The paws are round, closed, pads are full and resilient. Nails must be darker than the hair's ground colour.

Body:

Well marked, long withers. The back is straight, short and well muscled. Loins medium long, very solid, broad, well muscled croup. Breastbone somewhat prominent, moderately broad. Chest deep and long, not too barrel. Ribs moderately arched, the belly is slightly lifted.

Tail set somewhat low, medium thick. It is docked, two thirds of its length is left. When the dog moves the tail is carried horizontally.

Hindquarters:

The hind limbs somewhat strong angulated, cover much ground. Thigh bone is long, at the knee an angle of 110-120°. Hocks are placed low, paws closed, strong pads.

Hide and Hair:

Hair is tight, without wrinkles. Lips and eyelids pigmentated dark brown. Hairs short, straight, coarse, thick, close-lying and shiny. The coat gives a good resistance to weather. The colour of the coat is a vivid reddish yellow ("roll"-yellow), without marks.

The hairs on the muzzle are short and coarse. On the chin the hairs form a beard of about 2 cm. length. The skull is covered with short, hard, flat lying, not shiny hair. The hair on the ears is a little longer and thinner, like the shorthaired hungarian pointer. The hairs on the eyebrows are dense and hard, the single hairs pointing upwards and forwards. On the neck and body the coat has a length of 3-4 cm., rather close-lying, coarse, hard and not shiny. Under it, especially in the winter, an underwool. On the legs the short and hard hairs are lying close, but on the backside of the forelegs and the thighs there is a "brush" sticking out a bit. On the paws the hairs are shorter and softer. The hairs on the tail are dense, at the underside even more dense, but without forming a soft "flag" or "brush". The colour of the coat is a dark "roll"-yellow, without marks.

Size and Weight:

Height at the withers (measured with a stick): dogs 57-64 cm. (22.5-25.3 in.); bitches 53-60 cm. (20.9-23.6 in.).

The relative size of the single parts of the body as a percentage of the height at the withers (measured with a stick):

Length of trunk:	100%
Depth of chest:	44% min.
Broadness of breast:	33%
Girth	117% min.
Length of head:	42%

Length of muzzle = 46% of length of head. Length of ear = 76% of length of head. Weight of the body: 22-30 KGS.

Gait:

Lively, elegant gait. The beautiful shape of the body and the sound movement are in full harmony.

Faults:

Too refined or loose structure. Weak bone-frame. Coarse head. Head like a blood hound. Loose eyelids, pendulous flews. Dental faults. Thin coat. **Badly docked tail. Upwards curling tail.**

Wooly, soft hair on the head and when the hairs are longer than 4 cm. Soft, silky, curly or Griffon-like hair. A major fault is a parting on top of the back.

Disqualifying faults:

Not up to the standard are dogs under 56 or over 65 cm. at the withers, and bitches under 52 or over 62 cm. All sorts of spots. Breast patch larger than 5 cm, white paws. Spotted or black nose. Open eyelids. Pendent, slobbering lips. Undershot bite. Overshot bite which exceeds 2 mm. Pale or brown colour of coat.

Long coat.

Vizsla (Smooth)

Origin of Breed: The Vizsla (pronounced as if spelled VIZH-LA) is of Hungarian origin, where various records indicate its history as going back many centuries. It was the companion hunting dog of the early warlords and landed aristocracy who used it for general purpose hunting. It was known in Hungary as the "Yellow" Pointer. In North America it is used primarily as an upland bird dog, where its excellent scenting and retrieving characteristics have been widely acclaimed. It is a strong swimmer and also retrieves well from water.

General Appearance: The Vizsla is a short-haired, medium-sized sporting dog. It conveys the impression of an alert, muscular, well-balanced animal with a distinctive and aristocratic appearance.

Temperament: The Vizsla is intelligent, calm, obedient, and easy to train. It is a sensitive dog which becomes attached to its owner and develops a strong but not overly aggressive protective instinct. In the field, the Vizsla is an eager, happy hunter which is at home on land and in the water.

Size: The standard size, measured at the withers, for the Vizsla is 23 in. (58.42 cm.) for males, and 22 in. (55.88 cm.) for females. A dog of good bone and substance in this size range shall weigh from 50-65 lbs. (22.680 to 29.483 kg.). A bitch weighs about 10 lbs. (4.536 kg.) less. The length to height ratio should be approximately 1:1.

Coat and Colour: The hair of theVizsla should be short and dense and should lie close to the skin. Each hair should be thick and elastic and the coat should have a glossy sheen.

The correct colour is a golden-rust, sometimes described as the golden colour of the crust bread. In some strains slightly lighter or darker shades may predominate. A white mark on the chest under 2 in. (5.08 cm.) diameter is permissible but not desirable.

Head:

a) Skull — Should convey an impression of being lean and muscular, with a median line down the forehead. The top line of the skull should be straight. The skull tends to be comparatively narrow in relation to its length, with that of the male being slightly wider. The occiput is slightly visible. The stop should be slight and sloping rather than abrupt.

b) Muzzle — The muzzle should be approximately the same length as the skull. It should be narrow, end squarely, and have clean straight lines.

c) Mouth — The jaws should be strong and well developed teeth meeting in a scissor or even bite. The lips should be smooth and well developed and cover the teeth tightly. The lips extend in a level line 3/4 of the length of the muzzle.

d) Eyes — They should be almond-shaped, bright and intelligent in appearance. The colour is in harmony with or darker than the colour of the coat; they should be moderately deep set. The eyelids close neatly and cleanly with no overlap. The nictitating membrane should not be overly exposed.

e) Ears — The ears should be thin, silky and moderately tapered with rounded ends. They should just meet under the jaw, or reach to the corner of the mouth, but should not extend as far as the canine teeth. They should be set about 1/2 in. (1.27 cm.) below the level of the skull and hang close to the cheeks.

Neck: The neck should be of medium length in proportion to the body, it must be well muscled, with a definite arch at the nape and widened to blend smoothly into the forequarters. The skin of the neck should be smooth and tight.

Forequarters:

a) Shoulders — The shoulder blade should be of medium length and must be tightly held in place. The angle formed by the shoulder blade (scapula) and the humerus should be approximately 90°. The musculature should be firm, smooth and clearly defined.

b) Upper-arm (humerus) — The bone structure should be heavy, smooth and well covered by strong firm muscles. The skin should be firm, pliable and smooth. The upper-arm should be equal in length to the shoulder blade (scapula).

c) Lower-arm (Radius and ulna) — Strong big bones with good muscles. The legs should be straight whether viewed from the front or side. The angle at the elbow joint should be approximately 135°.

d) Pasterns — The angle that the pastern makes with the lower leg should be nearly straight (about 175° — 180°).

e) Paws — The paws should be cat-like with tightly closed toes and big rough pads. The feet should be webbed. The nails should be short, firm and well-curved, and their colour should be similar to that of the eyes, nose and coat. Dew claws should be removed.

Body:

a) Topline — The topline should be broad and smooth and is slightly arched over the loin and croup to the base of the tail; there is a slight depression at the juncture of the withers and the back.

b) Chest — The chest should be deep reaching down to the elbows and moderately broad. A cross-section of the chest is oval with well sprung ribs, narrowing between the elbows to permit free and easy leg movement. Width of the chest between the forelegs is at least 6 in. (15.24 cm.) for a male and 5 in. (12.70 cm.) for a bitch.

c) Loin — It should be broad, strong and well muscled.

d) Croup — It should be heavily muscled and smoothly rounded to the base of the tail.

e) Abdomen — The abdomen should be trim and neat with a moderate "tuck-up".

Hindquarters:

a) Hipbone (Pelvis) – This is the framework which forms the basic support for the hind legs. These pelvic bones should be wide and strong. The musculature attaching to these bones should be very well developed and gives strength to the hindquarters.

b) Upper thigh (Femur) – This bone should be heavy, straight, round and ᵛsmooth. Muscle attachments should be very powerful, broad and evenly distributed. The angle at the hip joint should be 90°.

c) Lower thigh (Tibia and Fibula) – Should be well muscled. These bones should be longer than the femur. The angle at the stifle joint should be 110-120°.

d) Hocks – The angle at the hock joint should be from 125-130°.

e) Paws – Same as the front.

Tail: The tail set is lower than on the other continental pointing breeds. In motion it is carried outstretched, at or above the horizontal level. A portion is docked, approximately 1/3 so that the tip of the shortened tail is level with the juncture of the upper and lower thigh. It should be thicker at the base than at the tip.

Gait: Viewed from the front, the dog's legs should appear to swing forward in a free and easy manner, with no tendency for the feet to cross over or swing wide. Viewed from the rear the gait should be true-tracking. The topline is level when dog is in motion, while the head is carried high and the tail "flags" constantly at the proper level.

Faults:

a) Very nervous dogs should be heavily penalized.

b) Very dark or very light colour coat

c) Hare feet

d) Light yellow, green, blue or "Pop" eyes

e) Throatiness

f) Dogs 10 lbs. (4.536 kg.) over or under the standard weight

g) Dew claws not removed

h) Roached, hollow or camel backs

i) Too steep a croup

j) Undershot or overshot bites

Disqualifications:

a) A dog 2 in. (5.08 cm.) or more over or under the standard height.

b) White markings over 2 in. (5.08 cm.) on the chest or white markings anywhere else other than the chest.

Vizsla (Wire-Haired)

Origin and Purpose — The Vizsla (Wire-haired) is of Hungarian origin that was formed by the crossing of the Vizsla and the German coarse haired Setter. In Hungary, it was used for general purpose hunting, but excelled as a pointer. Its keen nose and excellent swimming characteristics have brought it wide acclaim.

General Appearance — The Vizsla (Wire-haired) is a medium sized, all-purpose hunting dog bred to work both fur and feather. It is a noble dog, strong in bone and well muscled. Its tough wiry coat is dark yellow in colour. This breed is characterized by a lively and intelligent expression.

Temperament — The Vizsla (Wire-haired) is a sensible and docile dog, responding well to training, being sensitive to correction. Its keen nose allows it to be an enthusiastic worker in all weather.

Size — The allowable height for Vizsla (Wire-haired) when measured at the withers are males — 57-64 centimeters, (22.56 - 25.20 inches); females — 53-60 centimeters, (20.87 - 23.63 inches). Dogs and bitches of good bone and substance should weigh between 22 and 30 kilograms (48.50 and 66.14 lbs). The length of body from withers to tail set should equal the height from withers to ground.

Coat and Colour — The skin should fit the dog closely, showing no wrinkles or folds. The outer coat should be coarse and hard, about 3-4 centimeters (1.18 - 1.58 inches) in length on the neck and body. It is shorter and smoother on the legs forming a slight brush along the back of the forelegs and down to the hock on the hind legs. In winter, the body and neck should have an undercoat. Hair on the muzzle and skull is short and coarse but smooth-lying with the exception of the beard which is about 2 centimeters (.79 inches) in length, the eyebrows are prominent and bushy. The tail is densely covered with short, hard hair showing a slight fringe along the bottom. The colour is a dark sandy-yellow and should be even throughout, showing no marks.

Head — The skull is of good width and is slightly arched showing a shallow furrow rising from between the eyes toward a moderately prominent occiput. The supra-orbital ridges are of medium development showing a moderate stop. The muzzle is strong with a straight nasal bone meeting the skull at a 30-35 degree angle. It is slightly shorter in length than the skull and never snipey but rather blunt in appearance. Lips and flews are dry and not hanging. The mouth should close cleanly. The lips are brown in colour. The nose is well developed and broad with wide open nostrils and brown in colour. The teeth are strong and well developed and meet in a scissors bite. The ears are set approximately halfway between the top of the skull and the level of the eye. They should be of good length reaching 3/4 of the way to the nose, with thin leathers and hanging straight down in a rounded v. The eyes are not deep set nor protruding. The eye rim should be close fitting, showing neither white nor haw. The colour should always be a shade darker than the coat colour, but never black or staring. Eye rims are brown in colour.

49

Neck — The neck is of medium length, muscular and dry, showing a moderate arch.

Forequarters — The shoulders are well-muscled, showing good lay-back and must fit closely to the body. Elbows should be close-fitting and straight, neither turning in nor out. The upper arm should equal the shoulder blade in length, the lower arm is strong and of good bone, the pastern is short and strong. Feet are round and tight with a good depth of pad. Nails are short and strong, darker than the coat in colour. Dewclaws are considered to be a fault.

Body — Chest is of medium width, prominent and well-muscled. It should have a good depth and carry well back under the dog with medium spring of rib. The withers are prominent, sloping into a short level muscular back. The loin is strong of medium length and showing a slight tuck-up. The croup slopes slightly into the set on of tail.

Hindquarters — The hindquarters do not exhibit extreme angulation, the stifle joint having an angle of approximately 110 degrees. Hocks are well let down. Feet are tight with deep, resilient pads.

Tail — The tail is of moderate thickness and docked to 2/3 of its original length.

Gait — The gait should be brisk and smooth, indicative of sound conformation. The tail should be carried horizontally when the dog is in action. When coming and going the legs should move neither in nor out.

Faults — A soft, silky or curly coat or hair longer than 4 centimeters (1.58 inches) is considered a fault. Woolly hair on the head is considered a fault. Parting of the coat along the spine is considered a serious fault. Gay tail. Dewclaws.

Disqualifications — More than 1 centimeter (.39 inches) over or under the correct size range. Mixed colours, white feet, white mark or chest exceeding 5 centimeters (1.97 inches). Cream or brown colour. Spotted or black nose. Drooping eyelids, showing haw. Pendant flews. Long coat. Undershot or overshot more than 2 millimeters.

BRITISH VIZSLA STANDARD

Characteristics
The Hungarian Vizsla should be lively and intelligent, obedient but sensitive, very affectionate and easily trained. It was bred for hunting fur and feather on open ground or in thick cover, pointing and retrieving from both land and water.

General Appearance
A medium-sized dog of distinguished appearance, robust but not too heavily boned.

Coat
Should be short and straight, dense and coarse and feel greasy to the touch.

Head and Skull
The head should be gaunt and noble. The skull should be moderately wide between the ears with a median line down the forehead and a moderate stop. The muzzle should be a little longer than the skull and although tapering should be well squared at the end. The nostrils should be well developed, broad and wide. The jaws strong and powerful. The lips should cover the jaws completely and should be neither loose nor pendulous. The nose should be brown.

Eyes
Neither dark nor prominent, of medium size, being a shade darker in color than the coat. The shape of the eyes should be slightly oval and the eyelids should fit tightly. A yellow or black eye is objectionable.

Ears
The ears should be moderately low set, proportionately long with a thin skin and hang down close to the cheeks, should be "V" shaped, not fleshy.

Mouth
Sound white teeth meeting in a scissor bite, full dentition is desirable.

Body
Back should be level, short, well muscled; withers high. The chest should be moderately broad and deep with prominent breast bone. The distance from the withers to the lowest part of the chest should be equal

to the distance from the chest to the ground. The ribs should be well sprung and the belly should be tight with a slight tuck-up beneath the loin. The croup should be well muscled.

Forequarters
Shoulders should be well laid and muscular, elbows straight pointing neither in nor out, the forearm should be long.

Hindquarters
Should be straight when viewed from the rear, the thighs should be well developed with moderate angulation, the hocks well let down.

Feet
Rounded with toes short, arched and well closed. A cat-like foot is desirable, hare foot is objectionable. Nails short, strong and a shade darker in color than coat, dew claws should be removed.

Gait
Graceful and elegant with a lively trot and ground covering gallop.

Color
Russet gold, small white marks on chest and feet, though acceptable, are not desirable.

Tail
Should be of moderate thickness, rather low set, with one-third docked off. While moving should be held horizontally.

Size
Optimum weight 48½-66 lbs. (22-30 Kg) Height at withers 22½-25 in. (57-63.5 cm) Bitches 21-23½ (53-60 cm).

Faults
Any departure from the foregoing points should be considered a fault and the seriousness of the fault should be in exact proportion to its degree.

Note
Male animals should have two apparently normal testicles fully descended into the scrotum.

PHYSICAL MEASUREMENTS OF SELECTED LINE BRED VIZSLAS

Figures 3-2 shows the points used for measuring six of the author's Vizslas. Table 3-1 gives the selected measurements, and the weight and age of each one are included. The relationship of each dog is: Dog 1 is the sire of Dog 2 and Bitches 2 & 3, and grandsire of Dog 3. Bitch 1 is the dam of Dog 2 and Bitch 2. Bitch 3 is the dam of Dog 3. The sire of Dog 1 and the grandsire of Bitch 1 is one and the same dog. The grandsire Dog 3 is the same dog also.

The muzzle length is measured from a line (imaginary) at the front edge of the eyes to the tip of the nose. The skull length is measured from this same line to the rear part of the skull, and the length of the head is measured from the tip of the nose to the base of the skull.

The ear is measured from the forward point where it joins the head to the tip.

The Vizslas were in a show position for all other measurements, and it is important to note that the distance from the elbow to the stifle point, measured parallel to the ground, is a function of the position of the dog's hind feet.

Some of these measurements can be compared directly to those in the Hungarian Standard. One point of interest is the difference in the ear lengths in Table 3-1.

All six Vizslas are within the American Kennel Club standard and four have their Champion title.

These measurements are only intended to give the reader a better feeling of the actual dimensions of several Vizslas. It takes only a very slight difference in any one dimension to make a big difference in the relative appearances of a Vizsla.

TABLE 3-1

VIZSLA MEASUREMENTS

	Ref. Pt.	Dog 1	Dog 2	Dog 3	Bitch 1	Bitch 2	Bitch 3
Skull Length	B-C	5½	5	5	5	4½	4½
Skull Width	E	5	4½	4¾	4½	4¼	4¼
Muzzle Length	A-B	4¼	4¼	3¾	4	3½	3½
Muzzle Width (Top)	G'	1-5/8	1½	1-3/8	1½	1¼	1¼
(Bottom)	G	3	2½	2¾	2½	2½	2½
Muzzle Depth	G'-G	3¼	3¼	3¼	2¾	2¾	2¾
Length of Head (Nose to Skull Base)	A-D	11	10½	10¼	10	9¾	9
Ear Length (Stretched out)	F-H	6¼	6	6	5½	5¾	6
Neck Length	D-J	9	9	8	8	9½	8½
Front Leg	Q-O	13	12	12½	11½	11½	12
Pastern	P-O	4	3½	3¼	3¼	3¼	3¼
Height at Withers	J-O	23½	22½	22¾	22½	22¼	22¼
Chest Depth	J-Q	10½	10½	10½	11	10¾	10¼
Elbow to Stifle Joint	Q-S	15½	15	14½	14	14	15
Stifle Joint to Hock Joint	S-M	10	9	8	8½	9	9
Hock Length	M-N	7	6-7/8	7	7	7	6¾
Withers to Tail Set	J-L	18½	17	16¾	19	16	17
Skull Circumference	E	16½	15½	16	15	15¾	14-7/8
Muzzle Circumference	G	9¾	9	9	9	9	8½
Neck Circumference	I	16½	16	15	14	14½	14¼
Smallest Part of Foreleg	R	5	4-7/8	4½	4½	4¾	4¼
Chest Circumference	J	29	27	27¾	26	26½	27
Loin Circumference	K	21	19	21	20	20	18
Width at top of Shoulder Blade	J	3¾	2	2¾	2¼	2½	2¼
Weight (Pounds)	–	60	48	48	46	48	45
Age (Years) at measurements		6	1	3½	7	1	5

All measurements taken with tailor's tape measure.

FIGURE 3-2

REFERENCE POINTS FOR VIZSLA MEASUREMENTS OF TABLE 3-1

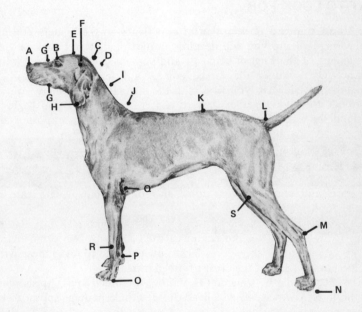

CHAPTER 4

Vizsla Conformation

WHAT TO LOOK FOR

The Vizsla standard does not offer experience to the reader. You can read the standard and you will develop an idea or picture based on your understanding of the English language and perhaps your past dog owning experience. Once you see the Vizsla, you get a different picture from the one first perceived when you first read the standard. Eventually you are able to put the two together and it is at this time that you begin to understand the Vizsla breed. To reach this point requires exposure and experience with a number of different Vizslas.

The Vizsla should have a pleasing and enjoyable temperament that exudes happiness, pleasure, desire and confidence. While hunting he moves with power, endurance, stamina, intelligence and tireless determination. These traits and characteristics *must* also be combined with ease of handling and the desire to please.

The color should be the same rust-gold overall with a slightly darker shaded narrow band down the center of the back with two symmetrical lighter spots behind the shoulders. Vizsla owners tend to favor those with hair color like the color of the crust of bread (sarga).

The muzzle should be squared off without too much upper lip showing below the lower jaw when viewed head-on. It should perhaps appear to be a triffle longer than the skull but is not. Looking down on top of the skull it should have a slight taper toward the front. The median line of the skull should join the muzzle in a smooth faired line with the eyebrow bulged forward of the sloping line of the skull to give the appearance of a stop when viewed from the side. The crown of the skull has a furrow in it. The set of the eyes is important, as is the color of the iris which should not vary more than a shade from the coat either lighter or darker. The ear set should be back and set slightly below the top skull line. When one watches some Vizslas listening intently, one may be reminded of an

56

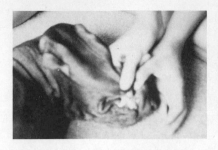

The photo at left shows a Vizsla ear that is too long; the tip of the ear reaches the canine tooth. The photo at right shows correct ear length, reaching to the corner of the mouth.

elephant preparing to charge; his large ears pushed forward. The neck should appear short and strong — not long and lean like a giraffe in appearance, not too short and blocky.

The breast bone forward of the shoulder should be prominent and the upper arm have a distinct backward cast as related to the shoulder blade and set back with the breastbone showing rather than appearing as if the neckline continued down forming the forearm and front leg. Viewed from the front, the chest is wide and the front legs parallel with the front shoulders giving a blocked appearance as opposed to a barrel or rounded appearance where the two front legs appear as if they are almost together (note standard "legs and feet"). The chest cross-section should be somewhat oval or heart shaped. The chest, viewed from the side, slopes down from the breastbone, passes in line with the elbow, with an upward sweep to the loin where a slight tuck-up should be evident.

The top line of the back should slope slightly downward from shoulders to tail. Because of this, many Vizslas appear to have a slight swayback when standing naturally. The length of the body should be the same as the height at the withers (front shoulder), and the length of the front legs from the elbow should be about equal to the depth of the body (chest) at that point. The Hungarian Standard gives exact measurements for important parts of the Vizsla.) Looking down on the back, the front portion should be fairly wide at the shoulders and they should be tight and the top of the shoulder blades relatively close (approx. 2 in.) with a narrowing at the loin and then the hip being wider with heavy muscled hind legs. The tail set should be lower than a straight line extended along the back and the tail docked leaving two-thirds of its original length still on the dog for good balance, and it should be carried high when active.

(Docking and cutting variations could be important factors relative to the carry of the tail.)

Looking from the rear, the width of the muscled portion looks as wide as the chest behind the front legs and the hind legs are set parallel to each other. As it gaits, the distance between the hind feet should appear to decrease so that it appears to single track, but not so that they appear to cross or come together, yet retain the illusion of being nearly parallel. The dog which hind legs almost meet at the feet when moving will spread with an increase of space between them until eventually at full driving power are parallel. It should be noted that the best balance and the most striking movement develops from single tracking. A wide spread of the hind legs induces a rolling motion of the body. When viewed from the front, the front legs should have the same type appearance as the hind legs in motion.

Locomotion and gait of the Vizsla are important to both show and field conformation. Both defy analysis except by an expert. In-depth scientific studies have been made on working dogs, such as sled dogs, for locomotion relative to energy used and endurance. There are good books available on dogs in motion which describe the mechanics of their motion and balance. Dr. Bernard McGivern, AKC judge, states that a good front combined with a good rear makes for good balance in movement as does a straight front with poor angulation. All dog breeds do not have the same standards for locomotion, and each one must be studied according to its individual idealized standard of perfection. They should now be compared to the Vizsla description which I have presented only as a general working guide.

A Vizsla with this physical description will have a striking appearance from any angle it is viewed, and will, when compared to others, look to you such that you derive a feeling of contentment or pleasure—call it

Angulation of the front shoulders, rear legs, chest, muzzle and head proportions can be seen on this young puppy. These proportions remained when the Vizsla was full grown, in this case.

showmanship or style for the lack of a better expression. *Do not* expect to develop an "eye" for Vizsla conformation overnight as it will take both time and observation to see that no two Vizslas look or act the same.

Whenever you can tell definite differences in body structure and can identify different Vizslas easily, this is the point where enough experience has been gained to recognize proper conformation in the breed. But it will take practice before you can develop confidence. The quickest and easiest method is to own several Vizslas at the same time, for being with them and seeing them constantly enables one to recognize their differences.

Sketch No. 1
It is difficult to visualize the perfect Vizsla, but Nancy M. Heinold, D.V.M. has made the effort with a female. Generally, females in the United States have better conformation and uniformity than males. This seemed true in Hungary, but their males were better than those in this country.

ILLUSTRATED CONFORMATION

All Vizslas are alike, yet none are. Strange statement? Yes, but is generally true. The standards do not make clear the differences between male and female characteristics, and there are several of these in the breed which are not related to sex. Differences between male and female characteristics in the animal world in most cases are significant.

Not all breed standards make distinctions between males and females. Then the only reference is to height and weight differences. There are also differences in heads, bones, bodies and muscles. A male and female Vizsla standing side by side are expected to be different — one is expected to have a masculine appearance. This difference is not always evident.

All Vizslas have minor and/or major faults which do not relate to the problem of sexual appearances. There is incomplete agreement between clubs responsible for generating breed standards as evidenced by the different breed standards. The problem is for you to sort out the *real* Vizsla, if you can.

Sketch No. 2

The narrow skull and short neck are illustrated. These two faults are not normally found together. Most Vizslas tend to be short in the neck based on my own observations. That being true, one could consider it more representative of the breed.

60

Sketch No. 3

The lack of a defined brisket makes the shoulders appear farther forward than normal. You will often see Vizslas that are pigeon breasted. Neither are typical.

Photographs do not help too much, for they are very misleading. My daughter, Nancy M. Heinold, D.V.M., was weaned around Vizslas. Since that time she has been having difficulty deciding whether to devote her life to the breed or to the veterinary practice. While in veterinary school, she must have spent much of her time sketching Vizslas. She made all the sketches in this chapter so that you might study both the good and bad physical features as they relate to the standards.

Some owners, breeders and judges are criticized for being "head hunters," meaning that they put more emphasis on a dog's head than anything else. The connotation is that they are prejudiced meaning there is more to a dog than the head. That is true, but I tend to defend their right to reject the entire dog if it has a bad head. That is the first thing one sees when approaching a dog and it is the most beautiful thing about one other than its temperament. That cannot be seen, but must be experienced which is what is meant by the statement: "All Vizslas are alike, yet none are." There are differences in temperament, but not

61

enough to keep you from knowing you own a Vizsla. Some owners let their emotions and sentimentality get in the way of their objectivity.

There are several malformed skulls in the breed. They have won show, field and obedience titles and some are just personal companions never campaigned. They should have been culled no matter how much potential they had or performance they accomplished in the name of the breed. It is very difficult to write standards for a large numer of imperfect representatives of a breed and their owners. This may be part of the problem in all the different standards in use, yet none indicate the desirability of a bad head (or eyes).

Some breeders are first time owners who bred their dog because they owned it. That dog, in their mind, represented the standard and they wanted another one without regard to its acceptability to the written standard.

Whenever a judge awards a blue ribbon to dogs having serious faults, he only encourages that owner to become a breeder of that dog and so, perpetuates the problems. We cannot improve the breed by using different standards or standard writers. Only conscientious owners, breeders and judges can help eliminate those problems illustrated in the accompanying sketches.

Sketch No. 4

The badly formed head. The sketch is an extreme example, but serves to illustrate what the head should not look like. While "running gear" is important to function, a dog's head is probably the first thing anyone looks at. There is no reason why it should not be true to type.

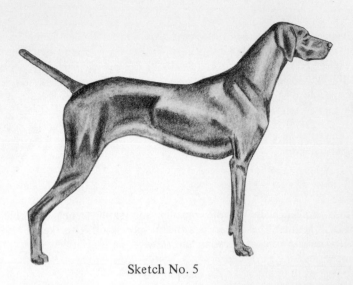

Sketch No. 5

The Vizsla should have a straight back. This sketch shows one with a dropped back that is also too long. It is not unusual to see this in the Vizsla breed.

Sketch No. 6

Long legs. This is most often accompanied with a shallow chest. The depth of chest and distance from the elbows to the ground should be the same.

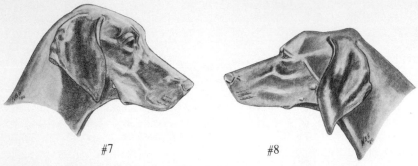

#7   #8

Sketch No. 7

A non-parallel plane of the muzzle and skull is not desirable. The Canadian standard best describes the proper skull. This sketch also shows the dog having excessive dewlap and flew.

Sketch No. 8

The enlarged frontal skull bones makes for a very ugly dog. This is just one example of the skull problems in some strains in the breed. They range from the look of a zebra to a Denny Dimwit skull. It is probably a recessive characteristic.

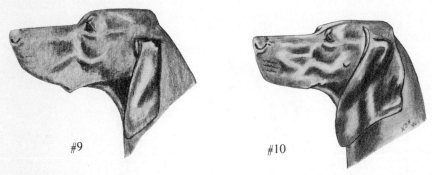

#9   #10

Sketch No. 9

A low ear set with excessive flew. This gives a hound appearance. There are a few dogs having this problem.

Sketch No. 10

Long ears are not characteristic of the breed. The Hungarian standard appears to be correct. Also see the photograph in this chapter showing correct and incorrect ear length.

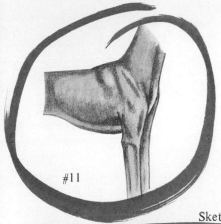

#11

#12

Sketch No. 11

Sketch No. 12

A normal shoulder angle. This is the most desirable shoulder structure on the Vizsla and other similar breeds. The layback angle is about 54 degrees with a 90 degree angle between the scapula and humerus.

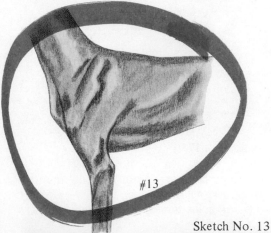

#13

#14

Sketch No. 13

The chest must reach the elbows and this one does not. A common problem perhaps in bitches more so than males.

Sketch No. 14

The front feet are turned out. This may not be of any concern in a puppy, but is faulty in the adult.

65

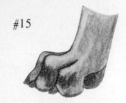 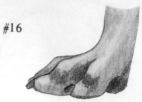

Sketch No. 15

The cat foot is preferred.

Sketch No. 16

The hare foot is not preferred. Splay feet can be a problem that is generally caused by environment. This kind of foot may not seriously affect the dog's field ability for short periods, but will not help it win blue ribbons in the show ring. The one most important asset to a dog's running ability is found between the ears which translates into **desire**.

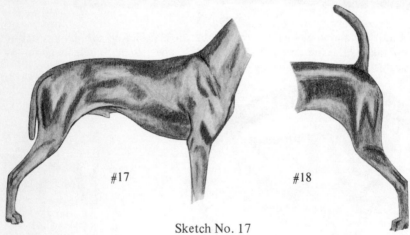

Sketch No. 17

The correct tail length for the adult Vizsla. In any litter, there will be differences in each puppy. Removing exactly one third generally results in most puppies in the litter having long tails. Each puppy's tail should be individually measured and one half joint removed in addition to the one third measurement so that most of the puppies will grow up with the proper length.

Sketch No. 18

The gay tail is a problem in some show strains. Some individuals in litters have high tails which may not be so desirable relative to the standard either. They do show much better than those with their tails at horizontal which often end up tucked while in the ring.

Sketch No. 19

Sloped croups often give a greyhound appearance to the Vizsla. This probably has nothing to do with the mention of greyhound in the Hungarian standard. These dogs run differently, perhaps with less effort, than one with the proper slope to its croup. The dog with a sloped croup has no problem with a high tail and is less animated than one with a normal slope.

#20

#21

Sketch No. 20

The straight stifle is not uncommon and with a dog like this it is not unusual for the hock to knuckle over. Vizsla stifles are not normally this straight, but range between this and normal. There is an occasional one that is over-angulated. It is difficult to present a dog with straight stifles in the show ring, but they adapt and compensate for this in the field.

Sketch No. 21

Not everyone knows a cowhocked dog. This is not a problem in this breed and seems to be a rare occurence.

CHAPTER 5

The
Vizsla - Owner
Relationship

CLOSENESS OF THE VIZSLA TO THE FAMILY

It is a traumatic experience for the Vizsla owner to learn that what he believed was a most uncommonly bright dog is a common occurence in the breed. It has been said by those who are not breeders, or have not owned show or field trial dogs that no man can own more than one good dog or one good wife in a lifetime, and he is fortunate to be that lucky. A new owner cannot believe that almost every Vizsla could satisfy the criteria of his "one good dog."

The Vizsla expects to be part of the *total* family life. He prefers to be treated as a member of that family. While this often does have disadvantages, the Vizsla strives to please in every way. He develops exceptional poise and a personality like behavior (imprint) that at times seems almost human which is seemingly reinforced by his ability to sense and understand the communication processes.

But the time comes when you must be away from home and your Vizsla cannot go with you. For this reason, it behooves you never to let your

Vizsla gain control over you during his early growth and development. The dog must learn to be left behind and, also, learn that you are always going to return. Control and discipline should be gentle, yet firm, but not physical in nature. Discipline is best accomplished with the trained use of words and voice inflection. Your Vizsla must understand what you expect from him by repetition. The dog soon learns the difference between a command and the asking or talking type request as a substitute command. Proper response is only gained through constant repetition, patience, kindness and reward. No other system will produce results without losing a great amount of confidence from the dog in return.

This is not to imply that the Vizsla is a sensitive dog, but he responds somewhat differently than you might expect. Normally we think of temperament as meaning predictability of his behavior in different situations although it is likened to personality in people. The Vizsla is different in that he will not generally take or accept rough treatment or physical abuse while being trained. Chances are that he will lie down, and roll those big rust-gold eyes at you and want petting although steadfastly refusing to obey any command. For the owner with vengeance, a hot temper or the thought for physical punishment, it is a lost cause.

The Vizsla is a discriminating protector. He does not possess an aggressive or vicious nature and will not normally go out of his way to look for trouble. A problem can occur when you think your dog is so friendly and gentle that you fail to recognize that his basic protective instinct does exist. Some exhibit it and others do not which is probably influenced by their environment, but most all Vizslas make good doorbells.

THE VIZSLA WITH CHILDREN

Just how does a Vizsla behave with small children? This important question has a different answer for each Vizsla you own or will own. All good, mostly, and for those who can, it is a very pleasant and rewarding experience to be able to enjoy a Vizsla and small children at the same time.

The Vizsla will tolerate considerable punishment and cruelty from a child and will often form a close and tolerating relationship with some qualified exceptions. I know of a few circumstances where children have been bitten after much torment by a particular child in the family, but one could not hold the dog accountable.

One common objection to the Vizsla can be noted when no children are present and the Vizsla becomes the center of the couple's affection. Then when a baby is born to them the dog is suddenly faced with a screaming "NO" at every turn. The dog expects to be first. Once given this position it

69

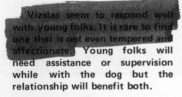
Vizslas seem to respond well with young folks. It is rare to find one that is not even tempered and affectionate. Young folks will need assistance or supervision while with the dog but the relationship will benefit both.

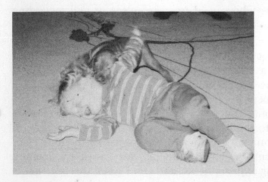

is hard to satisfy him with anything less than what he previously enjoyed. The best practice is to never allow your Vizsla to dictate under his own terms, but you should recognize the traumatic adjustment required for him with new situations.

Some Vizslas develop a deep sense of loyalty and protective feeling for the small child, but not for other members of the family.

It is normal for a baby to try to gouge or push a finger into the dog's eye, and he can do this with enough force to hurt the dog. This is probably the most difficult time for the Vizsla and small baby.

One of our Vizsla pups could and did drag a twenty pound sack of dog food across the floor before she weighed as much. A few weeks later while trying to play with my 4½ year old son, she jumped on him and knocked him down, and then playfully took him by the clothes and dragged him down our driveway. Up to that time we had admonished him that he should not fight back or hurt the puppy, but that type of play was too much. It was finally time for the boy to take his part, and the puppy soon quit when he started getting rough also.

Do not get a dog or puppy for your children and then expect them to understand proper care or to practice it. If you want a puppy for the children—fine—you should be prepared to care for it and supervise its freedom as well.

HOW MUCH FREEDOM

One might wonder how the Vizsla can tell its own kind, and this can be said of other breeds too, or how it can tell that some dogs are actually dogs and not some other animal. The Vizsla will generally accept other Vizslas in unfamiliar surroundings as if they had always been together. This may not hold true in a place in which it is possessive about such as its own home. The Vizsla is basically friendly and sociable with all breeds, but prefers his own. Vizslas will get into dog fights.

Actually one must not lose sight of the fact that a dog is a dog. That while they are predictable for the most part, each one can revert back to the feral stage of a fighting, teeth slashing wild animal which can be caused from either fear or injury. An owner would be naive not to recognize this possibility. The Vizsla can be provoked to this point with a lot of deliberate tormenting.

I once listened to a discussion between two breeders of a working dog breed talking about their dogs. One, evidently more experienced than the other, and who also raised other breeds, insisted that this particular dog breed was a born killer. He said that some innocent little happening could instantly provoke him to attack and kill—like a situation where a child, or animal, got hurt and was crying in pain. This is what I refer to when saying that "a dog is a dog," no matter what breed it is, any dog has a certain

71

potential for destruction—as well as the capacity to do so. It would be foolhardy to say that a Vizsla could not be provoked in a number of different ways to cause injury to another dog, person or some other animal. It is normal and natural for the Vizsla to kill fur type animals. Fear biting is also a normal provoked protective reaction.

Control your dog! This statement will be read time and time again. It means many things, but in every case it also means just one thing. No matter what else, the owner knows (or should) better than anyone else what his dog is or is not capable of doing. In a crowd, at a dog show or if there are strange noises, or any unusual experience, the owner should be aware of just what will disturb his dog, and he should be conscious of the need for restraint and correction at the proper time. Each Vizsla owner should know that his friendly dog might sometimes try to bite a person for no apparent reason and that it is a coward and sneak as well.

How much freedom? Allow your Vizsla just enough to maintain a healthy attitude, some exercise and under your control at all times. It is just that simple. Whenever your Vizsla is outside the house unattended he will eventually leave the premises. The chance that he will bother your neighbors is no longer in question—he will. From this point on you have lost control, but caught early it is not difficult to regain. If you do not regain the control and authority over your Vizsla he develops bad habits and will then become a neighborhood nuisance.

The respect or consideration that you have for your neighbors in the local community, or street, where you live will always be revealed by how you control your Vizsla. There is not a better neighbor than the dog owner who properly cares for his dog.

Mother will soon be telling these young "hoodlums" to "buzz off" as they are about ready for weaning. The diverse activity in this photo illustrates the potential trouble young active curious dogs can create when left entirely on their own.

Some states have leash laws and most cities do, but these are sometimes very poorly enforced—if at all. These laws are designed to protect you and your neighbors from the dog owner who has no respect for others living in the neighborhood.

A typical example of just such a dog owner appeared in my local newspaper under the column: "People's Forum"

To the Editor of the News:
To the Humane Society:

> I have always been under the impression that if your dog had its license tag, rabies tag, name and address tag on his neck, it was permitted to run and play freely. How wrong I was! I found out that a dog cannot be out of its yard without a leash. If they are not permitted off of your property, then why must you have a license?
>
> On a Saturday, our dog and several other neighbor dogs were out playing, one-half block from our house. These dogs play together late each afternoon for a short while, then come back home. They are properly tagged and ours is a snowy white and tan German Shepherd. Not a dirty, stray dog. Along came a dog catcher . . . . Well we had to pay $5 for the release of our dog.
>
> I have no idea what the money from the sale of dog licenses . . . . but you will never get another cent from me. I don't need a license for her to run and play in the house.
>
> People just don't put up a fence to keep in a friendly house pet, perhaps a mean dog it would be necessary.
>
> You see . . . our dog, likes to run and play as do your children. Also . . . .

If dog owners only could realize the number of stray and wild dogs that exist and the amount of damage done, they would declare war on all loose dogs themselves. No person is safe from a pack of wild dogs, and it has been proven time and again that such "pets" as described in this letter often turn out to be the pack leaders.

Many people are extremely afraid of dogs and some are petrified when confronted by even the friendliest dog. Your Vizsla can also cause car wrecks, so keep it under your control at all times.

The Vizsla owner should spend the time that is required to make his dog an asset to the community and welcomed by all—that is by seeing to it that his Vizsla stays home. Positive control is essential at all times.

If you are using your Vizsla for hunting, this positive control will prevent many problems in training it. It will also save many young rabbits in the nest, and protect the young quail and pheasant. The longer your Vizsla is allowed to have unlimited and uncontrolled freedom, the greater his desire will be to hunt for himself, and soon he will not hunt for you in the field. This is called self-hunting, or bolting when seen in field trials.

Control of your Vizsla inside the house should be just as positive as outside. An unattended dog can cause a lot of damage to articles of clothing and furniture, or raid the food shelves, table and whatever else is interesting and amusing.

THE TEMPERAMENT OF YOUR VIZSLA

Aside from the fact that the Vizsla's instinct and genetic make-up are for performing as a pointer and retriever, it seems that each one develops some special interest, and some develop more than one. You could call them idiosyncrasies.

Whatever the favorite interest, or pastime, that develops spontaneously, aside from hunting and retrieving, by your Vizsla you should develop it as much as you can. That is as long as it does not cause other problems or endangers its general well being.

It is important to recognize these individual traits as they occur and make the most of them. They manifest themselves in a number of ways, but usually in a form which suits the Vizsla's own entertainment and amusement. Some chase shadows and light beams, stalk and point houseflies, dragonflies, and other insects, climb upon some object, climb ladders, walk on narrow boards, talk or vocalize and any number of other things.

One of my male Vizslas would duck his head and go between my older boy's legs and rub his back while pushing upward at the same time. My son would try and keep the dog from dumping him sideways at first, but before long the two had together perfected their game. By this time my son was 11½ years old and weighed 69 pounds, and the Vizsla dearly loved to come in between his legs, arch his back and carry him off. This sounds inhumane and impossible, but in this situation it was neither. This was different than that of a boy riding a dog. **One cannot over stress the fact that this should never be permitted.** For the most part a dog will not permit it, but a reader should not think this is a cute trick and try to imitate it.

Whenever you notice one of these spontaneous acts—that is not harmful to the dog—use it as a take-off point to work with your Vizsla in play. If it is nothing more than your using a fishing rod with a hookless plug. The Vizsla soon learns the difference between play, amusement and business.

The Vizsla is an interesting and amusing dog to watch, and all seem to enjoy life from puppyhood to old age. It is easy to picture a young puppy playing, but it is more difficult for one to picture this in a dog after its prime of life. This is the Vizsla. He will play, chase, roll, play hide and seek, crouch and stalk, toss objects in the air to catch, lunge and run like a young puppy. Some will remain aloof and indifferent around other Vizslas who are playing in this manner.

The Vizsla uses his front feet to do all sorts of things in his play and living, and can use his mouth equally well. It will search and find some object on the bottom in shallow water and work with it just like a raccoon. Its love for water is fantastic. It will swim for hours searching for moving objects on top of the water, and even go under in an effort to catch fish, snakes, frogs and other water life; or, stay on the surface pointing and chasing all types of insect life.

It is never a surprise to hear from owners who tell about the different things their Vizsla does for play adaptation. It will not stay bored for very long because of owner neglect. This behavior is very refreshing and causes the owner to renew his love and appreciation for his Vizsla as time goes by, rather than ignoring him for the most part and tiring of dog ownership.

THE VIZSLA AS AN ACTOR

The movie of the Vizsla, a Dachshund and a falcon was purchased from Hungary and adapted for television by the Walt Disney Studios. Dr. Istvan Homoki-Nagy produced this and other excellent movies of the Vizsla. The Disney studios titled this one "The Legend of Two Gypsy Dogs", "Three Gypsies" and also "The Companions." This was a fantastic production and a moving story.

As an amateur movie photographer myself, I have tried my own hand at this work and am convinced that it is a very easy job to train and work with Vizslas. You need only to find one that has some ability, likes to ham it up, and one that will respond to and do many different things with his owner or trainer.

Most adults look upon a dog as just something else they own and consider it as being nothing special, but the young children are always somewhat in fantasy land and expect *their* dogs to perform as a Lassie or a Rin-Tin-Tin. The owner who thinks along these lines will certainly be rewarded for his efforts.

For the most part, story acting and movie production should be left to the professionals, but amateurs have made outstanding documentaries. The Vizsla is used in movies in Hungary and no doubt will be used here sometime in the future.

THE VIZSLA AS A GUIDE DOG

The happiest man that I have ever met was a blind man who found a suitable replacement for his deceased guide dog. Such a handicapped person is rendered helpless and is lost upon losing his dog, for he trusted it with his life completely. There is no depression or self-pity when a blind person has a dog that can take him, or her through the busiest downtown traffic, pedestrian traffic and through stores.

Of the several schools training dogs for the blind, Pilot Dogs, Inc., 625 West Town Street, Columbus, Ohio is one that fulfills this need for sight. It is a non-profit organization formed in 1950. It utilizes the state 4-H youth to raise the puppies and then takes them back for training at approximately one year of age. Vizslas are included in its training program.

Pilot Dogs experimented with many breeds of the proper size for suitability and trainability, but have yet to find the **ideal** dog and for this reason wanted to use the Vizsla. Pilot Dogs raises a few of their own dogs, mostly Doberman Pinschers, but also use German Shepherds, Laborador Retrievers, smooth Collies and mixed breeds.

Aside from a dog being trainable and of good disposition, at least one other factor is important. The appearance and cleanliness of the blind person. Loose dog hair of the long haired breeds musses up their clothing. Short dog hair might go unnoticed. It is difficult for the blind person to

The first Vizsla guide dog works with her owner, Linda Cunningham of Elyria, Ohio. Draga .was donated to Pilot Dogs, Inc., Columbus, Ohio by Ernie Davies of Columbus.

76

Linda Cunningham Giese of Lorain, Ohio poses outside Pilot Dog headquarters after receiving her second Vizsla guide dog which she received when her first Vizsla guide dog had to be retired. Mrs. Giese specifically requested a Vizsla replacement. Snoopy was raised by Jackie Rupert of Columbiana, Ohio.

Joseph Matthews of Columbus, Ohio works his Pilot Dog Vizsla donated by Dr. and Mrs. Paul Rothan of Cincinnati, Ohio. This was the sixth Vizsla Pilot Dog to graduate successfully as of February 1972.

properly care for and groom a long haired dog. The Vizsla easily meets all of these requirements but is unproven, since not enough have completed the program yet.

Pilot Dogs has taken a strong interest in the Vizsla breed, but not every one will make a trained dog for a blind person. It will require more than just a casual effort of random owners donating puppies. It has been proven by the people at Guide Dogs in California that better success was obtained by breeding for specific characteristics that were most important to this type work, and then utilizing a puppy training program before putting the dog with 4-H boys and girls. The puppy training program helps the young dog to adjust to the several transfers of ownership, and this is the biggest drawback to the Vizsla when it has not been properly prepared.

The Vizsla is sensitive to the change from a woman to a man and vice versa. It would also appear that the male Vizsla is better suited for this type work although there are no meaningful statistics to prove this assumption. Pilot Dogs prefer the female dog based on its experience.

The program is based on bringing the dog into training at approximately one year of age, and usually Pilot Dogs will not accept a dog for training that is over two years of age. The Vizsla seems to be too immature for this training at one year of age although a few have been successful.

One such Vizsla was donated from one of my litters and my wife and I were invited to visit with its new owner, Martin Lyons from Colorado at the Pilot Dog Center. He was an experienced guide dog owner, and was definite in his ideas of what he expected from his dogs.

At the request of his trainer, Dennis Jones, Mr. Lyons and Gypsy took a walk around the block for us. My family and I were just interested in talking with this remarkable man, but both he and his trainer were rather excited about the match-up, so we obliged.

No wonder they were so excited! As soon as the harness went on what appeared to be a playful puppy, Gypsy was all business. Never before had I witnessed such a performance—absolutely flawless and somewhat unbelievable. The occasional doubts I had in the past for the success or failure of this breed as a guide dog were gone.

Mr. Lyons was apparently aware of the tremendous potential of his dog immediately and said so. A few months later, I was in Colorado where he was invited to attend the Vizsla Club of America's spring field trial banquet to put on a demonstration. One of those attending the banquet had visited Mr. Lyons at his home earlier and told of the two crossing a narrow plank laid across an irrigation ditch as if both had sight.

After such a short association, Mr. Lyons was even more impressed with his Vizsla. He even stated more emphatically than ever before that the Vizsla was the perfect dog for a blind person.

A female Vizsla finished Pilot Dogs training program before this male did. It was donated by Mr. Ernest Davies who had a kennel near Columbus

78

Martin Lyons came all the way from Colorado to train with a Vizsla guide dog at Columbus, Ohio. Mr. Lyons had owned guide dogs previously and had a good idea what he wanted.

Mr. Lyons downs his Vizsla, Gypsy after she indicated the chair in which he was to sit. These photos were taken the last night of training in Columbus.

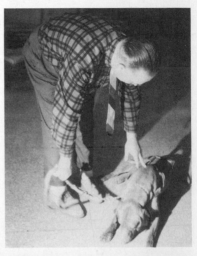

Mr. Lyons confers with Dennis Jones, Pilot Dogs trainer. Once a dog is trained by the staff, he is placed with the blind student to finalize training at the center.

While Gypsy playfully relaxes, Mr. Lyons tells the donor of his Vizsla how pleased he is with the progress he and his dog have achieved at the Pilot Dogs center.

at the time, Linda (Cunningham) Giese and her Vizsla, Draga, lived in Lorain, Ohio, until it was put to sleep because of an arthritic condition. She requested and got another Vizsla, Snoopy, which had just finished training. This dog was from the author's Ch. Szekeres' Kelet Szel and Dual Ch. Behi's Csinos Csiny, C.D. Another has finished in 1971 and is with Marcia Springton, Hudson, Ohio. She calls him Cosmos and he was from Ch. Rothan's Betyar Gaza, C.D. and Dual Ch. and Amtr. Fld. Ch. Rothan's Rozsda Kisanya, C.D., donated by Dr. Paul and Shirley Rothan of Cincinnati, Ohio.

Pilot Dogs, Inc. has continued to use Vizslas in their program and will continue this practice. They were absolutely amazed with the intelligence and progress made by a male donated from one of our litters. He completed the program in less than normal time, and was impressive while doing it.

Patti Overholt, Kettering, Ohio has completed training at Pilot Dogs. Josh, her Vizsla, was donated by the author and his wife. Josh was then raised by 4-H member Christina Puckett of London, Ohio. On completing the 4-H training phase, Josh went to Columbus for additional training with a Pilot Dogs instructor. This training is completed by the new owner with supervision from the Pilot Dogs instructor. Josh was sired by Behi Csecse Kovacs out of Ch. Behi's Jeri Redef.

CHAPTER 6

Housing
And
Care

THE VIZSLA IN THE HOME

Many Vizsla owners choose to keep their dogs in the house. These people agree that the real value of ownership comes with the association and experience gained in living with their dog. The task of educating the Vizsla while inside is a continuing one. The dog must learn that one place in the house is his "room," "home" or "sanctuary" where no harm or punishment will befall him. This could be a wire cage, basket, box, old chair, closet or anything permanent.

Many breeders prefer to use a wire crate for the dog's **home** in the house. Then, whenever the dog is left for short or long periods of time, he can be placed in the crate without his discomfort or your risk to clothing and furniture.

The age that a Vizsla can be trusted with the run of the house varies with each dog. Some puppies never show any destructive tendencies, though others are terrors. Once the Vizsla has matured enough to leave everything belonging to other members of the household alone he can be given his total freedom. But the wire crate (cage) always comes in handy whenever the owner wants privacy from his dog, has company, or does not wish to have the dog involved in some activities.

The Vizsla, as are all dogs, is prone to becoming spoiled and revels in it, so it is wise to always keep a firm hand on all situations to maintain positive control. Do not allow the Vizsla to become so stereotyped in his living and activity that he decides what is agreeable, or not agreeable.

Some owners have always claimed that keeping a hunting dog indoors ruins its nose. This is false — at least when related to the Vizsla being kept indoors. The worst possible situation would occur in the winter months where aritificial heat is used without adding moisture to the air. Moisture is important to the internal nose functions and operation, but there is no evidence that the lack of it prevents the dog from using his nose effectively.

One instance which was of concern to me happened when going to a field trial where the dogs were enclosed in the station wagon for a single stretch of 16 hours with heavy smoking. The next day my Vizslas exhibited superior scenting powers while dogs that had traveled less than an hour had difficulty finding birds. After that trip I was convinced that if my dog had problems that there had to be other reasons.

There is evidence that an apparent loss of scenting ability can occur if you keep your dog kenneled next to a pen of game birds or pigeons. It apparently causes the dog to lose its sensitivity to those particular odors or else he later refuses to associate that odor with hunting.

Whatever one might believe about the hunting dog and scenting problems related to the dog being kept in the house, there are more important considerations that should be evaluated first.

THE VIZSLA IN THE KENNEL

The serious breeder must make use of a kennel. While the Vizsla has little, if any, coat for real winter protection he seems to fare well in the colder regions. With no other choice, he will adapt to just about any situation. The kennel serves a basic need for the "big time" breeder. A kennel may not be used by the owner who is primarily interested in using his dogs for his own recreational interests or for an occasional litter.

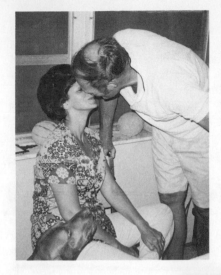

Above Rozsda "kisses" Dr. Paul Rothan. At left, Gaza protests the exchange of affection between Dr. Rothan and his wife, Shirley.

Every family must draw a line and decide when their Vizsla ceases to be "cute" or entertaining and becomes a pest. A little "begging" at the table can get out of hand. The author does not really have this problem, but arranged for a photo to illustrate that a Vizsla will make himself as at home as possible.

Even though you've had a hard day at the office, if your Vizsla expects a run when you get home, you'll get little peace until you have performed your obligation (or chore, depending on point of view).

The kennel can be difficult to manage in winter if it is not heated. Kennel run cleaning is a chore in warm weather and impossible in cold freezing weather. Excess food in the run is a problem in any season. Rats are attracted and may urinate in a dog pan which if not properly cleaned and disinfected can cause sickness and death to the dog; in the summer there are flies and other insects that are a nuisance. In some climates kennel screening is essential to the health and general well being of the dog.

Sometimes the choice between keeping the Vizsla in a kennel and the house can be just the difference in the amount of work and inconvenience. Keeping one in the house is usually cheaper.

Whenever a litter of Vizsla puppies becomes active, there is no other place for them except in some kind of kennel or enclosure. They will destroy a house. But they do need individual attention in their critical formulative weeks. The object is for the puppy to have other puppies for play and companionship and the mother serves the function of the older dog association for awhile. Approximately at seven weeks of age the puppy should begin its permanent association with man more so than with dogs or littermates. By three months of age it should be kenneled separately for best results, but should be allowed to play with other dogs (puppies) every day for its exercise.

The practice of chaining a Vizsla to a barrel on the outside is in violation of leash laws and city ordinances in some areas. Anytime that a child can walk into the area where a dog is kept in such a manner, there is the chance that the dog can cause serious injury to the child and the dog's owner is responsible for damages.

Any dog so restrained, or in an enclosed kennel, has a tendency to develop habits which are undesirable and over which the owner has no control. When more than one dog is kenneled together they have a tendency to become anti-social, and usually establish a pecking order over their kennelmates. This is not good for the Vizsla. Each Vizsla should have a place all to itself that it can call "home"—a safe place from man and dog so that it has a better chance of not developing bad habits.

FEEDING AND CARE

The reader will not be told how to care for and raise, *per se*, a puppy or older Vizsla. There are many good books and monthly publications on this and other useful subjects presented in great depth. This information can be obtained free by writing to most dog food companies and asking for it.

Here are some of the reasons why so many Vizsla owners prefer to have their Vizsla join in the family life rather than keep him confined to a kennel except when hunting.

Pleading at the door, a Vizsla just doesn't like to be left behind.

Even a Vizsla will be well-behaved on Christmas morning if there is a goodie likely under the tree.

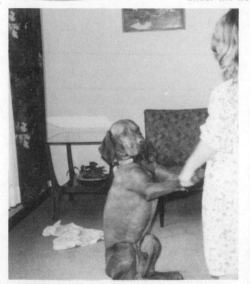

"Prayers" bed may not fit the dignity of a noble bird dog, but they help remind a little girl.

The Vizsla is athletic; especially when suitably inspired.

The reader should be interested and observant enough to tell if his dog is not healthy or is losing weight for no apparent cause. A dog is susceptible to many ailments and diseases, and most of all internal parasites. Some internal parasites are caused by external parasites. So when you feel that your dog is not up to par take him to the local veterinarian. Some owners take a stool specimen once or twice a year so the veterinarian can check microscopically. This is the best practice for the inexperienced owner, and in time, with experience, he will learn when not to call in the veterinarian, for minor ailments.

Once a Vizsla reaches his mature growth and weight, there is no reason why his weight should vary during its useful life span. His weight can usually be controlled with food alone, or a combination of food and exercise.

Every owner in time will settle on his own favorite commercial dog food for any number of personal reasons. Most like to think their decision is based on practical considerations. My Vizslas are fed a commercial dog food that is as complete as any on the market for providing the essential vitamins, proteins, fats and minerals (Crude Protein 26% minimum, Crude Fat 15% minimum and Crude Fiber 3.5% maximum). My Vizslas eat this food dry from the time they are puppies three weeks of age and are given no other solid foods except an occasional dog biscuit product. The fat content is most important to the Vizsla's weight, energy and coat condition. It seems to improve the skin's resistance to dermatitis also.

Some dog owners have and need just a vague knowledge of nutrition as they are close enough to their dog to tell when he needs more or less food. For a particular brand of food he may need supplements from time to time. Fat, protein and carbohydrates help the dog convert fat energy more efficiently and helps keep the protein (meat) in its digestive tract longer for improved utilization of energy sources. My dogs are given chocolate or hard candy in the hope that it will improve their energy for better endurance while hunting or field trialing, or to improve the utilization of stored fat. A lot of dog owners have various practices that they believe help.

An annoying problem with some Vizslas when used in field trials and to a lesser degree when hunting is excessive bowel movement while on a high bulk diet. For most situations it is important to have the bulk, but for the field trial work they should get a high protein feeding a day or two before competition and continued while in competition. It is also better to use a high protein and high fat diet while the dog is in hard training or hunting. Some owners claim that meat and spinach solves the problem of

86

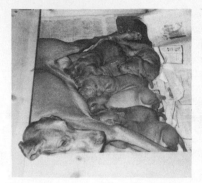

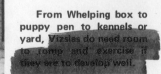

From Whelping box to puppy pen to kennels or yard, Vizslas do need room to romp and exercise if they are to develop well.

excess bulk and excessive bowel movements when the dog becomes excited when first starting to hunt. A low bulk diet will reduce the chance of irritation to the anal gland which can cause a dog extreme discomfort and nullify his effectiveness as a hunter or field trial competitor. If in doubt and inexperienced you would do well to experiment with the commercial dog foods when this appears to be a problem.

When your Vizsla's coat looks like it is losing the luster or sheen, a supplement of polyunsaturated corn oil obtained from the local grocery store can be added to its food. The skin and hair condition is an indicator of several different skin problems in the Vizsla. Sometimes the dull coat is the result of internal parasites.

No amount of food will correct a physical health problem. The mature Vizsla must be of the proper weight and conditioning to perform normally, and his weight should never vary by more than five pounds. Abnormal fluctuations are a sign of poor health, sickness, improper diet, improper exercise, internal parasites, and too much or too little food. It is wrong to always give the same amount (weight) of food at each feeding with no consideration to the dog's health, weight or the amount of exercise he is given. For example, it has been determined that it takes about 31 calories per day for each pound of the dog's weight, and for some dogs this might be too much or too little causing a subsequent increase or decrease in the weight if practiced without any other consideration. With a change in the dog's weight, the amount of food should be increased or decreased accordingly.

As an example, my puppies are started off with four feedings a day when weaned with the actual amount of food regulated according to their individual needs until only a *cup* per day is fed the mature bitch on a maintenance diet with a little more being required for a male because of his greater weight. Excellent results have also been obtained in the early growth stages using a self feeder.

It is difficult to comprehend how a dog can turn so little a quanity of food into so much energy when you observe the many many miles he covers while hunting.

The worst offense an owner can make is to overfeed, and the next is to underfeed. A working dog needs to be in better health and fed more than one that is worked only occasionally or not at all. While food not eaten should not be left for the dog to eat later (unless a self feeder is used), fresh water should always be available and the dog should normally be allowed to drink all he wants. The exception is that some of the dry foods cause an unusual craving for water that seems to bloat the dog, perhaps caused by the dry food swelling in the stomach with the added water.

Small pup benefits from early human experiences like playing with the author's son, Carl. This early association with humans is a great help in developing temperament as the dog grows.

Vizslas have the capability of entertaining themselves or engaging in group play if given half a chance. Of course supervision is still necessary to a degree lest the play get out of hand.

Young man realizes too late that a couple of Vizsla pups can be more than a match once he got down on their level.

Since some owners use self feeders they should be alert for this situation. It can be usually corrected by changing to another dog food.

When I was a boy living in the hills of West Virginia the feeding of my father's coon hounds was a chore in itself. My dad worked up all kinds of "dog food" mixtures and cooked them in the kitchen stove's oven much to the chagrin of my mother. He believed that a proper and balanced diet was extremely important to the dog's ability to hunt as well as its endurance. This job was very seldom left to anybody else except when he went off deer hunting every year for a week. During this time my mother

did the feeding and dad usually made sure that enough of his special food had been prepared before he left. She sometimes fed his dogs potato peelings and we kidded him about how well his dogs looked when the hunting was over with. His formula was successful, in fact too much so, for many times it took us a week to find his hounds. Usually they would be found in the woods still trying to hunt.

Before commercial dog foods were available, a lot of people had no desire to own good dogs because of the extra work of feeding them. Some breeders still prepare and mix their own food for economy, but it is no longer necessary, and the day is gone when feeding dogs homemade biscuits causes them to have "fits."

GROOMING

The practice of cutting toenails should be started shortly after birth and continued at regular intervals throughout the dog's life. While in the nursing stage trimming nails protects the bitch's breast area as well as the puppies from being scratched. As the puppy grows this practice helps foot development and in older Vizslas helps prevent broken or torn toenails. This is the most important requirement in Vizsla grooming.

Whisker trimming used to be done for show purposes but is no longer required so this practice is becoming increasingly rare.

Brushing of the coat helps remove dead hair and stimulates the skin and this should be done at regular intervals. At the same time the ears should be checked for mites and cleaned, then the dog checked for fleas, wood ticks and dog ticks.

Caring for the Vizsla is really not complicated or especially involved. The above problem areas and conditions are not the only problems possible but are pointed out to make the owner more aware of a potential problem. Certainly if you suspect that your Vizsla is not in good health, you should contact your veterinarian.

Occasionally mother will not be able to handle all her litter or her milk will not be acceptable. Then the breeder is faced with the tedious job of force feeding. It is time consuming and must be done often but for a well-bred litter it is well worth it.

Happy healthy 10 week old pup seems to reflect a proper attitude just sitting.

"Vizsla rash" is not especially pretty and it certainly can discourage a prospective puppy buyer even though the condition is only temporary.

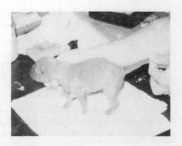

SKIN PROBLEMS

The Vizsla like all dogs, is susceptible to skin problems. An understanding of those affecting the Vizsla will help owners solve most of them.

The first problem may show up a few days after the puppies are born. Whatever is the cause, this skin affliction has been nicknamed the "Vizsla rash." Some puppies are affected less than others, but they break out in pimples, then sores that run, and later these dry up and scab over if the scratching can be controlled. It is not a very pretty sight especially when sores cover the entire body. This hurts sales for many weeks, if not permanently. Numerous breeders have come up with their own solutions, some cure it by internal treatment and some using external treatment. Each veterinarian gives different recommendations, and if he does not know that it is common in Vizsla litters, he should be told. Our best success has been using internal treatment first recommended to us by a friend, but more recently we get a prescription of antibiotics from our veterinarian.

If absolutely nothing is done about this problem with puppies, it seems to eventually correct itself except with an occasional puppy that has difficulty with one or two spots. Some breeders attribute this problem to the bitch being a poor mother, and not properly caring for her puppies by not licking them clean enough at birth and then later on. Others claim that this is the same as cradle cap on a baby. Whatever the cause is, there might be less of it with the dam that cleans her puppies exceptionally well and often. But a litter of mine was delivered by Caesarean operation and the dam was an excellent mother. All the puppies developed Vizsla rash. It was found when the puppies were about a week old, medication was started and they had a very mild case. This tends to disprove the claim that a poor mother or unsanitary conditions at birth causes it.

As the Vizsla grows older, it has other skin problems. Usually the veterinarian diagnoses it as mange, and more often as red mange that is "inherited" (actually infected at birth) from the dam. There are many different types of mange and other forms of dermatitis that the Vizsla may become infected with. It is true that a healthy dog with a healthy skin is more resistant to every disease. Further, the dog's diet is as important in the prevention of skin disorders as any other single factor.

One of the first signs of an ensuing problem is the appearance of dandruff behind the shoulders and on the back. This indicates dry skin which is easily noticed on the Vizsla, and especially with those kept in the house which could also be a contributing factor. Action should be taken immediately to restore the natural oils to the skin.

92

Bathing the dog in various chemical solutions for dermatitis of various types is sometimes recommended by veterinarians, but this only treats the sympthoms and provides temporary relief from itching. Most of all these skin problems will normally disappear by using the proper vitamins, oils and minerals in the dog's food. In spite of dog food advertisements that all the dog's daily requirements are added, the individual Vizsla's digestive system shows that some foods are better than others.

Once the proper skin and coat is restored to its natural color and luster, it is a very simple task to correct any skin condition.

A strange thing happens to the color of a Vizsla's hair in that it turns gray and then white. It happens at different ages from as young as two years to most any age. Usually a Vizsla begins to get gray around the muzzle and toes at around eight years of age. Since there is a wide variation depending on care, health, genes and others, it is impossible to predict when it might happen with the individual Vizsla. It is normal and there is no need to look for its cause. With a few Vizslas, this color change will cover its entire body.

EVERYDAY HAZARDS

Just about everything is hazardous to the general health and well being of a puppy. In many cases these hazards continue to exist for older dogs. The more active a puppy is, the more chance for a serious injury. The automobile is responsible for more injuries and deaths than any other single cause. The best performing field Vizslas come from the most active puppies, and no doubt caused their owners the most problems.

Next is the ingestion of objects and materials. Poisonous materials are the most serious, followed by ingested objects or parts of them. Poisonous reptiles and alligators are at the bottom of any list except where there is a chance of more frequent contact. Anyone living in such areas must take their chances when hunting and field trialing, but should use good judgment.

Active puppies can break bones, cut pads, lose eyes, tear or cut skin and muscles and lose teeth. The solution is not an easy one. Close confinement will not always prevent injury.

Toys are available for dogs that are nearly indestructible. They help relieve boredom which is the catalyst for getting puppies and older dogs into serious trouble. Never leave dogs unsupervised for very long and confine them in crates when you are not at home.

Owners like to make their puppy or older dog more comfortable by giving something soft to lay on. Bored dogs seem bent on self destruction, even if unintentional, and many will tear up such material and ingest some of it. Some material will not appear on x-ray film. Exploratory surgery is usually necessary to save the dog. I had one eat most of a bath

93

towel which was removed through exploratory surgery. Although her chances of recovery were slim, she did survive.

Dogs can get wood splinters lodged in their teeth, gums, throat and stomach from chewing on objects made of wood. Some materials and objects can be passed through their digestive system and some cannot.

There is no limit to what things dogs will chew and/or eat — such unlikely things as nylon hosiery, steel wool, electric wires, pot scrubbers, feces and the list goes on. Many of these common items can be life threatening. Dogs will also drink harmful substances which can cause serious toxic reactions over which you have little control.

Most plants are poisonous to dogs. The list is quite long. Never ignore toxic symptoms. Many owners do not know what poisonous substances, plants or animals kill dogs. The Florida toad has a 100 percent death rate. Snakebite need not result in death when properly treated.

Common plant stems, bark, leaves, berries, flowers, sap or bark poisons dogs. The list of these is long.

Lead poisoning results from the puppy or older dog chewing on something painted with lead base paint, soldered parts or lead in any form. Zinc and thallium are two other metals which are poisonous and are found in rodenticides. Avoid using any container coated with zinc.

Great care should be taken when using pesticides and herbicides where dogs can be exposed by walking in it, drinking, or eating it. Avoid field training where farmers are known to use these materials or dispose of the containers improperly.

The more active (frequently the dogs with the most potential) seem to fall victims to everyday hazards. A dull, lazy, puppy may be satisfactory for the apartment dweller, but is not suitable for field work. The best bred puppy for this work should have almost unlimited desire to play or otherwise be involved in some kind of activity.

Hye Tanya, owned by Sarkis Paparigian, California is one example. He said, "Tanya is so birdy that she would go through the camper screen window and work birds with screen and frame hung around her neck. Even in 90 to 110 degree weather; if I didn't stop her she'd work until she dropped." Tanya was in season and squeezed out of her kennel run April 1975 when she was hit and dragged by a car and severely injured. Her injuries were so extensive and serious that the veterinarian recommended euthenasia. Sark would not give up. He attended to her night and day even though she was expected to be a cripple if she lived. Tanya survived and whelped a litter of black puppies. After eight months of therapy by Sark, she was back near normal. She was later bred, and went on in competition to win her field champion and amateur field champion titles and in 1980 became winner of the Vizsla Club of America's Amateur National Championship.

Brush with the hair and regularly is all that need be said with a Vizsla. Really the breed is easy to care for in this respect.

There is no dew claw here and that is how it should be. If a Vizsla pup is born with dew claws, they should be removed at the same time the tail is docked.

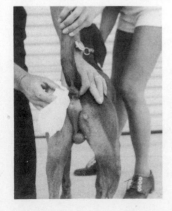

Expressing anal glands is not a pleasant job but if there is a problem, you will want to take care of it. These glands are located just below the tail and by gently "pinching" them an unpleasant smelling liquid is removed. If you prefer, a vet can do this or show you exactly how.

95

ANAL GLAND

The anal glands are a source of irritation for certain Vizslas and seem not to affect others. The problem can be detected by the carry of their tail, odor, scooting their rectum on the ground and excessive attempts at a bowel movement (especially when running in a field trial or at the start of hunting). Many dogs are able to relieve the fluid build-up with their bowel movements.

The owner should make a regular practice of expressing the anal gland once this problem is noted and is persistent. Males seem to be bothered more than females, and once the problem starts it never seems to go away permanently. The anal gland gets infected quite frequently and when it becomes a nuisance it can be removed by a simple surgical process.

A Vizsla bothered constantly with this problem may never carry its tail high. If it is in the habit of carrying a high tail and then you notice that it has dropped its tail and behaves as if its tail is broken or bruised this is usually the problem.

HEARTWORM

Heartworm is a relatively new problem for dog owners in the northern United States and parts of Canada. It is suspected that dog owners attending southern shows and field trials are responsible for its spread north.

Control of this problem requires that preventive medication be administered dogs all year in some areas, and during the warm months in all other areas whenever mosquitoes are active. Control can be provided for the dog with liquid or tablet medication each day. This prevents infection of Dirofilaria immitis and aids in the treatment of ascarid infection. These products may be obtained from your veterinarian after your dog's blood has been examined, and is negative.

Adult heartworms seriously impair the operation of the heart and they migrate up the pulmonary artery and clog the blood vessels of the lungs. This results in loss of body weight, dropsy, chronic cough, shortness of breath, muscular weakness, disturbances of vision, chronic heart failure and death.

Heartworm can be cured using chemical therapy when diagnosed early. These chemicals are toxic and must be administered with care.

96

Trimming toenails is not difficult. Get the dog used to it young and you will have less trouble. Once in a comfortable position, the obedient dog will behave allowing you to make quick work of this chore.

Whisker trimming can be done easily with a curve blade sissors and takes only a few minutes. For the companion dog this isn't necessary, but it helps improve appearance, especially for show competition.

Little Vizslas all in a row. This crew is just about ready to leave the whelping box and move into a roomier puppy pen.

Dogs thus treated have reduced lung capacity and are worthless for field work.

A blood test detects the microfilariae which appear within nine months of infection by a host mosquito. If medication is discontinued at the end of the mosquito season, new blood tests should be made before starting again.

Keeping a dog inside all the time, or in a screened area outside may be helpful, but not foolproof in preventing heartworm. The best solution is to have your dog's blood tested regularly and give preventive medication every day.

CORONAVIRUS

Coronavirus is not a mutant form of parvovirus or vice versa. This disease was isolated in 1971 and reached epidemic proportions in 1978. Drugs are not effective in its treatment, and there is no vaccine yet that provides immunity.

This disease is mainly transmitted through direct contact with infected dogs. Airborne transmission is considered possible. It is highly contagious and with immediate veterinary care most dogs recover in approximately one week. It has a lower fatality rate than parvovirus and is seldom fatal unless the dog has parvovirus or other bacterial infection. Coronavirus and parvovirus cause enteritis which is an inflammation of the intestinal lining.

Symptoms of this disease, that occur after an incubation period of one to three days, are diarrhea, depression, lack of appetite, vomiting and loose mucoid stools. Feces are usually orange, foul smelling and may contain blood. Vomiting lasts one day, but diarrhea may last for several days or weeks. Any dog having these symptoms should be taken to the veterinarian.

The virus can be killed by a solution of one part Clorox and 30 parts water when used as a disinfectant. Shoes should be treated, as well as a dog's feet when returning from dog activities.

PARVOVIRUS

Parvovirus is a new and deadly disease discovered in dogs for the first time in 1977. It is highly contagious, deadly and fast acting.

This disease is mainly transmitted through the feces of infected dogs, but can also be spread from saliva, urine and vomitus.

Most fatalities occur in young puppies less than six months of age with death occuring in less than two days. Entire litters have been wiped out. This disease causes enteritis.

Symptoms of this disease that occur after an incubation period of three to 12 days are diarrhea and rapid dehydration. The feces may be light gray or yellow gray with streaks of blood, or may be bloody. The dog's temperature is usually high. Affected dogs are susceptible to secondary bacterial infection which may result in death that could have been prevented. Drugs are not available to treat parvovirus. A dog having these symptoms should be taken to the veterinarian immediately.

All dogs should be vaccinated with killed or modified live feline panleukopenia vaccine. Two vaccinations are required to produce immunity for short time periods of two to six months with varying levels of immunity. Pregnant bitches should be vaccinated with the killed virus with vaccinations planned properly before pregnancy.

Bacterial enteritis has similar symptoms as parvovirus and requires the same treatment. Such things as internal parasites, poisoning and distemper also show similar symptoms.

The virus can be killed by the same solution as used for coronavirus. Preventive measures such as isolation, keeping your dogs away from the feces of others, changing clothing and treating shoes and dogs feet after returning from any dog activity or boarding kennel, and cleaning food and water containers with the solution are helpful in control.

CANINE BRUCELLOSIS

A bitch I own had one puppy the first time she was bred. She had none on the return service. She had ovulated the day before she was bred. Why did she fail to conceive? She was normal and healthy otherwise, although her estrus cycle seemed shorter and her vulva swelled less than others.

I never had been concerned with, or checked any of my dogs, for canine brucellosis. Since sterility in males and abortion in bitches results from this disease, I had her tested. She tested negative.

This disease is caused by a small bacterium, Brucella canis, recognized in 1966 at the James A. Baker Institute for Animal Health at Cornell University.

Both male and female dogs should be tested for this disease before used for breeding. Dogs with canine brucellosis appear healthy and lead otherwise normal lives. Infected dogs experience breeding problems and can infect the mate when bred and in other ways. Males are rendered permanently sterile.

Other diseases cause reproductive problems, but canine brucellosis should always be suspected whenever a bitch fails to conceive or aborts a litter.

The disease is transmitted through aborted puppies, placentae, uterine discharge following abortion, copulation and nursing primarily by ingesting the organisms from such contaminated materials or surfaces. Males shed infected urine for long periods of time.

Infected dogs should be neutered only after proven conclusively by all available tesing procedures. Any attempt to cure this disease is doubtful, but very, very expensive. There are no vaccines available yet. A kennels' breeding stock can be wiped out from this disease.

You should have your bitch checked several weeks before you expect her to start estrus and breed only to dogs proven free from this disease.

Should your bitch abort, keep her isolated, wear gloves when handling the soiled materials and disinfect everything with a good germicidal detergent, and consult your veterinarian immediately.

Each new dog should be tested before bringing it into your kennel or household. Few, if any, owners practice this. Since all dogs like to lick each other's vulva and anal area on occasion, and this disease can be transmitted to humans, it is safer to never allow dogs to lick humans in the face. Fortunately, people do respond to treatment and can be cured while dogs cannot unless a new drug is developed.

CHAPTER 7

Dog Shows

TRAINING FOR THE SHOW

The training of your Vizsla for the show ring should start earlier than any other training. It takes very little time and effort to handle and set up a puppy in a show position and to give it gaiting exercises. He should be taught in such a way that he really learns to love being handled. At this time it is important to take the puppy into crowds and enter sanctioned puppy matches in order to help build up the early experience so essential for a show dog.

The young puppy soon learns what a pleasant experience it is to have strange people come up, say a few nice words, and feel him all over. Delay this training and experience with people, and he may show distrust and be reluctant to allow a judge to touch him.

This training can begin the day the puppy is bought, for just a few seconds at a time, one or more times a day, but never in a forceful manner. The time for this work can be increased as the puppy grows older. Teach the puppy that by just being handled he is pleasing you and this will

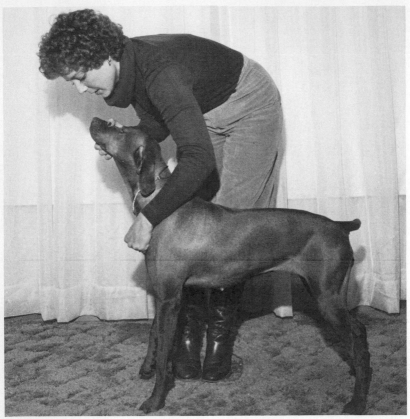

Setting up a Vizsla for show. Lifting front feet off ground to let dog know what is to come and what is expected of him.

encourage him to like the attention and relative immobility. This will require firm force from hands and voice both at certain times.

When setting up your Vizsla for the judge's inspection as described in the training situation, you should place the front legs perpendicular to the floor using the proper frontal spacing such that the normal angulation of the front leg and shoulder shows. The Vizsla's hind legs are then moved into a position such that its hocks are nearly perpendicular to the floor. This will vary with each dog for the best appearance. The dog should be held by the muzzle firmly with the right hand, or with the fingers in the hollow of the lower jaw and the thumb against the muzzle with the muzzle parallel to the floor. The back should be straight and with the proper rear angulation it should have a slight downward slope at the hips. The height of the rear end in this position will indicate, in part, whether or not the

102

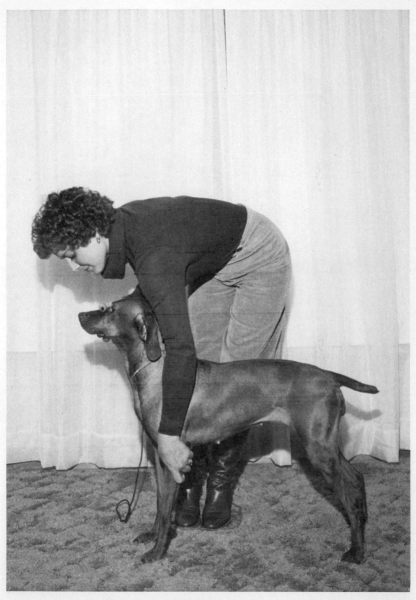

Setting up a Vizsla for show. Holding muzzle to shift dog's weight, slide hand down to set left foot. Repeat for right foot.

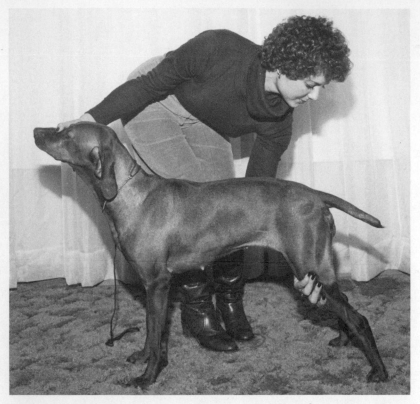

Setting up a Vizsla for show. Still holding muzzle, place left rear leg by reaching under. Be careful to keep front legs still. Repeat for left rear leg.

Vizsla has too much or too little rear angulation. None of these characteristics mean much until a puppy is over six months of age. You can see one part grow, seemingly so, while another stays unchanged temporarily. The puppy's progress is not too important until he is approximately a year old, although some Vizslas have completed their champion titles by this time. They were exceptional and were moved along at a faster rate.

In starting the set up position, the show lead may or may not be removed. In most cases the judge does not care in class judging where time is a factor. The judge, in class judging, cannot spend on the average more than two minutes examining and gaiting each dog. In Group and Best In Show judging the handler should use whatever time he needs to present his dog in the best manner and the lead is usually removed.

A good signal, which lets the dog know what is expected from him, in

Setting up a Vizsla for show. With all legs in position, handler steps to front and pulls ear leathers up to show judge the neckline.

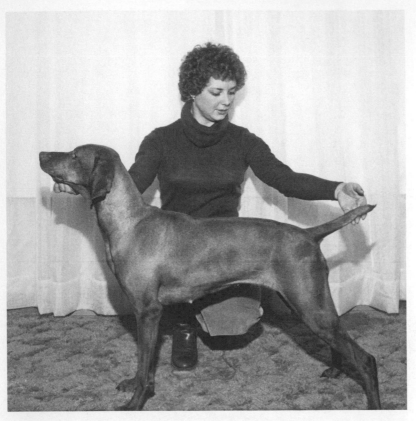

Setting up a Vizsla for show. Final position is shown. Optional method is to hold muzzle with right hand and tail with left while handler is on both knees.

starting the set up for show position, is to lift the dog bodily at the front until both legs are off the floor using both hands, or by just using one hand between the front legs, and then place both feet back on the floor firmly in the approximate position desired. This can be followed for the rear legs by placing your hand between the legs from behind. For some reason, this has a psychological effect on any dog and helps put his brain on the right track for what is ahead.

Then with the right hand still holding the muzzle, push the muzzle to the right, slide the left hand against the left shoulder and down the leg to the forearm and grasp it firmly, and then place the leg and foot in the proper position and position the toes straight forward; then with the right hand still grasping the muzzle push it to the left and then switch hands and repeat the same procedure for the right front leg. The moving of the

106

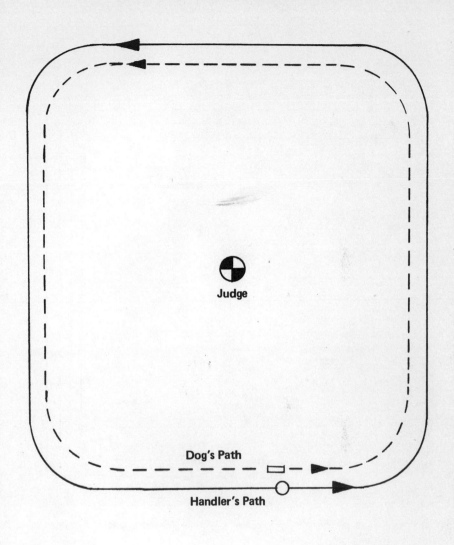

Judge

Dog's Path

Handler's Path

**GAITING DOG AROUND THE RING FOR THE BEGINNING
AND FINISHING OF JUDGING**
FIGURE 7-1

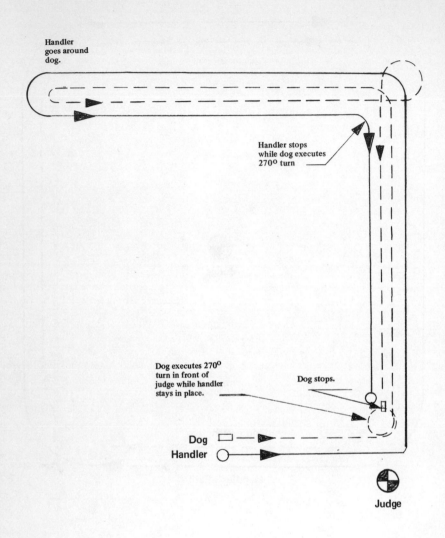

Handler
goes around
dog.

Handler stops
while dog executes
270° turn

Dog executes 270°
turn in front of
judge while handler
stays in place.

Dog stops.

Dog

Handler

Judge

GAITING DOG IN FIGURE "L" PATTERN
FIGURE 7-2

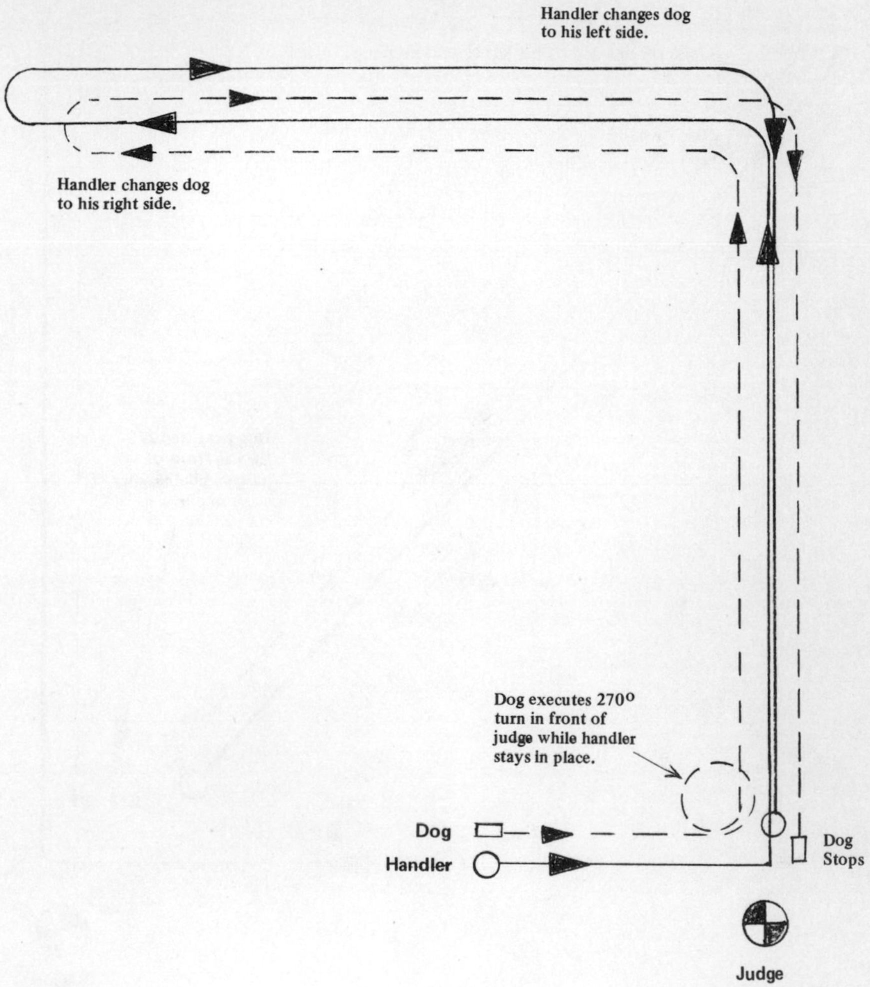

Handler changes dog
to his left side.

Handler changes dog
to his right side.

Dog executes 270°
turn in front of
judge while handler
stays in place.

Dog

Handler

Dog
Stops

Judge

GAITINGDOG IN FIGURE "L" PATTERN
FIGURE 7-3

109

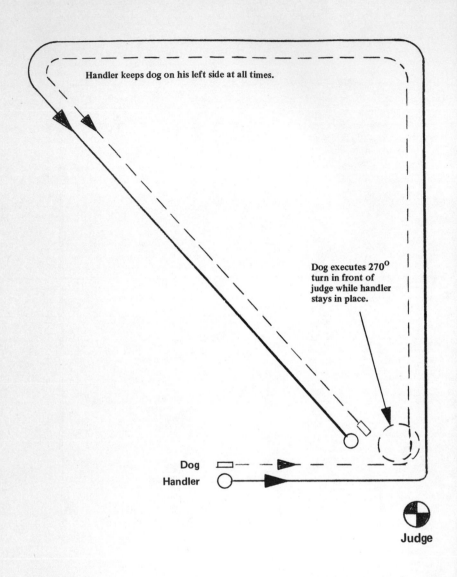

Handler keeps dog on his left side at all times.

Dog executes 270° turn in front of judge while handler stays in place.

Dog

Handler

Judge

GAITING DOG IN TRIANGULAR PATTERN
FIGURE 7-4

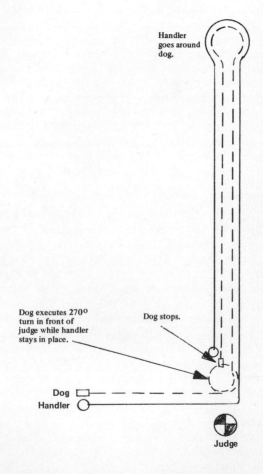

Handler
goes around
dog.

Dog executes 270°
turn in front of
judge while handler
stays in place.

Dog stops.

Dog

Handler

Judge

PACING DOG UP AND BACK

GAITING DOG IN UP AND BACK PATTERN
FIGURE 7-5

muzzle left and right shifts the dog's weight to that foot and insures the handler that it cannot be moved. As each of these procedures are completed the weight is shifted back to both feet equally.

Then squat on your haunches, or get down on both knees, and reach under the dog using the left hand, still holding the muzzle with the right hand, and position the left rear leg again with the toes straight forward; now position the right leg using the left hand. While still holding the muzzle with the right hand, stroke the left hand down his back ending it by raising the tail and back stroking it on the underside (against the hair.)

Once satisfied that all feet are in the proper position and the back line is good, while holding the muzzle with the right hand, step directly in front of the dog; then with both hands pull the ear leathers forward and with a movement of both hands move the head and neck laterally in both directions without displacing any of the feet; then return to the normal position at the right side of the dog and stroke the back again.

Talk to the dog in a nice voice while doing this if you wish. The handler should now be on *one knee* and the dog should be fixed in both physical position and mental attitude such that he will not move until allowed to do so by its handler.

Gaiting in the ring begins in a circular counter-clockwise pattern as shown in **Figure 7-1** with all other dogs in that class. Then after examination, they will be gaited individually as shown in **Figure 7-2**, **Figure 7-3**, **Figure 7-4** or **Figure 7-5**. One pattern not shown is the "T" gaiting pattern which is similar to the "L" patterns shown in **Figures 7-2** and **7-3**, except the handler continues the same distance in the other direction. The "L" pattern may be executed either way as with the triangular pattern in **Figure 7-4**. The up and back pattern, **Figure 7-5**, is usually requested of certain dogs after doing one of the other gaiting patterns. It is also the pattern which takes the least amount of time.

In the ring remember to listen carefully to the judge's instructions for the type gaiting pattern he wants. The angulation from the side, front and rear, and the general attitude and style (showmanship) of the dog are determined partly from the gaiting exercise in addition to individual comparison to all other dogs in the ring.

The object in training for the gaiting exercise is to produce (develop) a good stride or movement of moderate speed, with the hind legs being the driving force with the front legs in perfect harmony. In gaiting, the trainer can do much to improve the style and prevent such things as paddling with the front feet, padding, crabbing, bolting, body roll and otherwise not going in a straight line. The dog should be next to the handler without a taunt lead and oblivious of anything else except to demonstrate that he enjoys what he is doing. Normally the dog is on the left side of the handler while gaiting for the judge in such a position that the dog's side

Various scenes of Vizslas being shown in the ring. Both gaiting and individual inspection is shown.

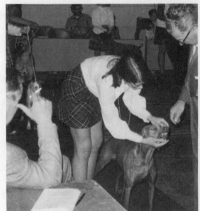

It is not uncommon when the judge has a close decision between two dogs, to have them shown side by side so he can more clearly compare them.

AMERICAN & CANADIAN CH. JOSHUA MELTO
by Am., Can., & Mex. Ch. Johnson's Titian Charger out of
Am. & Can. Ch. Taunee's Cariann

Breeder: Lynn Worth   Owner: Cheryl & Joel Feldman

profile is not obstructed from the judge's view. The handler should try to keep his dog's top line in line with the judge's eyes when moving straight away or coming directly toward him, and then stop the dog (without being told) at least six feet in front of the judge on finishing the gaiting pattern. Sometimes the judge will request that the dog be *walked* in one of these patterns.

As long as the dog is in the ring under judgment, the handler should never be between his dog and the judge whether it is gaited, set up, at rest or while other dogs are being judged. Exceptions will be noted usually in Group judging which has a large number of dogs.

This describes the basics to teach the Vizsla the show position and subsequent examination by the judge or a helper. It takes time and patience to train your Vizsla without causing him to hate the show. This training is completed by having a helper, and preferably different strangers, examine the dog in the same manner as the judge would. This

CH. GREAT GUNS RIDING HIGH
by Ch. Brok Selle Son of a Gun out of Olca Barat Gunners Mate
Breeder: Dr. & Mrs. Maynard Wolfe   Owner: Thomas F. Kepler

CH. TAUNEE'S LOKI SANTANA, C.D.
by Ch. Glen Cottage Loki Barat, C.D.X. out of Ch. Cariad's Gaybine, C.D.
Breeder: Linda Greenfield   Owner: Marion I. Coffman

person should approach from the front in a direct manner with the back of his hand extended for the dog to inspect (smell). The handler should then show the bite and always maintain positive control over his dog while the helper inspects the muzzle, ears, neck, shoulders, chest, belly, back, hip pressure resistance, rear leg muscles and testicles. As the helper approaches the rear end of the dog, the handler steps in front of his dog and pulls the ear leathers forward for the helper to examine the neckline. As the helper returns to the front, the handler steps to the rear of his dog while insuring overall control. Then the helper should step back and look at the profile (side view) of the dog while the handler establishes the normal set up (show) position.

Whenever this entire operation can be done without the dog moving its head, body or feet and looks happy just doing it, then this part of the training is complete.

Gaiting should be taught when the Vizsla is still a puppy. It is just a matter of getting the puppy to walk at first and later run along on a show lead. Allow it to get used to something on its neck beforehand by putting a collar on for a few days before this training is started, and then continue the lead training on a regular basis. Using the gaiting patterns of Figure 7-1, Figure 7-2, Figure 7-3, Figure 7-4 and Figure 7-5 work with each one for the perfection of both you and your dog. Practice gaiting in both clockwise and counter clockwise directions. This work is more difficult for the handler than it is for the dog.

ENTERING A DOG SHOW

The most descriptive rules for showing a dog in competition are published in booklet form by the American Kennel Club. Each owner should have a copy of this pamphlet obtained free by writing and requesting it. Join a local all-breed kennel club, so that expert help is available to you.

Showing begins wth the various classes such as Puppy, Novice, American-Bred, Bred by Exhibitor and Open mostly with a division of sexes. Each class winner in each sex is judged for **Winners** (dog or bitch) and **Reserve Winners** (dog or bitch which will win the points in case the **Winner** is ineligible). After this judging sequence is completed, the two **Winners** go into the ring for competition with **Specials** (Champions) and the sexes are mixed from which the judge picks **Best of Breed, Best of Opposite Sex** and **Best of Winners**.

The **Best of Breed** winner then joins all other winners in the sporting breeds in Group competition where four placements are awarded. The

CH. RENBROK'S SAND PEBBLE
by Ch. Great Guns Riding High out of Renie's Amber Gypsy, C.D.
Breeder: W. S. Brown & W. S. Brown, III   Owner: Linda Promaulayko
Photo: Nica Lyons

CH. MARY MAC'S RUSTY BABE, U.D.
by Ch. Buda's Pest of Zanger out of Visse's Mihaly Draga, C.D.
Breeder: Sandra & Richard Visse   Owner: Mary V. Blank

Group Winner then joins representatives from the other Groups for **Best in Show** judging where the judge selects from the seven competitors.

Points are awarded for **Winners Dog** and **Bitch** and in Group and Best in Show when the points awarded in the breed are less. It would be very unusual for a dog to win points for Best in Show for usually the maximum number of five points will be represented by some breeds in the Group.

DOG SHOW COSTS

All-breed dog shows are big business. Some owners show dogs for a business (breeders and handlers), others for a hobby and still others just to have something to do on the weekends for recreation. Then, too, it is a wonderful family sport when the children also participate in Junior Showmanship classes or regular class judging.

The cost to show a Vizsla varies considerably. Only after learning the finer art of showing and the dog's conformation can the owner-handler be considered proficient.

There is also the extra benefit of personal satisfaction derived in showing your own dog but some owners seem to get nearly the same satisfaction (some even more) when they hire a professional handler to do all this work for them. Perhaps some owners just get too nervous in the ring and cannot show well.

The professional handler charges a fixed fee for showing a dog in a class. Additional charges are incurred as the handler proceeds from the **Breed** to the **Group** and on to **Best In Show** competition. Also, the professional handler earns and is entitled to all prize money.

The professional handler usually takes the dog and keeps it with him for part or all of his show career. He will charge for board, and may also charge other fees for grooming, although very little grooming is needed for the Vizsla. The toenails require regular trimming.

Whenever the cost of the professional and the owner-handler are compared, the professional handler has some definite advantages. First, he will usually win more often than the owner-handler, he fares better in the Group for the added distinction of competing for Best in Show honors.

The professional handler, through his constant exposure on the show circuit, is usually at the right place at the right time. He makes an individual dog look better than the owner-handler does as a general rule.

An estimated cost for the professional handler to finish a Vizsla Champion, including entry fees, handling charges and board while competing where other Vizslas are being shown on a regular basis is under

AMERICAN & CANADIAN CH. VALHI'S STICK TO YOUR GUNS, C.D.
by Ch. Great Guns Riding High out of Magda Szereto
Breeder: Patricia Kepler   Owner: Julia & Ron Bonar

AMERICAN & CANADIAN CH. CARIAD'S ALYDAR LOKI SANTANA
by Ch. Taunee's Loki Santana, CD out of Ch. Eszaki Cinka Panna
Breeder: William E. Wion   Owner: Judy Harvey

$1,500, with some dogs finished for much less. The cost of a champion will vary with the inflationary and deflationary trends in the general economy, and with the frequency, number and quality of the competition.

The professional handler's cost might appear high at first. But no matter whether the owner or professional handler does the showing, it requires a minimum of three shows, under different judges, with each one having five point majors to finish a dog. It does happen in three shows occasionally. A handler could finish two dogs at the same time by one taking the major for Winners Dog or Winners Bitch and the other dog taking Best of Winners. It requires a minimum of two majors of three to five points each and an accumulated total of fifteen points under three different judges. The two majors must be under different judges and any additional majors under these judges count only as points toward the champion title. At some time in the future these American Kennel Club rules could be changed or modified in the best interest of the sport, but the basic framework for the rules would not change.

The cheapest cost to the owner-handler would be if he finished his dog in three shows which would amount to less than $100, and a professional handler's cost would be based on the three shows and the time he had the dog in his care, but it would amount to less than $350. Some Vizslas have finished in four shows and others at one year of age or less, but so much depends on how many Vizslas are being shown at a given time in one's area and the overall quality.

The professional handler should properly inform his customer of his total fees and show practices. For example, sometimes there is no advantage of showing a dog where there is only the one Vizsla entry, and in this situation the owner pays the entry fee, but not a handling fee.

Some sanctioned puppy matches offer constructive help and training for the novice handler, and it is recommended experience before going to the all-breed point shows. The cost for entry of each puppy in a sanctioned match is small when compared to a point giving show.

The all-breed show entry fee is $12 - $14 per dog and more for the first entry in a class. An additional entry fee for the same dog in other classes is less than the initial one. The first entry fee usually entitles the dog and owner admission to the show. Some of the prestige or larger shows have higher entry fees.

The point rating is scaled different relative to the number of dogs being shown in specific sub-divided geographical areas in the United States. The Vizsla point scale varies from less than ten dogs for all areas for the five point major; but mostly is as follows: 2 dogs, 1 point; 3 dogs, 2 points; 4-7 dogs, 3 points (major); 5-10 dogs, 4 points (major); 6-16 dogs, 5 points (major). Dogs as used here refers to male or female,

CH. CSINOS V HUNT, C.D.X.
by Ch. Csisckas of Goncoltanya out of Asta V Schonweide
Breeder: Joan Hunt   Owners: Paul & Shirley Rothan
VCA Hall of Fame, 1980

CH. SZEKERES' KELET SZEL
by Ch. Hunor out of Ch. Szekeres' Kezdet
Breeders: John & Priscilla Carter   Owners: B. C. & Hilda Boggs

AMERICAN & CANADIAN CH. TAUNEE'S CARIANN
by Ch. Glen Cottage Loki Barat, C.D.X. out of Ch. Cariad Gaybine, C.D.
Breeder: Linda Greenfield   Owner: Lynn Worth

CH. PARADOX RAKETA KEP
by Ch. Great Guns Riding High out of Behi Csecse Raketa, C.D.
Breeder/Owner: Drs. Nancy & David Heinold

CH. SAGEACRE WHISPERING WIND
by Ch. Miklos Heliker out of Ch. Sageacre Vidam Gazember
Breeder: Connie Johnson   Owner: Francine A. Gorman

DUAL & AMTR. FLD. CH. VICTOR OF HOLZWORTH FARM
by Fritz of Connlly Dale out of Sally Creek
Breeder: Patricia Connolly   Owner: Sheila Holzworth

CH. MASHA'S SUPER SARA
by Ch. Maximillian-Ridgewick Clan out of Ch. Sascha of Kislany
Breeder/Owner: Cynthia & Frank Hibler

CH. BRAHMS GOLDEN EXODUS
by Brahms V Redway out of Golden Miss
Breeder/Owner: Beryl K. Taylor

CH. GRETL VON TATABANYA, C.D.
by Debreceny Magyar Red out of Ch. Aranyos Adeleen
Breeder: Dale Piper   Owner: Valerie Piper

AMERICAN & CANADIAN CH. VIZSTA'S MAGNUM RYDER
by Ch. Miklos Heliker out of Ch. Vizsta's Jezza V Exodus
Breeder: Beryl K. Taylor   Owner: Gail Sanford Uprichard

CH. FUTAKI NYIR OF POPPLE DUNGEON
by Bratt's FK Crackerjack out of Fld. Ch. Futaki Lenke
Breeder: Mrs. Alice Hadik & C. M. Smith, Jr.   Owner: Betty & Carlo Zezza

CH. BEHI'S RHINESTONE COWBOY
by Dual & Amtr. Fld. Ch. Victor of Holzworth Farm
out of Fld. & Amtr. Fld. Ch. Behi Csecse Csiny
Breeder: Bernard C. & Hilda R. Boggs   Owner: Shirley Rothan & Hilda Boggs

CH. DEBRECENY DEZSO
by Herzog Schloss Loosdorf out of Ch. Besa V. Debretsin
Breeder: Art & May Carpenter   Owner: Gary Carpenter

CH. REDEF'S J-PACES RUSH, C.D.
by Fld. Ch. & Amtr. Fld. Ch. Randy Duke
out of Fld. Ch. & Amtr. Fld. Ch. Behi's Piri Csiny
Breeder: Jerry & Carol Feder   Owner: Fran & Pat Johnson

although there are from time to time slight variations in major point scales for the two sexes in a few areas.

The number of points earned relative to the number of dogs competing in each designated area is revised every year by a formula designed to make competition meaningful when compared to the other geographical areas and the total dogs shown each time.

The equipment needed to groom a Vizsla for the show need only consist of toenail clippers, file (optional) and brush. Some owners never groom their dogs before a show — and win. It can be a matter of choice, but the well-groomed Vizsla looks better, has better eye appeal and in the long run should have a better chance of winning.

It is essential that the handler be neatly dressed when showing his Vizsla. Dog shows are not sloppy and hap-hazard by any stretch of the imagination and those who attend one for the first time will be impressed with the general good appearance of dogs, owners and spectators. When showing, pay attention to the manner and dress of the judge and pattern after him. If the judge is working with his suit coat off, then it is acceptable for the handler to do likewise. Shorts and slacks are strictly in poor taste for women handlers, and so should the micro-mini-skirt, but some women do wear them. It is a good idea to observe the professional women handlers dress habits and pattern somewhat after them. Wash and wear suits are best for men. Show the judge the courtesy he deserves by proper dress in the ring — and remember, no smoking.

Another item of expense involved in the dog shows is usually a night or two in the motel at each one. If one considers the extra cost of motel, food and banquets involved in going and showing his dog, along with the other incidental car and out of pocket expenses, then the cost of using a professional handler would begin to look cheap when just one dog is involved. It is more expensive whenever the entire family goes. Then there is always the lure of going to prestige dog shows like Westminster, the International, Bermuda and others. Many show dog owners like to consider these shows as their "vacations." Whenever this point is reached, the cost of showing by counting pennies has long been forgotten.

Each owner will perhaps reflect back at times on what a championship title cost — or what is this Vizsla champion worth? A friend, for example, might be interested in showing and wants some information, and depending on whom he asks, he can get several different answers — all true, but no Vizsla owner has a good estimate of his total investment — whether it be tangible or intangible costs incurred. The investment could be as little as $350 or several thousand dollars.

128

DUAL & AMATEUR CH. PIROLIN
by Dual Ch. Futaki Darocz out of Wag Inn's Kedish
Breeder: Elizabeth Zezza   Owner: Carlo & Elizabeth Zezza

CH. BOLEN'S GEZA BELL
by Am. & Can. Fld. Ch. Ripp Barat out of Bolen's Athena
Breeder: Robert & Helen Butts   Owner: Mrs. Connie Johnson

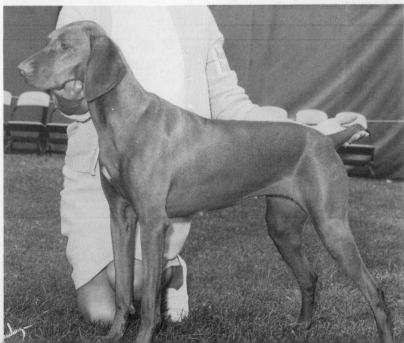

VIZSTA'S MAGYAR WARRIOR
by Ch. Miklos Heliker out of Ch. Vizsta's Jezza V Exodus
Breeder: Beryl K. Taylor   Owner: Jack, Marcia & Tracy Hanson

CH. VIZSTA'S JEZZA V EXODUS
by Ch. Fleckes of Sageacre out of Ch. Brahms Golden Exodus
Breeder/Owner: Beryl K. Taylor

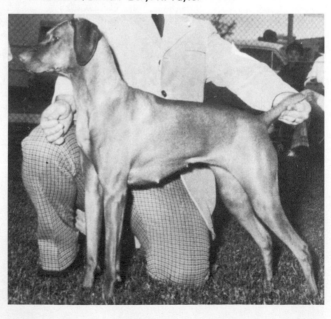

130

CH. MISS MIDGE OF BEHI, C.D.
by Dual & Amtr. Fld. Ch. Victor of Holzworth Farm
out of Fld. Ch. & Amtr. Fld. Ch. Behi Csecse Csiny
Breeder: Bernard C. & Hilda Boggs   Owner: Patricia & Wayne Leis

AMERICAN & CANADIAN CH. FIELDSTONE'S NAGY EGY
by Dual & Amtr. Fld. Ch. Brook's Willie Whompum
out of Dual & Amtr. Ch. Rothan's Rozsda Kisanya, C.D.
Breeder: Shirley Rothan & Hilda Boggs   Owner: Sandra & Keith Lasure

CH. PIPER'S PEPPERMINT PATTI
by Fld. Ch. & Amtr. Fld. Ch. Earl's Red Rogue out of Piper's Lady Lucy
Breeder: Valerie S. & Harry Piper, III   Owner: Linda L. Kelly

CH. PARADOX MAGAS SZALAD
by Ch. Great Guns Riding High out of Behi Csecse Raketa, C.D.
Breeder: Drs. Nancy & David Heinold   Owner: Carol Croninger

CH. SCHNAPSNAMEN SPEAK-EASY GIN
by Ch. Sogens Fussy Fellow, T.D. out of Ch. Schnapsnamen Apricot Brandy
Breeder: Susan Flowers & Susie Goldberg   Owner: Susan Flowers

CH. POPPLE DUNGEON TOLGYFA
by Dual and Amtr. Fld. Ch. Pirolin out of Ch. Uropuyka, C.D.
Breeder: Elizabeth S. Walton   Owner: Betty & Carlo Zezza

133

CH. CARMEL SAGE
by Ch. Trisha's Bogart by Loki out of Starvonn Von Schonweide
Breeder: Carl Schleh   Owner: Bonnie & Mike Letscher

CH. SCHNAPSNAMEN APRICOT BRANDY
by Ch. Golden Boy Tito out of Lauri Lee
Breeder: Jon B. Held   Owner: Susie Goldberg

CH. MIKLOS HELIKER
by Ch. Sandor V. Debretsin out of Tina V. Debretsin Macias
Breeder: Vivian & Mike Macias   Owner: Jeannie & Herbert F. Heliker

CH. MELTO'S CSABA ZENESZ
by Ch. Johnson's Titian Charger out of Ch. Taunee's Cariann
Breeder: Lynn Worth   Owner: Nica & John F. Lyons
V. C. of A. Specialty Winner, 1979

CH. FIREBRAND'S CONSTANT COMMENT
by Ch. The Magician of Melto's out of Ch. Firebrand's I Dare You Darling
Breeder: Pam Pierce   Owner: Elizabeth Anderson
First female Best In Show in the United States, 1980

CH. RUSSET LEATHER WILD EMBERS
by Ch. Russet Leather's Ricca Luna out of Ch. Rotkopf's Dancing Wheat Seek
Breeder/Owner: Beverly Sartor Wanjon.

136

CH. RENBROK'S TARA HEGYI
by Ch. Great Guns Riding High out of Renie's Amber Gypsy, C.D.
Breeder: W. S. Brown & W. S. Brown, III   Owner: Carol Vola

CH. FLOWERS FORGET-ME-NOT
by Ch. Rotkopf's Dancing Wheat Seek out of Ch. Schnapsnamen Speak-Easy Gin
Breeder: Susan Flowers & Susie Goldberg   Owner: Susan Flowers

Some owners are overly attached to their dog and will spend money for a long time without getting the required points for a champion title, and fail to recognize that they are showing a very bad specimen of the breed. Most owners will give up and get another Vizsla, or even a dog of another breed, for very few dog owners like to lose in show competition.

ADJUSTING TO DOG SHOWS AND JUDGING

While all breeders should avoid "fads" with a minority breed, such as the Vizsla, handlers and breeders should especially refrain from merely showing or trying to breed the dogs the judges put up consistently even when they know for a fact that the judging is incompatible with the Vizsla standard.

For example, breeding large Vizslas just because that is what most judges seem to prefer. Breeders and owners must recognize that at the time the breed was first recognized and judged at dog shows by the American Kennel Club that few, if any, of the judges licensed for the breed had ever raised Vizslas — and most had probably never seen the Vizsla outside of the ring before their first judging assignment.

It is important to recognize that these judges did influence the size of the Vizsla breed for several years. But judging even in the field must start using relative unknowns of one particular breed. Further, the language

Bear in mind that these first Vizsla breed judges were the "old timers" developed through other breed ownership. Their preferences were based on such experience and their concept of the proper gait and corresponding motion of the dog's body had been fixed.

The difference in the trunk and gait of the Vizsla breed, as opposed to other pointing breeds, can be observed at dog shows. The majority of the Vizslas still single track as opposed to double, or wide, tracking (placement of the feet). In the Group judging the same situation prevails. It is extremely difficult to consider that single tracking is a serious fault in the Vizsla breed. Once a handler decides that single tracking is his dog's problem in not winning, he may decide to try breeding for a wide rear gait. All other factors being equal, the single tracking Vizsla shows the best grace and poise.

From left to right are Am. & Can. Ch. Vizsta's Magnum Ryder, by Ch. Miklos Heliker out of Ch. Vizsta's Jezza V Exodus, owned by Gail Sanford Uprichard; Am. & Can. Ch. Vizsta's Tazz V Exodus, by Am. & Can. Ch. Vizsta's Magnum Ryder out of Vizsta's Inga Krishna, owned by Beryl Taylor and Am. & Can. Ch. Vizsta's Shannara V Exodus, by Ch. Miklos Heliker out of Ch. Vizsta's Jezza V Exodus, owned by Beryl Taylor. All three were bred by Beryl K. Taylor.

Some field trainers use roading harness to develop a dog's lungs and muscles, thus causing the dog to double track due to the force needed to pull the load and maintain normal balance at the reduced speed. By removing the load the speed increases, but the muscles have been set more or less to pull the load.

A Vizsla that single tracks while gaiting and then stops without placing his legs in a firm supporting position could be faulty. A dog that either single tracks or double tracks and produces motions wrong for that type gait such as rolling, fishtailing, bouncing or others could indicate faulty angulation. Other indicators are loose shoulders and paddling while gaiting.

It should be understood that the Vizsla show "Champion" title has been earned by some not so perfect Vizslas; look at the dog, not his titles.

There will be moments of happiness and disappointment in dog shows. No matter what the difficulties are, and there will be many, the owner-handler must learn to take most everything he encounters in stride. Whatever one hears (from the losers) about the crooked business, the novice handler should stick it out until he reaches the point where he is able to evaluate for himself both the good and bad features of the sport. The owner-handler who does not learn to find a sense of satisfaction and enjoyment after this point should quit.

SHOW WINNERS AND BREEDERS

The general clean looks and aristocratic bearing of the Vizsla could eventually make it one of the winningest short haired dogs in both Sporting Group and Best in Show. It will require that his owner go to every show all year long and use the best professional handler. This will take a lot of money and wealthy Vizsla owners will have to be the major source of this exposure. The average owner is fortunate if he can show his own dog at those shows within a three hour drive from his home.

Rating systems are invented from time to time and used to tell the owners how successful their dogs are. The one used most in shows is the Phillips Point System developed by an American Kennel Club licensed judge. It is based on a dog winning its respective breed judging first, a win or placement in Group and Best in Show. The system is based on the number of dogs defeated at each show and for the year. A Best in Show win gives the dog credit for beating every dog entered in that show. A Group win would give the dog credit for winning over all the dogs shown under the breeds represented by the Group. Lesser placements in the Group results in subtraction of the number of dogs in the breeds that were

140

CH. GOLD STAR'S VALDAR
by Ch. Brok Selle Son of a Gun out of Ch. Gold Star Kandi
Breeder: Virginia Tinnesz   Owner: Mr. & Mrs. Anton J. Tinnesz

CH. SZEKERES' CSILLAG
by Dual Ch. Futaki Darocz out of Szekeres' Kezdet
Breeder: John & Priscilla Carter   Owner: Alexander F. Tolgessy

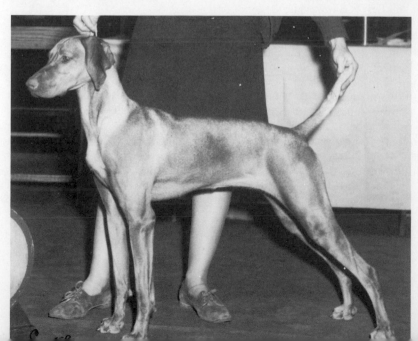

not defeated in the placement. Top producing sires and dams are determined by the number of their offspring that earned champion titles for that particular year.

Any rating system has its limitations and does not measure the actual worth of a dog. So many variables are involved such as the number and quality of Vizslas being shown, the subjective opinion of the judges, and how often an individual dog is shown. Once a dog is declared the winner in the breed, group or show, in a rating system all these intangible factors are forgotten. It is purely statistical from that point on and many people interpret the standing as sacrosanct.

Before national Vizsla show specialties came into being, the best prestige win in terms of publicity for the breed was the Westminster dog show in New York City, and probably still is. Ralph Wilson and his Ch.Pal Joey received a great amount of publicity for the breed before he was retired from the shows after failing to win at the first Vizsla Specialty (1965) at the Chagrin Valley Kennel Club in northeastern Ohio.

Mrs. Ann DeBarr of Mexico City brought her Champion Piros of Mile High to the Specialty in 1966 so she could compare her Best in Show (Mexico) winner with other Vizslas.

The first Best in Show title in the United States and Canada was won in 1970 by American, Canadian and Mexican Champion Napkelte Vadasz Dalos which failed to win at the 1970 Specialty in Illinois. He was the biggest winner in the shows since the breed's acceptance by the American Kennel Club. These included 22 Group placements and three Best in Show wins. His performances have since been surpassed in breed, group and Best in Show wins.

Ch. DeBreceny Dezso owned by Gary Carpenter of California had 15 Group placements and one Best in Show win in 1970. He was the only United States Bred Best in Show and the only one to win a specialty show which he did in 1968 and 1970.

Two of the most prominent breeders from the early 1950's to 1970 are Osborn's Kennels in Minnesota and Hunt's Kennels in Tennessee. Both have produced a large number of Vizslas of which many were owned by show people who campaigned them to their champion title. Mrs. Joan Hunt was active in shows and finished the second Vizsla champion just after the breed was recognized with Ch. Csicskas of Goncoltanya. It is probable that Dr. Osborn has been the most expert breeder of Vizslas in the United States and he produced some of the best dogs for show and field while never becoming interested in anything other than field competition himself.

A review of past breeders who contributed to the breed's success in dog shows indicates that most have come and gone without having developed a strong line of winning dogs.

142

Showing your dog in motion is as much a part of exhibiting as "stacking" your dog to advantage. Since locomotion is so important to the function of the dog, most judges will put a careful eye on this aspect of judgement.

Although Dual Ch. Behi Csecse Gyor Lab is not being exhibited along the ocean, her natural gait is an excellent example of good extension.

Several owners in California have maintained a good record for several years of breeding on a low level and of getting their dogs into the hands of people who have shown them. It is this group of owners who have earned the highest ratings in show under the Phillips System. Art and May Carpenter have been active since before 1960 with their Vizslas and have an outstánding record of Breed and Group wins. The Best in Show winner is owned by their son, Gary.

The Futaki line started by the late Bela Hadik, of Chester, New Hampshire has an impressive record of show champions. He was one of the most serious and successful breeders with emphasis on the dual dog for field and show.

The Vizsla breed did not progress with just a few large breeders, but with the unpublicized hard work and dedication of a great many people. The names of its breeders are constantly changing. Some are getting too old to continue, some have died and some lost interest.

The once rapid growth of the breed has leveled off for several years, and there is no indication that this will change in the near future.

We are beginning to see a more pronounced polarization between show and field owners, although there is a high interest in a dual dog. With the new title of "Obedience Trials Champion" maybe other owners besides Robert Costa will make their Vizslas Triple Champions as he did in 1980 with Cariad's Kutya Kai Costa.

First Vizsla

to be shown in the U.S.

SARI
by Tomy Szeged out of Boeske
Arrived in U.S. October 7, 1950

Shipped by Emmett Scanlan, who obtained the Vizsla from a Hungarian refugee, to his friend, Frank J. Tallman of Kansas City, Mo. While waiting to be shipped, Sari had two puppies, Shasta and Tito.

145

American & Canadian Field Champion Ripp Barat, owned by Betty Kenly, was trained and handled in open competition by Paul Sabo, Jr.

Reilloc's Tyke, CDX demonstrates form during an informal training session. Tyke is owned by Dr. Linda L. Collier.

146

Fieldstone Duke's Fanny, owned by Kristin Keller, is ready to play ball . . . she must be a Pirates fan.

Vizslas stand heat well allowing that proper conditioning has been accomplished. These hunters are at the Gladwin Recreation Area in Michigan taking advantage on an August "put and take" pheasant season to maintain the conditioning of their dogs.

These four Vizslas "ready to load up" are owned by Dr. Paul and Shirley Rothan. From left to right are Ch. Csinos V Hunt, C.D.X., Ch. Rothan's Betyar Gaza, C.D., Rothan's Csinos Tuzijatek and Ch. Rothan's Rozsda Kisanya, C.D.

Catching and fetching frisbees has caught on as a pastime for a number of dogs. Vizslas are no less quick to pick up on this fun "game" and it is a good way to keep dogs active off season. Fleeta shows her style here during a demonstration at the "Wonderful World of Dogs" exhibition.

Everyone is taken in by a puppy. These two are no exception.

Barsony Hobbit Vadasz, C.D.X. shows how easy executing a jump can be. He is owned by Jayne and Howard Coneybeare.

This is a breeder's dream. A contented mother and a healthy litter of nice uniform puppies.

Ch. Melto's Csaba Zenesz is pictured with Karen Lyons. The Vizsla is an adaptable companion taking all members of the Vizsla family group as his.

Reilloc's Piri, C.D. points with style. Piri is by Dual & Amateur Field Champion Victor of Holzworth Farm out of Field Champion & Amateur Field Champion Behi Csecse Csiny. She was bred by B. C. & Hilda Boggs and is owned by Dr. Linda L. Collier.

Am. & Can. Ch. Sandor Miklos Ishi Debretsin, C.D.X., by Ch. Sandor Miklos Heliker out of Brute's Kipper Z Ravenwood, was bred by Pat & Gene Burleson and is owned by Hazel & Gene Tisdail. He has the distinction of being the first owner handled Best In Show.

Buffy's Kopr Jena Luv, the personal gun dog of Sandy Brygider of Norcross, Ga. has received a unique tribute from her owner. Her photograph (above) has been engraved on a custom made .410 double manufactured by A. Francotte & Co., Liege, Belgium.

Manov Selle Olca shows the white which characteristically appears on a Vizsla in advanced years.

The author's Vizsla, Trixie gets to know Snoopy a little better during the Ohio State Fair. Trixie demonstrated some of the capabilities of her breed at the "Dog House" which is a focal point for dog activities in Ohio.

153

CHAPTER 8

Training
And
Communicating

INTRODUCTION TO TRAINING

The novice oftentimes cannot restrain himself in his eagerness to prove, to himself or others, how his dog behaves or performs. Maybe it is because he thinks and wants to believe and prove that his Vizsla is the best and it might have that potential. But this cannot be proven, or demonstrated, the first time out in competition. Neither can it be proven by taking the dog into unusual or strange surroundings and expect him to behave normally. Most important of all, an owner should never be so eager to win that he would turn over his dog to a professional handler, or experienced amateur, the *first* time he enters him in a dog show or field trial.

When we expose a Vizsla to new things and experiences, it is better if he has the "crutch" of a friend. In this way he can better react and behave in a rational manner without fear from being among, or only with, a stranger under disturbing situations. Such experiences, if traumatic, as this

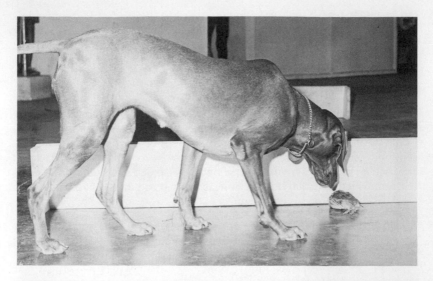

Above Trixie "does her thing" at the Dog House and below she completes her retrieve to the author. While demonstrations are often very artificial, they do make the public aware of the breed and they show what can be accomplished with a dog.

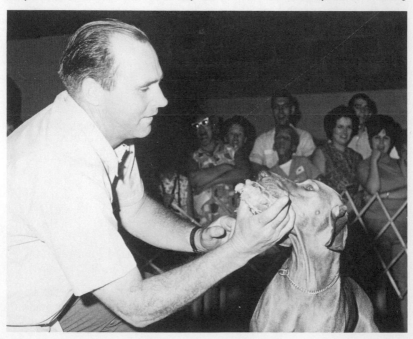

can result in fear biting, gun shyness, cowing, tucking tail, running and hiding and many many others. Each owner or new handler should establish himself as a friend and protector to his Vizsla first and foremost—develop his trust. Then and only then can the dog be expected to challenge new situations.

Once trained sufficiently, it is no problem for the dog to do this same thing with other people who may not know him so well. The Vizsla *reacts* to commands then in much the same way he does with his owner. Certainly there are situations and individual dogs that will not require such caution, but the novice will not usually recognize these. It takes experience in each activity and knowledge of dog behavior (each dog's temperament) such that it is possible to estimate a good or bad reaction to every given situation immediately.

Alone, in a friendly environment (atmosphere), a Vizsla may do many wonderful things, but remove him from this and he may do nothing. This serves to demonstrate a common fault with most dog owner-handlers. They will train under very limited conditions, then expect performance at the same level in a strange area, strange surroundings, and among strange people. Even we cannot do this! To further complicate the matter, the Vizsla has an excellent nose, so when his owner secretes an odor that he has long ago recognized as one indicating that the owner is mad, nervous or in a strange situation he may react unfavorably.

The best practice is to treat your Vizsla as you would a developing child and learn to expect a reaction to every new situation. What age child? Below the age where it knows the meaning of your words and while depending on the tone of voice rather than a generic meaning and understanding. Or below the age that reasoning commences, whichever is preferred. Only with extensive exposure to the same repeated situations that involve commands of some type will the handler develop his dog into a trained one.

A good example for visualizing this type of behavior is for the owner to take his dog before a strange group in strange surroundings and attempt to put on demonstrations that involve previously trained tricks, variations of obedience exercises or field pointing demonstrations for the first time. Unless previous training has included this type audience the owner should not expect his dog to perform well. There may be the exception of the showoff or the extreme intensity of involvement in the act that will exclude all else.

This same behavior can be expected at the first field trial, or dog show even though there may not be the audience and closeness involved. The

Training for demonstrations or hunting starts here. Puppies "point" a pheasant wing on the basement floor. This is more constructive play than training per se.

The author still uses the bird wing outside and for more advanced lessons. The procedures are more formal and more is expected of the dog, but the plaything of puppyhood becomes a bridge to the Vizsla's mission in life.

157

dog must learn to ignore some distractions and like the activity that is being done under those conditions.

Because of the lack of understanding of the training principles and dog psychology by the owner, this is often a cause for him believing that his dog is stupid, shy or has a poor disposition. The real problem was that the dog's owner did not know how to train and control it, control his own emotions or did not realize the real cause for the initial temporary or undesirable form of behavior.

The owner must be patient, have understanding, and offer both controlled good and bad experiences for training, but never good and bad experiences for the same command. Care must be used such that bad experiences contribute to the positive development of the Vizsla. Always be able to control the dog while under training such that its training is always in a positive sense. This is quite difficult and is not to be underestimated by the new trainer. Later on, after the training is fixed and disobedience is in evidence, then physical punishment can be a useful tool for control and correction when properly applied.

It is better to ignore incorrect performance, than to compound it by taking the wrong action. No two Vizslas will react the same way. Timing of corrective action is extremely important. It is false to believe that a Vizsla can associate correction or punishment at any time other than the *exact* instant it has done wrong.

Once the general physical surroundings are fixed and accepted in the dog's mind, then additional training is possible. Each situation and command can be a building block for the next. The handler should always watch his dog's reaction for the telltale clue that something in its behavior or performance is about to go wrong.

Forced training is not a solution, whether physical punishment is involved or not in accomplishing a particular objective with the Vizsla. It is wrong to beat and physically abuse one's Vizsla to vent off anger and lack of self control when training him. This cannot accomplish training purposes and will destroy any build up of *desire to please* which is so important to performance, class, style and good manners in a Vizsla. Stop—cool off.

Another common fallacy is the belief that one Vizsla can learn from another one while under uncontrolled conditions. While it is normal for a young dog to steal a point early in his development, it is not normal to expect self correction of this fault. Respect for the other dog's point must be taught either by the trainer or the dog that first established the point.

Demonstrations and performances are fun and can be very satisfying. This is also an excellent way to show our breed to others.

Top is the MVVC booth at the Wonderful World of Dogs in Dayton, OH in 1979.

This shot was taken at the Dog House at the Ohio State Fair in 1979.

This booth was at the International Folk Festival.

Performing at the International Folk Festival.

A Vizsla must be faced with a large number of repetitions (rote) such that he learns to respect that training where the most need for restraint is required. It is entirely too much to expect the completely trained Vizsla to continually undergo intimidation by a bunch of young pups, for example, playing havoc with his point. Soon, the best training is lost for that pointing dog. *Caution* must be exercised in training two, or more, bird dogs together. It is very easy for each one to learn to *depend* upon the other, or for one to develop a leader pattern and the other a follower pattern and never learn to hunt and perform independently and intelligently. They will develop as many bad habits under these conditions as when hunting alone without supervision.

There is no practical method for separating different trained commands for obedience, hunting, field, water or home use because they overlap. A distinction is made between obedience and manners for the Vizsla. Obedience is doing what is ordered, and manners is the way or style of performance associated with the order or trained behavior. The trained ordered requirement is the obedience part of a Vizsla, but the manner and style is that esthetic part that is so important in obedience, hunting, field and water work. Some owners train for all of these while others simply train for subservient behavior.

Vizsla owners can find many books that give precise step by step procedures and training methods for every test required in all levels of obedience training for trials held under the rules of the American Kennel Club. But *obedience* for the Vizsla breed is a complete schedule of training since it is essential for use in control and direction of the dog while hunting and doing other functions for his owner.

This chapter treats the training requirements for activities and provides a schedule essential for developing and training a Vizsla. It is important to note that there is a distinct difference between what is ordered and what is not ordered but developed by certain handling, petting, grooming or living association.

"Go to bed!" This is an order and requires that the Vizsla obey it. It is also a command and must therefore be enforced any time the dog does not reasonably obey the person giving that command. The Vizsla must be taught that a *command* is to be obeyed and the trainer must learn not to use a command that he does not intend to enforce, or is in no position to enforce. Obedience to specified commands is the only proven method effective for dog control.

Whether a person owns a hunting dog, cattle dog or guard dog, there are certain basic commands that the dog must learn to obey without fail.

160

Vizsla has advanced to field work on live birds. The wires in background insures that dog will not "dive in" and grab bird. Preventing bad habits is easier than curing them.

Above Vizsla points pigeon. These birds provide a good substitute for the real thing for training.

Author and son approach a point. When breaking a dog it is important that the first birds be downed. So two gunners properly placed are good insurance of training success.

The hunter, using a Vizsla, does not want it to jump up and grab a mouthful of tail feathers just as he is preparing to shoot; the cattle man or sheepherder does not want his dog to move or chase his stock without some useful purpose; and, the dog being used to guard or protect must learn that only certain things under given conditions are to be attacked as well as to what degree sometimes.

CORRECTION OF THE DOG

Entirely too many owners make their dogs come to them and then administer punishment for some misdemeanor and believe that the dog should understand why he is being punished. Some trainers use slingshots as a means of extending their arms, others use the check cord and still others use the electronic shock collar. Yes, some trainers use their shotguns for this purpose. In the house where the crate is used, or for that matter if the dog is loose, a kitchen detergent plastic bottle can be filled with water and used to squirt a harmless stream of water on the dog followed by the command "No!" for undesirable behavior, and this method is very effective. It is especially effective in stopping undesirable barking. The dog does not ordinarily associate the person using such corrective devices as harming him as he does with close contact physical punishment. The command "No" is by far the best and most universal command for effective control. Some other methods of correction are no better than the person using them.

VIZSLA OBEDIENCE TRAINING

Obedience trials offer tests that most any owner can do reasonably well after his initial training under formal instruction given by obedience clubs, and these clubs are not restricted to just a few breeds as are field trials but are open to all American Kennel Club recognized breeds and the miscellaneous class of dogs.

These trials offer the only opportunity for direct comparison of all different breed performances under a given set of rules and conditions. They provide the environment for the handler to train his dog, or more exactly to determine how well the handler has done his training. There are rewards given for both the dog and handler.

The Vizsla is easily trained. He is also a dog that is respected in obedience trials and has made a perfect score of 200 in this competition.

Author's wife is working on honoring or "backing" which is essential manners for field trial work. The woven wire barrier is still protection for the bird being pointed to insure the dog will not be successful in catching game if he breaks point. This allows attention to be diverted to the backing dog or the pointing dog without having to worry quite so much about the other dog.

Vizsla owners have not heralded it as any "wonder dog" in obedience yet, so very little attention has been focused on it by the news media.

Some Vizslas appear to be extremely bored in the obedience ring as if it insults their intelligence or alters their purpose in life. If so, it can only occur because *that* Vizsla is not sure in its own mind that what it does is pleasing to its master (handler), for this breed is basically happy in whatever pleases it and its master.

In 1968 approximately 112 Vizslas competed in obedience trials. Of this number, 52 (46.4%) placed in their class (first to fourth), and this cannot happen unless the dog breed has a high trainability quotient. Then in 1971 there were 118 Vizslas competing with 40 (34%) placements of which 10 were for first place.

Titles were won in all categories of obedience work in 1968: Companion Dog (C.D.); Companion Dog Excellent (C.D.X.); Utility Dog (U.D.); and, Tracking Dog (T.D.). Usually a dog in competition will get his "leg" (a term used to indicate that he scored over 50% on all required exercises with no less than 170 points total out of a possible 200), but the competition for the four placements is always very keen and requires nearly a perfect score. Often a score of 195 will not earn the dog an obedience class placement.

Not every owner is capable of accepting the obedience training himself at first so that he can train his dog, but all dog owners should try, since the real measure of success must be evaluated by the owner receiving the training.

In obedience training, as with all kinds, firmness in voice is learned properly or it is never learned. This is one of the major weaknesses with the owner in training his dog. He does not develop the voice command indicating authority for ease of training and control, or else his dog develops a mental block once he knows he can take advantage of the situation.

It takes a Vizsla no time at all to learn that first he hears a command and if he does not respond immediately, the correction comes through the training chain, followed by praise, which is a very important point, no matter how poorly the dog just performed. Far too many owners think that the chain collar is a device with which to choke their dogs into submission, but this only teaches a dog to continually strain against it. The Vizsla learns that the choke chain collar causes him no undue hardship considering that he does not *have* to obey. The *owner* must learn that the noise of the chain collar is what the dog hears before he is choked, stopped or else he feels the pain of the very quick jerking action by the trainer.

Convincing a dog that he doesn't want to go with the bird can be a handful. Training your own Vizsla to a finished performance is a great feeling.

Having one's dog steady at the break-away is essential for field trials. Many hunters observe the same discipline before casting off their dogs for a hunt.

It is not so much a matter of great strength as it is timing and forcefulness on the part of the owner. The secret of using the training choke collar at first is quickness with force—not strength. If the normal training choke chain collar does not work with the Vizsla, the spiked collar will not substitute for the owner's inability to properly apply the above principles.

As training in the various exercises progresses and the dog becomes proficient, he will begin developing the tendency to anticipate commands or will start performing carelessly. At this point in training, the Vizsla is ready to undergo variations in his exercises to keep him alert and sharp, as well as keeping him impressed with the idea that a command is just that—that the initiation must first come from his owner. As training progresses, vary the routine in any manner that you choose, but vary it. But do not confuse the dog in this effort.

Descriptive rules for obedience work and trials are published in booklet form by the American Kennel Club. The standard of performance for each type obedience exercise is given and how it is to be judged. Each owner should have a copy of this pamphlet and study it carefully from time to time while training and competing.

Vizsla owners interested in obedience training should join a local obedience club. These are well established in every major city and advertise in the local newspaper for new obedience classes at some specified cost for the several weeks of training. Obedience competition is also the cheapest one of the competitive activities for the Vizsla.

It is possible to learn how to do obedience work from any one of several excellent books on the subject that are specially written for each level of obedience. But the better trained dog crystallizes what it learns in the presence of other dogs in training, and the owner becomes a better trainer in the company of experienced trainers and teachers.

FIELD OBEDIENCE

The most difficult training for the owner and his dog is the field training, which again is a different form of obedience training involving many uncontrolled variables between dog, game, terrain, cover, weather and others. And all of these variables are further compounded in competition by new or changed rules and by subjective opinions of those judging.

Rules are quite essential to every form of competition. Sometimes it is hard for the judges and trial officials to apply them because interpretation among judges varies. It is further complicated in that those involved are both "players and officials" at one time or other during the field trial season.

While the enthusiasm and drive to obtain these awards in obedience trials and field trials are undiminished, they nevertheless do not mean as much as they could. The rules are stronger and more exact for obedience trials and the judging seems to be more exacting in this competition than in field or show by comparison.

Much of the discussion in the training and communicating with the Vizsla is directed toward hunting and field trialing because these two areas of activity offer the potential for developing the maximum from both the dog and handler, but of equal use in all other dog training. It is covered in more detail in another chapter.

PUBLIC DEMONSTRATIONS

Our Behi Vizslas have been used in demonstrations involving field work and specialized acts at the Clark County and Ohio State fairs, schools and in 4-H work.

For these demonstrations a simple routine is used and is important in that it shows people that a Vizsla will accept a variety of training.

The field demonstrations involved live coturnix quail, but in a non-selected audience such as is found at fairs, a small percentage of people do not like the sound of blank pistol shots or to see a dog retrieve a live bird. Retrieving raw eggs creates general acceptance and a high level of interest. The pointing demonstrations are better accepted when a hookless fishing plug or bird feather is used on a fishing pole.

One female learned and enjoyed working at a variety of acts and audience appalause made her ham it up to everybody's delight. Most acts are not difficult although not every Vizsla is suited to doing them.

The most gratifying experience we had in doing these public demonstrations was from one we did at the Steele School in Colorado Springs, Colorado while attending the national club's field trial in the spring of 1969. Mrs. Shirley Rothan helped and we used Trixie, Dixie, Pete, Csinos and Rozsda in the show before the fifth and sixth grades. Trixie was the only one with experience at this type of work, but the rest seemed to sense the spirit of things and entertained just as well.

Later, one of their teachers (and our friend) Mrs. Phil Brown, mailed a large number of letters from the students expressing their appreciation and enjoyment. A few are presented to show their reactions.

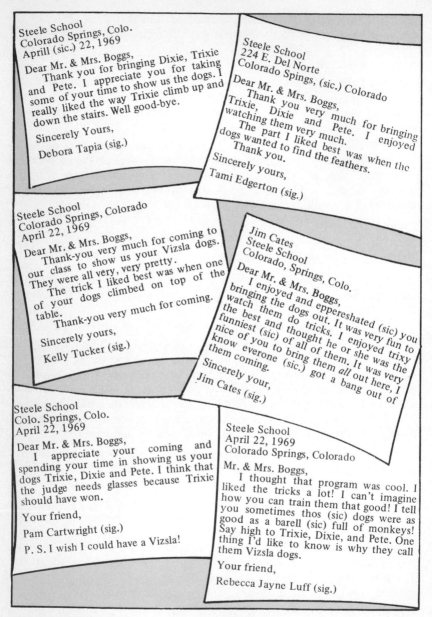

Steele School
Colorado Springs, Colo.
Aprill (sic.) 22, 1969
Dear Mr. & Mrs. Boggs,
Thank you for bringing Dixie, Trixie and Pete. I appreciate you for taking some of your time to show us the dogs. I really liked the way Trixie climb up and down the stairs. Well good-bye.

Sincerely Yours,

Debora Tapia (sig.)

Steele School
224 E. Del Norte
Colorado Spings, (sic.) Colorado
Dear Mr. & Mrs. Boggs,
Thank you very much for bringing Trixie, Dixie and Pete. I enjoyed watching them very much.
The part I liked best was when the dogs wanted to find the feathers.
Thank you.

Sincerely yours,

Tami Edgerton (sig.)

Steele School
Colorado Springs, Colorado
April 22, 1969
Dear Mr. & Mrs. Boggs,
Thank-you very much for coming to our class to show us your Vizsla dogs. They were all very, very pretty.
The trick I liked best was when one of your dogs climbed on top of the table.
Thank-you very much for coming.

Sincerely yours,

Kelly Tucker (sig.)

Jim Cates
Steele School
Colorado, Springs, Colo.
Dear Mr. & Mrs. Boggs,
I enjoyed and eppereshated (sic) you bringing the dogs out. It was very fun to watch them do tricks. I enjoyed trixy the best and thought he or she was the funniest (sic) of all of them. It was very nice of you to bring them all out here, I know everone (sic.) got a bang out of them coming.

Sincerely your,

Jim Cates (sig.)

Steele School
Colo. Springs, Colo.
April 22, 1969
Dear Mr. & Mrs. Boggs,
I appreciate your coming and spending your time in showing us your dogs Trixie, Dixie and Pete. I think that the judge needs glasses because Trixie should have won.

Your friend,

Pam Cartwright (sig.)

P. S. I wish I could have a Vizsla!

Steele School
April 22, 1969
Colorado Springs, Colorado
Mr. & Mrs. Boggs,
I thought that program was cool. I liked the tricks a lot! I can't imagine how you can train them that good! I tell you sometimes thos (sic) dogs were as good as a barell (sic) full of monkeys! Say high to Trixie, Dixie, and Pete. One thing I'd like to know is why they call them Vizsla dogs.

Your friend,

Rebecca Jayne Luff (sig.)

Such demonstrations are almost as enjoyable as finding one of my Vizslas locked up on point while hunting where the thrill never diminishes.

Ch. Glenogen's Gift of Gold, owned by Valerie and Roger Birkel (left) and Ch. Reilloc's Draga Leany, CDX (right) perform the "stand for examination" requirement in Utility obedience competition.

Dr. Linda L. Collier and Draga perform the obedience exercise "heeling on lead."

OTCh. Gold-In-Hills Janos, owned by Melissa and Blaine McGaughey, shows how a bar jump should be executed. This exercise is required for Utility competition.

Draga selects by scent the appropriate article required. Scent discrimination tests are a part of the Utility degree in obedience competition.

SCHEDULE OF ACTIVITY, CARE AND TRAINING FOR COMPLETE VIZSLA DEVELOPMENT

This schedule is a general guide and need not be followed exactly. Some of the training can be done when the Vizsla is younger than indicated, but better results will be obtained by the amateur by following it. Not every facet of a dog's training and usage is given in the items listed. With experience each person can improve upon it.

One point cannot be emphasized enough: **DO NOT OVER TRAIN OR TRAIN FOR TOO LONG OF A PERIOD OF TIME ON ANY ONE EXERCISE OR ANY COMBINATION OF EXERCISES!**

| Vizsla's Age | TYPE OF PERSUASIVE EXERCISE OR COMMAND |

Vizsla's Age   **TYPE OF PERSUASIVE EXERCISE OR COMMAND**

6 - 12 weeks

1. *Provide* puppy a permanent place to sleep so that he will learn it is his *home* and a sanctuary where no harm or punishment will occur.
2. *Choose a call name,* preferably one syllable.
3. *Housebreak* and use much praise.
4. *Come* and use much praise.
5. *No.*
6. *Kennel,* meaning to go inside and praise.
7. *Handling* for conformation and praise.
8. Play with adults and children.
9. Positive control. Put puppy in wire crate to stop undesirable play, chewing, accidents or to get out of the way. The crate can be his permanent home.
10. Sight *point* live birds only occasionally and praise.
11. *Introduction* to strangers, appliances, cars and etc.
12. Trim *toenails* regularly as needed.
13. *Avoid scolding* to stop puppy from undesirable activity. Use only "NO."
14. *Play* with *fishing pole* and *wing* both inside and outside of the house.
15. *Use dim flashlight* to play so puppy will point spot or use shadows.

3 - 6 months

16. *Use leash* and praise.
17. Provide toys for puppy.
18. *Obstacles.* Talk in reassuring manner.
19. *Swimming.*
20. *Retrieve* objects in play.
21. Take *car rides* regularly.
22. Expose to unusual *noises.*
23. *Trim whiskers.*
24. *Clean* and *inspect* ears.
25. *Bathe* only as necessary.
26. Introduction to sanctioned *puppy matches.*
27. *Whoa; Sit; Stay; Stand;* and, *Down* inside house and praise.
28. *Water retrieve* objects and praise.
29. *Jump* into water from shore or floating object.
30. Introduction to *boat.*
31. Take *swimming with people.*
32. Take into *city* or *shopping center* on *walks.*

6 - 12 months

33. Start in *novice obedience* at local club or at home.
34. *Water retrieve* dead *pigeons* and praise.

Trixie made it up the ladder in fine style and enjoys the view so much that the author is moved to encourage her that fun's fun and that Snoopy deserves a private platform.

Many things can be accomplished with a trained dog. Not that a dog would really want to see a parade in this fashion, but it demonstrates that once the dog is trained to climb the ladder, he is perfectly at home, confident of his own ability.

Being able to perform such antics will amuse and impress friends and will compliment the breed. The person who really enjoys training a dog will never cease finding new things to teach his dog to do.

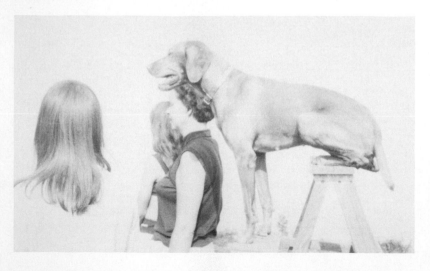

35. Accustom to .22 caliber crimp blank pistol shots.
36. Start *show* career.
37. Start in *water* trials.
38. *"Go Out," "Go Right," "Go Left,"* and any other command you wish to use in water work.
39. *Accustom* to *horses* and *livestock.*
40. *Accustom* to *strange dogs.*
41. Introductory *field training.* Yard work.

12-15 months
42. *Start* to *hunt* in field.
43. *Teach* to *point pigeons* by sight and smell and praise.
44. Formal start of *field pointing* on wild birds.
45. Stop on point and praise, at 15 months.
46. Field commands: "Whoa," "Stay," "Go Out," "Out Front," "Quarter, right or left," "Cut," "Swing Around," or any suitable command you prefer that works for you.
47. Cause dog to *chase bird* after point and praise.
48. Show desired *birdy objectives* to dog (if necessary put birds at these locations).
49. Teach dog to point coturnix quail and bobwhite quail after good progress using pigeons. Praise. Continue using pigeons also from time to time.
50. *Brace* with *another dog* only occasionally for *cast off* and to check individual *development* and *independence.*
51. Limited *force control* by handler.
52. *Independence* in hunting.
53. *Enter* in *puppy stake* in field trials. (Minimum age is 6 months to enter under American Kennel Club rules.)

15-18 months
54. Occasional *shot* with .22 or .32 caliber blank pistol when dog chases bird only.
55. *Teach* dog to *point pheasant* by smell and praise.
56. Start roading training and "E-E-Easy" command while following dog behind a walking pigeon and praise.
57. Call point by raising of hand and using "Whoa" and/or "Stay" command and praise.

18-24 months
58. Start *shooting* and *missing* bird with shotgun and praise if required.
59. Teach *"Whoa"* command at a *distance only* when dog is casting back. Go to dog and praise and pet.
60. After dog has *chased bird return him to place* bird was before flight, and praise, and kick weeds before sending him on.

61. Start *working dog from horse* if desired.
62. *Companion Dog Excellent obedience* work.
63. *Tracking obedience* work.

24-30 months 64. *Stay* on *starting line* for casting off.
65. Accelerate show career if not yet finished.
66. First breeding of a bitch (second time in season as a minimum).
67. *Open Obedience* work.
68. *Extensive exposure* to wild birds in the field.
69. *Shoot to kill occasional bird* and praise dog. (Wild birds can be shot much earlier. That is not considered training as used here.)
70. Use *dead birds* and practice "Whoa" and "Stay" and praise. Toss out bird, shoot and send dog on "Fetch" command and praise.
71. *Utility obedience,* provided Open is completed.

30-33 months 72. Begin steadying dog to flight of bird by blocking or other suitable method and praise when successful.
73. Begin bracing with another dog while training to *confirm independence* and *control.*

36-40 months 74. Begin steadying dog for purpose of *breaking dog to shot.*
75. Require *direct retrieve* on shoot-to-kill and praise.
76. Begin *teaching dog to honor* another's point or reinforce natural honor. (Opportunities prior to this should be avoided as much as possible.)
77. Start Amateur Gun Dog competition. (May be started sooner.)
NOTE: This is the first time that light physical punishment to obtain obedience or compliance to commands should ever be considered or practiced.

40-48 months 78. Completely *finish* (break) and *polish manners* of dog to shot. Do not miss any birds at this time until this training phase is crystallized in dog.
79. *Polish manners* on all other phases of field trials.
80. *Condition dog* for peak performance.
81. Start Gun Dog and All-Age competition and finish Field Champion and Amateur Field Champion titles. (may be started sooner.)
82. Keep dog sharp by working once in awhile on all previous training. Whatever training is initatied it should be continued from then on.

174

The first ever Triple Champion is photographed here at one of the memorable moments of his campaign. Cariad's Kutya Kai Costa was High In Trial at the VCA 1979 Nationals. From l. to r. are: Miklos Farkashazi, specialty judge; Merrill Cohen, obedience judge; Robert Costa with Kutya Kai; Marianne Costa and Trudy Lanman, obedience chairman.

Hilda Boggs and Trixie are about to execute a "figure 8" exercise. This exercise is found in Open competition.

Dr. Linda Collier's Draga clears the bar.

Mary Mac's Rusty Babe, owned by Mary V. Blank, shows her style taking a jump in obedience competition.

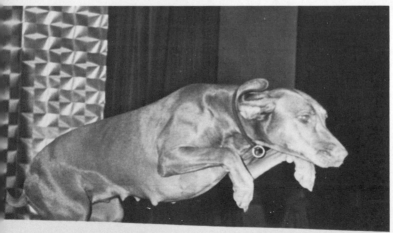

CHAPTER 9

Hunting
The
Vizsla

WHAT SHOULD THE NEW OWNER EXPECT?

The time is gone when the best use of a sporting dog is restricted to hunting. Hunting seasons are not long enough for the owner and his dog to really enjoy a continuous relationship at just hunting. Today's hunter is becoming more sophisticated in an affluent society and he does not really need the meat for his table as once was the case. Earlier, a hunting dog that could not produce meat for the table was not trained further, or hunted, and was probably sold, given away or destroyed. Now the hunting part of dog ownership is becoming, more and more, one of recreation.

The new Vizsla owner-hunter is a strange creature indeed! He oftentimes creates so much enthusiasm within himself that he finds it hard to keep from picking up his shotgun and taking his new puppy hunting right away. Then, unfortunately in many such cases, when the puppy grows to the age that he should be taken hunting, his owner has lost interest. Or, enough cannot be done quickly enough for his first Vizsla. He will get the best books on bird dog training and have his small puppy working overtime every day on exercises far too advanced for his little brain, but the puppy is always smart enough to tell when he is pleasing his master. Then, when this dog needs its owner to pick up those training books again, they are gathering dust.

My first Vizsla was less than five months old on opening day of pheasant season. I had lost my bird dog, of a different breed, that summer and although I looked for another like him nothing I found suited me. I had wanted a Vizsla since I first read about the breed in *Field & Stream* in 1954, so when an ad appeared in a local paper offering Vizsla puppies I bought a female that same day. This Vizsla was so young on opening day that my hunting partner and I debated on leaving her at home, but decided that she was small enough to carry in a hunting coat if need be and took her along. She hunted like an older trained dog and lasted the entire day. It was unbelievable. Talk about getting spoiled in a hurry? I did!

This was an excellent hunting Vizsla from that day on and just kept getting better with experience and age. Since that time, I have learned that the Vizsla must be evaluated and treated as an individual, and some even need training to search out game and point, but that is the exception.

It seems that for every breed that there are those who cry out the miracles for everybody to hear. The Vizsla is smart and has an outstanding

Some Vizslas will point close up especially in training situations although in hunting most points are not this close. When the dog is "right" you can expect him to get as close as possible without flushing his bird.

nose. Chokebore is an apt term. He learns fast, and assuming that his owner can hit a bird once in awhile, the Vizsla will darn near train himself steady to wing and shot. This does not mean that he will stay until sent like a trained dog for field trials—he won't.

The Vizsla needs no special training to do a good job of hunting, his owner does. The owner must understand his breed and his dog, and be willing to let his young dog learn by self-will rather than responding to the owner-hunter's will. In spite of the claims, no hunter can find birds better than a Vizsla when left to its own devices. But, the hunter can direct his dog in a number of ways to good cover other than by leading or forcing it.

The Vizsla will hunt any game bird without much prior introduction, and the more opportunity he has to work each kind the better all-round hunting dog he will become.

A Vizsla should never be allowed to hunt without being under control of his owner. Some hunters might like to cut a dog loose and never know when to tell the wife to have supper on the table. Who wants to go hunting and hunt for his dog? The Vizsla is not such a hunting dog. His forte is relay hunting where he checks constantly and comes to his owner's side if he stops very long in any one place.

The farmer's land has inviting domestic animals for the Vizsla. Whether the Vizsla likes pigs, or thinks that they smell like a big pheasant is hard to say, but some take a special fancy to them. Pointed pigs just do not fly! This would not be so bad in itself but some Vizslas will chase pigs and hogs at times like maniacs or fools. My Vizsla, Trixie, delighted in taking weanling pigs by the ear to hear them squeal—while ignoring my screams.

How does the new owner start his Vizsla hunting? You just take him into the fields and keep moving at a fairly brisk pace and cover all likely cover yourself. It is easy enough to go in any direction desired and the puppy will stay to the front. Stop and your puppy will come back to you. Slow up, or wander aimlessly about the field and your puppy will do much the same. If the puppy should by chance flush a bird, watch to see if he chases. If not, the next time encourage him to do so. As soon as he chases birds consistently, you may then start shooting at the birds. Allow the puppy to do as he chooses with the bird when killed until he loses interest or brings it to you, which he will usually do initially.

With this experience there can be no such thing as a gun shy dog, because he is chasing during the shot and thus learns to associate the bird and sound as one and the same pleasant experience. Some dog trainers recommend shooting a blank starter pistol around the pups, or banging the feed pans as they are being fed and experiencing something pleasant, but this method will not work for all owners and can cause gun shyness if not properly used. It seems to be an excellent way to teach a Vizsla to fear the shot of a gun since his ears are more sensitive to the higher frequencies of

Approaching the point is important. For a young dog, it is especially important to come from the side or the front. Only when the Vizsla is seasoned to the "ritual" at the point, should one approach from the rear. This helps prevent any tendency in the young dog to soften or blink the bird.

sound which are also more damaging physically. A shot in the wrong direction or too close in proximity to a dog's ear can be painful as well as do permanent injury.

Gun shyness is almost always a man made fault, and once made is very difficult to overcome. Blinking is much like gun shyness which can be caused in a number of ways such as when a dog gets flogged by a big rooster pheasant. That dog will change directions when he smells one afterwards.

One of my young pups was hunting one day and for some reason decided to sit down and rest or survey the situation when a covey of quail exploded out on all sides of her. I never did see that puppy sit again in the field, but she hunted quail with a passion from that time on. Another Vizsla in the same situation would possibly have been affected differently and would then blink quail after such an experience. Fortunately most of these faults can be corrected in time, but the owner who does not get or cause them is ahead.

DOG TRANSPORTATION FOR THE HUNTER

Good dog transportation is essential for the hunter, but a Vizsla is an easy dog to transport when loose in the car. Many times when out hunting your dog will be covered with mud and water upon returning to the car. The sedan is just not built for a dog in bad weather conditions. Some hunters with this kind of transportation use a car trunk which for the most part is unwise. The dog is confined in the event of a rear end accident, and the danger of exhaust fumes cannot be ignored. The hunter cannot leave one dog loose in his car while he hunts with another one without coming back and occasionally find the interior torn up. Then, while driving, the dog can be a hazard if he is not prevented from moving about.

A good form of transportation is the station wagon where wire dog crates are used. The pick-up truck with special dog compartments, as well as the van with interior crates or compartments, is excellent.

The dog trailer must by necessity always follow behind the automobile exhaust and does not absorb shock as well as the others.

The dog owner and hunter can appreciate the advantages in having his dog enclosed within his vehicle in some manner where he is always free to open the door, dress, assemble his gun and other equipment, and then take his dog from the compartment or crate and start hunting as opposed to fighting his dog all the time when he is loose in the vehicle.

WHERE TO HUNT WITH THE VIZSLA

With good dog transportation, the hunter should plan his trips in order to take advantage of all game bird seasons whether in his state or out of

Crates in a station wagon are probably the most versatile and still practical way to travel with a dog. The wire crates are light enough to be easily removed and allow the driver maximum visibility to the rear. Many crates are designed to fit side by side in standard size station wagons yet one need only use as many crates as he needs. Many fold up for convenient storage.

Newer on the scene is the van. There are many ways in which dogs can be housed in a van. These crates are built in and can be designed for maximum utilization of space. The forward part of this van has been fitted out to accomodate the hunters in the party.

state. He will find a different thrill in hunting with his Vizsla for grouse in the deep woods, quail in the shelter of brush and woods adjoining farm grain fields, woodcock in the wet swampy areas near creeks, and pheasant in the wide open grain and weed fields.

Even the shooting preserves have advantages, but the hunter should not content himself with such places where bird finding for his dog comes too easy, for his dog may never really learn to hunt. Most people using shooting preserves like to shoot or like the meat, and are not always interested in good dog work. This is a good place to go with a dog on occasion to build up his desire on birds. But only when the least number of hunters are present so the dog is not distracted by nearby shots as much.

One disadvantage in bird hunting too much where few birds exist is that the dog may learn to follow even an old pheasant track when he finds one. The hotter it gets the faster he runs to catch up. The next thing the hunter sees is the bird in the air and his dog has lost the track. It is unwise to allow a Vizsla to follow a cold foot track. He should be taught to follow the body scent; for if he does not, no matter how well he works the track, the odds are that he will push out the bird rather than cause the bird to hold for a point. Giving a Vizsla the necessary experience is mostly the art of striking a happy medium between a number of good experiences on different cover and terrain, and on different birds.

The predator call is sometimes used by some bird hunters to cause the wily pheasant and quail to quit running and to hide so the dog can find and point them. One sure way of getting a pheasant to flush wild is by talking loud to the dog or hunting partners. This loud talk may be useful in field trials to make sure all the birds are out of the way of the Vizsla so he cannot make a mistake on the back course. The quiet hunter is usually the most successful, especially with his Vizsla.

Hunting cornfields is extremely difficult with a Vizsla. If a bird does sit tight, the hunter may never know where his dog is, but birds usually fly out without the hunter getting much of an opportunity for a shot. The corn stubble fields can even be worse. Pheasants see the hunter come in one side of the field and they exit at the other end. Without cover to hide in, they have to find another place to hide from this danger. The sprays, fertilizer and corn density causes such a dense crop of corn that the sun cannot penetrate to support weed growth. The hunter wants to find the "dirty" corn stubble field along with the "dirty" farm for the best hunting success and fun. So do not waste time on ground so extensively farmed that the rotary chopper follows the sheller-picker, which in turn is followed by the plow, disc and planter.

During a cold rain or when the snow has been on fresh, the hunter should hunt the thick weed patches and fields where he knows there is a good population of pheasants. It is during these times that the pheasant holds best for the Vizsla. After the snow has set, these birds are harder to find. Another good time is just after the snow leaves the ground and the birds, being hungry, are active seeking food.

TRAINING THE VIZSLA FOR BEST HUNTING

When your Vizsla has progressed to the point that he is intensely interested in the chase after his point, you should wait at that spot until he returns, or call him back. Many times other birds will still be there and the chase is repeated, but it does not take long with these experiences for the Vizsla to think twice about chasing birds when he knows others might still be there. In this manner a Vizsla will practically train himself to stop chasing a flushed bird, and it even helps more if the hunter shoots the first bird to fly, then holds his ground until the dog has retrieved, and the Vizsla walks into another bird while bringing the shot one in. For this and other reasons it pays the hunter not to be too hasty in helping his dog with the retrieve.

As the Vizsla becomes more and more intense on his points, the hunter should talk to him in a soft voice when coming in for the flush, but not too much. Wild birds seldom allow the hunter to get too close to the dog before they run or fly. The hunter should try to approach from the right or left side of his Vizsla, but to one side enough that the shot will not blast his dog's ears. With two hunters, one should approach from the left side and the other from the right side and both walk at a brisk pace without hesitating, in line, to attempt the flush. Coming in from the front of the dog sometimes can be done, but this is more characteristic of the early training in field trials for steadying and blocking the dog to flush and shot. When hunting it is usually possible only when the dog establishes a point behind the hunters.

If the hunter desires to have his Vizsla both steady to wing and shot, he will actually have to do some type of formal training. Once the dog is trained he cannot be a meat hunter, for he must only have game shot over him whenever he does the job right. A free flushing bird, not worked, should not be shot.

The perfect hunting Vizsla is the one that hunts at all times under control of his handler, but takes the initiative in a forward manner to search out quickly all cover and the birdiest cover a little faster; find a bird's body scent and work it out happily and quickly, or casts beyond the bird and quarters back, to establish and hold the point. Upon approach by the hunter the Vizsla should never lessen his intensity and at the flush do whatever is necessary to accurately fix the bird's line of flight while the

The Vizsla is an excellent foot hunter's dog and he will have little trouble providing enough points so every hunter in the party fills his limit. He will also retrieve all those birds so there is no loss of game taken. Photo by Bob Foster.

gunner shoots. Once the bird is hit that Vizsla should be on its way quickly and arrive at the spot of the downed bird by the time it hits ground, catch the game on the first bounce, and quickly deliver the bird to hand. Thus, if the bird is wounded the dog need never follow the bird by track, but by sight or body scent. This insures that his owner can brag that his dog never lost a cripple. That is what the hunting dog is for, and the Vizsla does this well.

Whether a hunter wants one, two or a dozen dogs to hunt with, it is his choice. He will adjust his hunting with one or more according to their behavior and performance. Also, the hunter will quickly learn that just a few days of all day hunting in succession is more than any one Vizsla can take. By owning several Vizslas and hunting them one at a time the hunter

185

can make the most of his time for both hunting and training. Too many different dogs used singly or run double in a day's hunting over a period of several days begins to wear down the hunter, unless of course he does nothing else but hunt.

Owning a Vizsla bitch for hunting purposes has its disadvantages because she seems to have most of her seasons when it is hunting time.

It seems that male dogs are not as serious minded about hunting as the bitches, and usually even less so when he stays around a bitch that is in season near time for breeding. While hunting with the male he oftentimes gets the crazy idea (instinct) that his urine is so plentiful that he can stake off every weed and bush as his "territory" to the exclusion of all other males. This can become a bad habit but covering the bitch's urine at home is a blessing for it does serve to keep the attraction of other neighborhood males to a minimum.

FUR CONTACT IN THE FIELD

There is probably no one thing more misunderstood than that of a bird dog handling fur game in the field while hunting. The Vizsla is supposed to be interested in and should hunt the rabbit. In this sense he is a multi-purpose dog and is very capable on a number of species of small fur bearing animals.

The only animals of any consequence for most hunters while bird hunting are the rabbit, skunk, porcupine and groundhog. On some occasions the hunter will see his Vizsla make deer contact. Although the Vizsla is not much of a big game dog now, he will take up the chase. The Vizsla has been used by at least one game management official to track deer he shot with the hypodermic dart for tagging. The Vizsla followed the deer and when it was down the Vizsla came back and took the wildlife official to the drugged deer. The Vizsla has also been used by Nebraska game officials for finding (pointing) pheasant nests for game surveys.

The hunter may make a very bad mistake in trying to force his Vizsla to forget his natural instinct to point and chase the rabbit. It is not unusual for a Vizsla to give tongue for the chase—perhaps he should since many of them do this.

One of my Vizslas was used for rabbit hunting more than bird hunting and she barked like an idiot. My problem with her started after trying to use her for field trials. Being totally ignorant, and listening to people who claimed to know, I thought that for her to win that she would have to get off rabbits and be a bird purist. I tried to break her of rabbit chasing (her first rabbit point was in a field trial). After all else failed, I swore that I would never shoot another one for her. For the next four consecutive Saturdays while hunting, she deliberately (for spite) chased and caught a

Actual hunting points all too often look like this. On snow the Vizsla's coat color is an asset. In the early fall when the leaves are falling a white collar sleeve will make him easier to see.

The retrieve is as important today as finding game. In this era of conservation, no one wants to have game he has hit, get away. The Vizsla will virtually eliminate that problem. Not only will he retrieve, but he will track a wounded bird on the ground to insure it doesn't escape to fall prey to a predator or die wasted hiding in a groundhog hole.

187

rabbit on each of those days and delivered it directly to hand. She finally convinced me how foolish I was for trying. After that, I went on and enjoyed rabbit hunting sandwiched in with quail and pheasant hunting. Later on I gave up trying to field trial her. This problem is easily solved by training the Vizsla to point rabbits.

For field trials, I bought another bitch as a puppy and started teaching in another way. The training was directed toward a clean performance on both birds and rabbits. When the rabbit jumped from her point, she was taught to stay until sent on or the rabbit was shot. It is much harder for the Vizsla to remain staunch on a rabbit that takes off running than for a bird that flies. Most of the time the rabbit is not visible and the Vizsla, if nothing else, wants to see the rabbit (marking) for the retrieve. But once he starts the chase his training is forgotten.

Your Vizsla should show a natural interest in the rabbit because of being bred and used for that purpose in the past. Shooting rabbits over your Vizsla depends on many circumstances, but it is better not to if there is any chance your dog will be in the line of fire. For that reason he should be trained to point and stay at least until the rabbit is shot.

Precise and flawless performance and manners are not so important in ordinary hunting as in field trial competition. A rabbit properly handled in the field trial will not be credited against the dog, but will if not properly handled. No matter how artificial the field trial set-up may be, it still shows up a lot of the best in the Vizsla—or the worst. It is a pleasant form of recreation—but not necessarily intended to be a substitute for hunting. Good clean hunting with a bird dog all day long can be relaxing, exhilarating as well as tiring.

The Vizsla can be expected to point all game birds, retrieve all waterfowl and hunt (and point) all small fur animals. He will remember from one year to the next where he hunted and *found* game, and it is his uncanny memory that helps the Vizsla excel by going to the best bird cover and searching it out as well as to mark birds perfectly at long distances when shot.

Some Vizslas seem to have better eyesight than others and this is essential for a good squirrel dog as well as for marking shot birds. Their eyesight coupled with their memory is necessary for a retrieve under difficult circumstances.

TEACH THE HUNTING VIZSLA
TO OVERCOME OBSTACLES

The Vizsla will do anything he understands and knows will please his owner. After doing one particular thing enough times, he will learn to

Vizsla points pheasant in grass. The Vizsla is usually a good locator of scent; "chokebore" being an apt term describing his scenting ability.

There is still considerable controversy in America whether a bird dog should even touch or acknowledge furred game. Here the author's Ch. Behi's Csinos Csiny retrieves a rabbit shot while hunting. For the hunter who likes a mixed bag and his rabbit and bird seasons overlap, the Vizsla's ability to perform well on all game is important. The European hunter likes a versatile dog and the Vizsla was originally bred to function in all aspects of hunting.

The Vizsla points a groundhog. In this case the ground hog was not shot and the dog was not encouraged to fight and the groundhog was allowed to escape to his den. The incident did serve to illustrate the versatility of the Vizsla.

enjoy most work related to the man-dog association without even a token reward.

It is not difficult for a Vizsla to learn to go up or down stairs. He learns better as a young puppy at a time that he also fears some things and not others. He is more trusting. Put off certain training during this formulative period, and it seems to cause trouble later on. The Vizsla will overcome this obstacle himself since for the most part stairs represent something in the path that must be conquered to *stay* with his owner.

In the usual obedience exercises, the rote is sufficient when using the developed training techniques and such exercises cause little or no difficulty in the Vizsla's progress and mastery. But a hunting dog should develop certain experiences and habit patterns that will not hinder his ability to cover the ground, nor cause his owner to "wet nurse" him by showing him around and over the usual obstacles that will be encountered.

Consider the situation where the hunter must cross a fence. The fence is well built and in good condition and the Vizsla cannot find his way through. The hunter climbs the fence and goes on. What would the untrained or inexperienced dog do in this situation? The hunter might be unable to lift his dog over the fence safely. He will not want to involve his hunt with directed training of his dog. For maximum mobility of both dog and hunter, the Vizsla should be taught to crawl under, dig under, go in one direction or the other to find an easy crossing, jump or climb over under controlled conditions. The safest way for the dog is to go until he finds an opening. In crawling under, it is possible for the dog to get caught, but this is the easiest way to cross a fence for both the dog and hunter. Climbing is dangerous since your Vizsla could become entangled and injure a foot or leg, or even become firmly fast. Jumping a fence is the most dangerous because it is so easy for the dog to drop a hind leg between strands of barbed wire or between the barbed wire and the top strand of the woven wire fence and break a leg, hang until removed or die a terrible death. I had a bitch get caught once between the top two strands of barbed wire above the woven wire fence which put her leg in a half twist in the two strands that required considerable strength to release her, and I received a torn thumb in freeing her. She was there to stay, without my help.

An excited dog is always hard to control, or restrain, and in this case she knew the birds had run through the fence. There is always a certain amount of risk involved in hunting where there are fences, or for that matter in trying to lift a sixty pound dog over a fence.

In any event it is wise to select one or two methods and train the Vizsla accordingly. It seems most natural for a dog to go, or dig, under and this is usually a simple method. Sending a dog along the fence looking for a hole takes him away from you and this is more difficult, but it can be done.

The author's son is pictured with Vizsla and results of Ohio Youth Hunt program. A special season in a special area after a safety course and accompanying non-hunting adult supervision are features of this program designed to help stimulate future bird hunters.

A young Ripp Barat poses after a successful hunt.

A Vizsla can be taught to walk up one side of the fence and down the other. For this training it is better to start with a wooden fence, step ladder or rung ladder before advancing to the woven wire fence. Wood fences are also good to use in starting the dog to jump. For this training it seems more appropriate to use natural barriers, but for those who also have an interest in obedience training the standard jumps are helpful.

It is also helpful to teach the Vizsla to walk wide boards that are supported between two points and have him then advance to narrower boards more to develop his confidence than anything else, but this training can be very useful in the field later on.

For teaching a dog to go find an opening in a fence, I use a fence with an opening at one end or the other. The Vizsla is instructed to go around while I climb at the far end. If he comes back, I will then walk with him the necessary distance and then climb the fence. Holes are also cut in the fences in training to teach him to go through. This training can be done with just short stretches of woven wire with the use of food as bait to get started.

The Vizsla can be happy as just a companion to you and your family. But you are missing a real experience with your Vizsla if you do not take him afield. He fundamentally started as a hunter. Many feel as a hunting comrade, the Vizsla is at his zenith.

In many phases of training it is very helpful to have a buddie. Here the owner steadies the dog while his hunting partner works the flush. There are advantages for the hunter to have a steady, if not perfectly staunch, Vizsla.

193

CHAPTER 10

Field Trials

FIELD TRIAL TRAINING

Bird dog training is expensive and many owners will learn that it is beyond their means unless they can use public facilities and wild game. The additional training for field trial competition costs the owner much more money and short cuts do not normally work. For this reason, and others, the Vizsla selected should have good potential. An aggressive and independent Vizsla is required for competing in other breed trials.

It will be beneficial for the trainer to read books written by owners of Continental pointing breeds (European) on dog training and obtain some first hand experience before making a decision to engage in field trial competition. It costs nothing to go to one and watch or follow the braces in order to get a better idea of the sport. This practice is recommended.

During its first year, except for professional trainers, the Vizsla puppy should be worked sparingly in any field training. The whistle should not be used unless you are calling the dog in to stop hunting. Near the end of the first year of age, take your puppy into the field and walk straight lines initially at three to five miles per hour for ten to fifteen minutes at a session.

DUAL CH. & AMATEUR FIELD CH. MEHAGIAN'S PEPPY PALOMA
by Ch. Sandor Barat out of Hall's Desert Gypsy

Breeder: Ralph L. Hall
Handler: Denes Burjan

Owner: Marge Mehagian
Photo: M. Lanzim

V. C. of A. Amateur Field Champion, 1977
V. C. of A. National Field Champion, 1979
V. C. of A. National Field Champion, 1981

After several trips and after the dog stays forward all the time, zig-zag patterns can be used so the puppy will learn to change directions and quarter if he is not already doing so. Changes in direction by the trainer should be to some objective. Voice instructions are not necessary and for the Vizsla they should not be used yet. Many books say to start a dog's training early, and this is true, but the nature of the training is often misunderstood by the novice. (Refer to the training guide in a previous chapter.) Each person derives his own interpretation of what he reads and applies it differently. Keep the young dog happy and learn what the position of his tail or ears means relative to his desire to work as well as what is being telegraphed from his nose.

The young Vizsla needs other training before the field training which is useful and important later on in the field.

This pre-field training (yard work) is best given at a young age in order to prepare him for the role that we have to play in his life's work as a hunting dog. It is better that this young dog not be allowed to catch, or learn that he can catch live birds during this pre-field training as well as during his first two years of such training. Wild birds need not cause any concern for very few dogs can catch them.

When the time comes to start field *training*, the first training effort is to develop the Vizsla's intensity and teach staunchness on point if not already there. If there, then do not make a mistake and lose it. This is the most important thing that needs to be developed during those first two years of age. Most trainers do many other things too and the more experienced sometimes break their Vizslas to wing and shot. The Vizsla should be taught to whoa (stop) on command before he is two years of age, but this need not be done in the field until later on.

For competition in field trials, the puppy and derby age Vizsla should be introduced to and trained on pigeons and quail (coturnix and bobwhite). Pheasants and chukars can be used later on. Chukars are used by some trainers and they can be used just before pheasants—and they are excellent birds for working the dog on a moving bird (roading). Pigeons can be used exclusively for the total training process with good results ultimately demonstrated on all game birds. The trainer should plant (dizzy or use some other means to hold the birds in one place until found and pointed) birds and maintain proper control over his dog while he hunts for them. Extreme care should be exercised in this work to keep from teaching the dog to be dependent upon you.

It would help for your dog to have a strong desire for birds and also be staunch on planted birds before working him too much on wild birds. This may sound strange, but when a young dog learns to point wild birds first, there is enough difference that he will often refuse to point the birds that are planted because of the human scent on them. Pigeons used in this procedure may be used without additional scent added. This confuses the novice trainer and of course the exceptional Vizsla will not care what he points, how or where. Such a Vizsla will give his owner many wonderful hours of pleasure, but this type dog is not very plentiful, so owning and working one and developing him is gratifying.

Every trainer, in teaching his young dog to point staunchly and not grab the bird, has had his share of frustration. He will usually have tried every gimmick imaginable, and well he should, for this type of training is foreign to the Vizsla. A wild bird will usually be sick before a young dog will catch it, and consequently the Vizsla learns quickly to hold his pointing position so the bird will not fly away.

A list of some of the methods and devices used for training staunchness are as follows:

1. A wire mesh basket with a weight; wire mesh covering the size of a specific type of bird with the lower frame of heavy steel rod; mesh wire the size of the bird staked down; and other variations that cover the bird and prevents it from leaving.

196

Bird pin is a tool for stimulating desire in puppy more than teaching pointing. Pin in this photo is stuck in ground. Pigeon is allowed to flap and attract dog. Bird is released before pup can grab. Pup can be started with the pin at 12 weeks old.

Another pigeon holder basically consists of two clamps that hold each side of the bird's body. When released, the clamps spring away releasing the pigeon.

Below, a child's sock serves to keep a pigeon immobile. The principle is much the same as hooding a falcon and can serve the bird dog trainer very well.

197

Pictured is one type of bird releaser. This one does "launch" the bird into the air. The objective is to give the trainer the optimum control of the situation during the "breaking" process.

2. A circular section of woven wire farm fence about ten feet or more in diameter with the bird planted in the center or used with any one of the other devices preferred to hold birds. The bird in the smaller diameter section of wire will usually fly straight up and out without the dog having any chance of catching it. A larger version can be used where both dog and bird are inside to help break him of chasing.

3. Automatic and manual bird releasers where the bird is tossed into the air by a special design using spring hinged doors and a cradle of mesh screen as the thrower.

4. Bird enclosed in form fitted wire mesh or electrical trouble light (for small birds) and it can be dragged for roading exercises also. Hobbled and weighted birds can also be used for this purpose.

5. Plastic net container bags used for marketing oranges, grapefruits, apples or potatoes. Bird is placed inside with the bag tied using freezer bag ties.

6. Harnessed birds, bird put down with form fitted sock (hood) over its head, bird wings or fishing plug with hooks removed and used on fishing rod.

7. Dummy bird from any type of material with quail or pheasant scent used. Canvas covered boat bumpers are good.

198

8. Special designed pigeon holders.
9. Cage type containers with release.
10. Electric shocking collar and transmitter. (This device should not be used by an inexperienced dog trainer.)
11. Recall quail pens set up in the training area.
12. A twenty-five to fifty foot polyethylene cord, the type used for water skiing, or webbed horse tether to physically restrain the dog from going in on bird from its point. This should be used with caution as it can cause the dog to blink and the trainer never knows until too late.

Each one of these devices, or training aids can be useful to the trainer when properly used or applied, but all of them should not be used with each dog. Determine which one or two works best for your dog and yourself and stick with that. My own preference is to use a sock over the bird's head and it hidden inside the circular section of woven wire fence. I have also had good success with the wire launchers which "throw" the bird into the air when triggered. The plastic bag is equally as good but requires more effort to release the bird. Slept birds are also used after good progress is made, and the wire enclosure is not used all the time depending on the progress of staunchness. It is important to find some method to prevent the young Vizsla from breaking point and catching his bird.

When you get to your dog, all attention should be given him first before flushing the bird.

Another problem that concerns the trainer is how to plant (place in the

Vizsla is on point and handler is working to improve posture. More then that he is demonstrating to the dog that he is in no hurry and that the dog shouldn't be either. Hurrying to points frequently brings bad instead of good results.

199

field) birds so that a smart Vizsla will not learn to find the bird by tracking him to it. This is a serious problem and can cause bad training problems. It can best be handled by making a lot of tracks. Start by running one or more dogs over the general area with no birds planted. Then, after planting the birds, make numerous tracks in the general area to throw off the dog even more. Stay up wind from the bird when planting it. Since the freshest tracks are made after planting the bird, it is difficult for the Vizsla to establish the same association as when the planted bird has just one set of the bird planter's tracks leading to and from it. The Vizsla will then depend more on his own senses and judgment in finding the bird scent and the bird that he knows can be found by hunting.

A lot of trainers talk to their dog and encourage him to "find birds," and then do the same thing later on in field trials when in the bird field. However, it is better when the Vizsla seeks his game with speed and intelligence over that same bird field without encouragement. This looks better and when everything goes well it gives an unbeatable bird field performance that spells all class and will generally produce all of the planted birds in a minimum of time and the cherished win.

One might believe that the subtleties of training are unnecessary in training for field trial sport, but it is important to remember that a Vizsla will never perform like a machine. One day he may perform like a mechanical genius and the next day he will go crazy and act like an idiot without the first semblance of training.

Major faults develop without the benefit of training and are difficult to cure—sometimes impossible. So extreme caution is needed until the Vizsla is reasonably mature and well along in its training, but he need not be pampered or placed in isolation for this would be worse than the handler making his mistakes.

The best training philosophy is never to permit a situation to develop where positive control of the dog is not assured for the trainer. This will eventually come through the rote and the commands that insure obedience to the trainer.

A trainer's mistakes, or his neglect in training a dog for some constructive purpose, ruins most potentially good bird dogs. It takes work, and a lot of it, to train the dog to point steady and not to use his mouth on the bird for whatever the reason until told to do so.

Finally, the time comes when your dog is ready to be broken for shot. Do not initiate this phase until the *Vizsla* is properly prepared and ready. It is better to use another person to do the shooting so that your full attention can be given to keeping your dog in place while you flush the bird and your helper shoots. At first it is perhaps better to have your helper put up the bird too.

Blocking is a far better method for the Vizsla than using the check cord

TRI CH. CARIAD'S KUTYA KAI COSTA
by Ch. Glen Cottage Loki Barat out of Ch. Cariad's Gaybine, C.D.
Breeder: Marion Coffman & Linda Greenfield   Owner: Marianne & Robert Costa
First dog in A.K.C. history to win Field, Show & Obedience titles, 1980

FIELD CHAMPION KATAKI'S RIKI KNOH
by Dual Ch. & Amtr. Fld. Ch. Rippi of Webster Woodlands
out of Ch. & Amtr. Fld. Ch. Bratt's Fk Kataki
Breeder: Jean & William Lutz   Owner: Eugene Remmer

and allowing him to hit the end when first starting this training. It is better to hold your Vizsla by the collar and one hand under the flank while your helper produces the bird to flight. Some trainers are able to break a Vizsla with soft talk, and it helps to use this method in combination with others.

Once the Vizsla is steady under this situation, the helper should be left out from time to time, and the shooting done by the trainer. Then when the Vizsla is steady under this situation, the trainer should alternate the shooting from time to time to simulate types of field trial competition. The most important single factor in the breaking process is to kill every bird shot at cleanly until the Vizsla is *steady*. For example, a dog steady to a blank pistol and a flushed bird is not necessarily steady to the shoot-to-kill process. The training job is not complete until all possible combinations are trained for and proven by the dog's performance in a number of different situations in competition. Professionals may not be able to take but the minimum necessary training to get a dog broken to wing and shot. In most cases this depends on his client's wishes.

The amateur trainer-handler has a choice, and he can use any number of different techniques which by necessity prolong the breaking process. An inexperienced trainer can easily become frustrated and give up altogether. But it is a proven fact based on my experience and observation that a Vizsla brought along in proper timing at 3½ to 4 years of age can be completely broken to wing and shot with less than ten pigeons killed over him. Compare this with the estimate of 200 which is suggested for total training, by the beginner. A large number of these birds must be used in the shoot-to-kill process. Vizsla training in the shoot-to-kill process continues from the time of breaking until the dog is too old to hunt.

THE VIZSLA AND
THE PROFESSIONAL FIELD TRIAL TRAINER

The Vizsla does not seem to do his best in the regimented life of just a hunting dog. He demands and has every ambition to secure the bond of human affection if at all possible. As one professional who has much experience with several bird dog breeds said, "The Vizsla likes people better than he likes to hunt." This professional was Paul Sabo, Jr. and he spoke the truth. He piloted Ripp Barat and Ripp Barat's Rippy to both their American and Canadian Field Champion titles.

The Vizsla is not yet as successful in field trials under the training and handling of a professional as he will be eventually, perhaps, and it is no reflection on the ability of the professional trainers working with him. It cannot be stressed enough that the Vizsla will not respond to rough

202

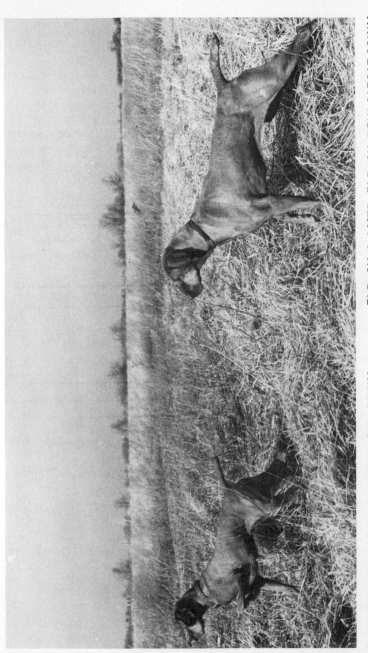

FLD. CH. & AMTR. FLD. CH. BEHI'S PIRI CSINY   FLD. CH. & AMTR. FLD. CH. BEHI CSECSE SCINY

Littermates by Ch. Szekeres' Kelet Szel out of Dual Ch. Behi's Csinos Csiny, C.D.

Owners: Jerry & Carol Feder (Piri) and Hilda R. & Bernard C. Boggs (Csecse)

Breeder: Hilda R. & Bernard C. Boggs

203

treatment. This dog will avoid situations which confuses it or when he does not understand what is expected of him which in turn compounds the problems for any handler.

Basically the Vizsla is both sensitive and contrary in training. Unless his owner wants to spend a lot of time trying to unravel problems, he should not get into the thick of competition through a professional handler where the dog is transferred back and forth without studying the situation first. It is better to turn the dog over to the professional completely and stay away from him, except to watch his dog at trials, and this is the way most professionals would prefer it. Dogs work best whenever their affection and loyalty is seemingly permanent although the Vizsla can do reasonably well in some cases with the switching of owners and handlers when properly indoctrinated.

Memories are poor, and we do not really know how other breeds reacted in the early stages of field trial training and development. It is possible that the Vizsla will fit into the plans of the professional better than he has in the past.

As in the breed, problems develop between the transition of doing something because of play or pleasure and that of being commanded through training routines. It is the psychoanalysis of the reactionary behavior which develops as a result of this that demands so much of a trainer's time and patience. To begin with, training under the professional set up does not normally allow the Vizsla to get close enough to satisfy his basic inner urge for affection, and he will sometimes waste too much of his time trying to obtain this as opposed to learning and performing.

A successful professional will certainly use most of the same training and handling techniques normal to his practice, but he may need to change slightly his approach and methods of discipline in many situations with the Vizsla.

As the Vizsla becomes more fixed in field trial circles, existing professional will trial them more and new ones will develop from the Vizsla amateur ranks.

Before the owner submits his dog to the professional trainer, he should first observe that particular trainer firsthand when he is training and in competition. The Vizsla owner who is financially well off usually cannot afford to spend his time to do all that he would like to do to improve the breed through personal competition and breeding and so must use paid professional services and kennel help. For this owner, the professional trainer and handler are essential for his dog work and pleasure.

It is usually the professional who raises the standards of performance of all breeds and it is not my intention to imply that the professional will not do a good job or will not be successful with the Vizsla. In dog sports,

At the 1972 Spring Nationals there were five Dual Champions. From left to right, Sir Lancelot (Hall of Fame, 1981) with Bill Goodman, Weedy Creek Lobo with Don Tade, Bobo Buck Selle with Hank Rozanek, Szekeres' Kis Szereto with Carole Smith and Behi's Csinos Csiny with the author.

205

the professional is successful or his job would cease to exist as a viable profession.

FIELD TRIAL COMPETITION AGAINST OTHER BREEDS

Up until the time an *all* Vizsla trial was held, Vizsla owners judged their breed in field trials according to almost every concept and standard we might imagine. The owners were mostly novice people interested in doing things with their Vizsla — and field trialing was just one. Field trials at first seem to be a difficult "society" to crack and a very close-mouthed one for the most part. The first novice and amateur owners had to compete against the all-breed professionals and experienced amateurs from the start. Some of these people were helpful, some sympathetic, some indifferent, but many were prejudiced against the new dog breed. Some were willing to defer their final evaluation and judgment.

Because of the situation facing the novice Vizsla owner, competing in field trials in the late nineteen-fifties and early nineteen-sixties, it was impossible for him to train his dog differently from the breed with which he was competing.

The judging corresponded to what was then the expected top performance for the Pointer and Setter in American Field trials, and the Continental pointing breeds in the American Kennel Club licensed or member trials. At that time there were no Vizsla trials for this breed and not one of the Vizsla owners could be considered for a judging assignment. Very few are yet, but this is changing with several specialty Vizsla clubs now holding trials. The Vizsla owners had to depend upon those who judged at the other breed trials to judge for them because few of them were knowledgeable enough to do it and others lacked the confidence. As a consequence, the Vizsla was judged as an inferior breed and more to other breeds' trial standards than any other. An unknown is always treated with reservation and aversion. To experienced field trialers this was just a new addition to the Continental pointing breeds, or just another competitor and could not offer anything different and nothing quite as good as already existed.

In spite of early doubt and distrust, the Vizsla is being trained adequately by several owners and is giving respectable competition in the open gun dog and all-age stakes in other breed trials, and is winning in increasing numbers and frequency. But, for *that* particular handler, and owner, he would experience less of a handicap if he owned and trialed the breed represented by the trial giving club. Not many Vizsla handlers can bring the Vizsla to this point yet simply because they either lack the ability to train a dog, cannot find training tips especially for the Vizsla, or they have insufficient motivation and desire to compete against the more

FLD. CH. FUTAKI JULISKA
by Ch. Hunor out of Piri

Breeder: Bela Hadik

Owners: Robert & Nancy Perry

FLD. CH. REBEL ROUSER DUKE
by Haans V Selle out of Fld. Ch. Weedy Creek Dutches
Breeder/Owner: Hank Rozanek

experienced dog handlers. These statements are not criticism of other breeds or people, but are made to present facts and educate those contemplating buying any bird dog.

The basic process to success is one of education of Vizsla trainers and handlers and those selected to judge the breed so that they will train and judge the Vizsla properly.

Some dog writers do not fully recognize the Vizsla's ability as well as its rightful place at this time as a pointing dog, and the only test course or method available to demonstrate the breed's capability is the field trial. How many dog owners put faith in the claims of the hunter who brags about his dog? They have to see for themselves and field trials excel for this purpose — along with many other reasons.

The Vizsla has more than demonstrated his ability to win against the best of competitors in the other breeds. All Vizsla Field Champions were earned from other breeds' trials until just very recently. At the beginning of 1967, of all the Field Champions only one Vizsla had earned his title from "Vizsla only" point trials under the rules of the American Kennel Club.

In 1971, approximately 1222 Vizslas were entered in the American Kennel Club point trials of which 276 placements were made and seventy of these were for first place. Fifty different dogs shared these placements. These statistics were taken from the January to December 1971 *Pure-Bred Dogs — American Kennel Gazette*.

Statistics in themselves do not prove a thing, but are used only to give the reader a reference point to assess opinions and claims being made about the Vizsla in field trial competition. Compared to previous years, entries and placements are on the increase as are the number of Field Champions. The breed had three in 1966, one in 1967, six in 1968, three in 1969 and one Dual Champion, and had two in 1970 and two Dual Champions, and in 1971 one Field Champion, three Dual Champions and two Amateur Field Champions.

Probably the biggest initial deterrent to the Vizsla has been the novice owners and handlers who are still in the process of learning, but they are the ones who deserve credit for the breed's progress. In spite of this handicap, the Vizsla is making its presence known for having an excellent (chokebore) nose and polished manners — along with many other worthwhile virtues including their running and hard hunting.

FIELD TRIAL COSTS

Field trials are a recreational sport of the highest order where the teamwork between man and his dog can be and is a remarkably thrilling experience.

DUAL CH. BEHI'S CSINOS CSINY, C.D.
by Haans V Selle out of Fld. Ch. Futaki Juliska
Breeder: Robert & Nancy Perry   Owners: Bernard & Hilda Boggs
VCA Hall of Fame, 1979

DUAL CH. BROOK'S AMBER MIST
by Ridgeland's Copper Gypsy out of Ridgeland's Olca Selle
Breeder: Joseph Cuthbertson, Jr.   Owner: Anthony J. Lucas

Let us suppose that golf or bowling, for example, does not suit your physical and recreational needs the year round, and you think maybe the field trial sport and its training might be just for you. How much does it cost to get started? How much to stay in it?

This sport is something like gambling. Once you have had a taste of it the value of your money loses its true meaning. As in gambling, money keeps you in the game, but does not guarantee any winning. This is *not* a sport for the person who has problems meeting his daily needs, but a person does not have to be rich either. Usually it turns into total involvement and oftentimes past recreational activities are given up entirely.

You already own a Vizsla or the idea would never have occurred to you. If you hunt or intend to hunt your dog, then transportation is not an added expense, and if you are wise the wire crate will have been purchased when the dog was first bought, so he can ride in it while in your automobile, station wagon, van or motor home. Guns are already acquired, and if not then a good over/under can be purchased for a moderate sum and it is like money in the bank. (This gun type is mentioned because it is one of the safest to use in training and competition.) The usual items like feed and water pans, brush, nail clippers, orange leather collar, choke chain, short and long (six foot) leather leashes, flushing whip, starter blank pistol, bells, whistles, check cord, retrieving dummies, bird scent, releaser for birds and other items can be acquired over a period of time for about $200.

Ammunition for training is expensive and for this reason the .22 caliber blank (acorn blanks) pistol should be the first training pistol. It costs about 10 dollars and the shells cost less than three cents each. Later on a .22 caliber starter blank pistol (long .22 blank), at least will be needed and it is expensive. Blanks for a .32 cost even more. Shotgun shells will average about 20 cents each for the low brass. The inflationary trend will keep every facet of this sport more expensive each year. It takes a lot of ammunition to train dogs effectively.

Pigeons are the cheapest and best birds with which to start training and they can be bought from 50 cents to whatever price the trainer is willing to pay. The cost of quail, chukar and pheasant has nearly doubled in the past 10 years. It is cheaper to train on wild birds wherever they are available, but the cost of gasoline will make long trips prohibitive.

The number of birds needed will depend on the training methods used and the progress and aptitude of your Vizsla and whether you have facilities to recall birds not shot. There is no accurate method of knowing how many birds are needed for each individual dog in his training prior to the time it is ready to break to wing and shot. It depends entirely on the success of the trainer and the progress of the dog. Once it is determined

DUAL CH. FIELDSTONE'S HEY DUKE
by Dual Ch. Rebel Rouser Duke
out of Dual & Amtr. Fld. Ch. Rothan's Rozsda Kisanya, C.D.
Breeder: Shirley Rothan & Hilda Boggs   Owner: Susan & Stanley Weiss

FLD. CH. & AMTR. FLD. CH. DOC'S SPOT
by Fld. Ch. Hubertus Aprod out of Sweet Pat
Breeder: Denes Burjan   Owners: Jean & Kelly Donham

Field trials are subject to change. Therefore, a part of them is illustrated as Ham Rowan, AKC representative, consults with Al Lucas, president of VCA, and Miklos Farkashazi visiting from Hungary. The search for the ideal structure for testing field dogs seems an ideal always just out of reach.

that your dog is ready to break to shot you should plan to use 20 to 30 birds a month. It is important not to miss any birds or the breaking time will be extended. If he breaks, he should be returned to the same spot he was pointing and praised, and this is true no matter how poorly the dog did. Start training with the cheaper birds first and do as much of the finishing work with them as possible, but also use the larger birds occasionally.

The reason for delaying training on pheasants is to prevent your Vizsla from getting flogged or spurred by a cripple which can hurt the dog's progress or cause it to kill the bird and ruin its meat in the process. This is the principal disadvantage in using pheasants for training. By the same reasoning, you should stop working your dog for several days the very first time you see him soften up on point.

Retrieving is an important part of this overall training process before and after the dog is steady to wing and shot. This too has a bearing on the number of birds you need to kill.

From the age of one to approximately four years (at four years of age your Vizsla should be steady to wing and shot) you ought to use a minimum of 200 birds in the training process. Using 125 pigeons, 50 quail and 25 pheasants, the cost to you will be approximately $300 for each dog. This means that in the three year period you should have trained with birds in approximately 100 sessions, and at least 300 times on non-planted birds or no birds at all. This should involve not less than 200 hours of actual running time.

Based on the initial cost of the Vizsla puppy and the cost of raising and training, and equipment purchases, the prospective field trialer could have a completely trained dog for $1,000 to $1,500 and this cost would include some field trial experience.

As long as the field trial owner does not go completely wild, the cost of campaigning his dog is less than $1,000 per year for each dog. If he enters

212

FIELD CH. WINDY DUKE'S REX
by Dual Ch. Rebel Rouser Duke
out of Dual Ch. & Amtr. Fld. Ch. Amber's Windy Autumn
Breeder: Phillip W. Rosenberg   Owner: Helen M. & A. R. Seelye
Handler: A. R. "Del" Seelye

DUAL CH. W.D. REGINA
by Dual Ch. Rebel Rouser Duke
out of Dual Ch. & Amtr. Fld. Ch. Amber's Windy Autumn
Breeder: Phil Rosenberg   Owner: Dana & George Roscoe
handled by Lisa Roscoe for this photograph

every stake his dog is eligible for, then the entry fee alone could cost $60 to $75 per trial per dog. Overexposure is not the easiest way to earn a Field Champion title.

The Vizsla field trial amateur who survives until he becomes moderately successful in his training and trial placements has surely been bitten by the "bug." He no longer cares about his investment in dollars or the costs involved in field trialing. Besides all the recreation, social enjoyment during and after the trials, new knowledge, better health, he also managed to keep fit and trim by "hunting" nine months out of the year and had the quail and pheasant he killed in training and field trialing for his table.

RETRIEVING

One common and perhaps the most perplexing problem in training the Vizsla is that phase where he wants to eat or tear up a quail, pheasant or rabbit, for example, rather than bring it to you. And this can happen even after the dog is fully trained to retrieve on command, although it will not be a problem with all of them.

What do you do about it? One way, and oftentimes the best way for the novice, is to do nothing that would aggravate the condition. The absolute worst action one can take is to punish him hoping to achieve proper response, but light scolding might help at times. (Any correction must be where and when the handler has positive control of the situation, and in this particular one he does not.) Many of my Vizslas have gone through this stage, even when they would retrieve live game without hurting it in training, then, all of a sudden it seemed, a change comes over the dog and he would pick feathers, chew the game to shreds and in some instances try to eat it.

You can have a Vizsla retrieving objects from land or water with absolute perfection and he will promptly eat the first quail you shoot and refuse to obey your command to fetch. Do not make the mistake of letting this command become associated with punishment. This act by your dog may be his method of getting back at you for something you have done that went against his "grain" without your knowing it. Any command other than "NO" is taboo at this time.

This dog's actions are not unusual and this is more normal than otherwise. There are many ways to correct the condition to one's satisfaction but it might require a slightly different method for each Vizsla.

Praise is the avenue to understanding and to willful obedience of your commands. The desire for your dog to please is already there. Make him proud of having the bird. The next step is to encourage this Vizsla to want

214

FIELD CH. AMBER-DUKE'S DANDY
by Fld. Ch. & Amtr. Fld Ch. Randy Duke
out of Dual Ch. & Amtr Fld. Ch. Brooks Amber Mist

Breeder: Anthony J. Lucas   Owner: Helen M. & A. R. Seelye
Handler: A. R. "Del" Seelye

FIELD CH. & AMATEUR FIELD CH.
EL CAZADOR'S RIP VAN WINKLE
by Ch. Sandor Barat out of Hall's Desert Gypsy

Breeder: Ralph Hall   Owner: Cal Leonhard
Handler: Bill Gibbons

to share it with you or to go and find another bird right away. There is no better or faster method of changing his one-track mind than to go on hunting and ignore it. Even better, is to arrange to kill another bird while he is chewing or playing with the one bird. The Vizsla will then leave it or carry it to the second bird.

Another way in training is to kill the bird and make your dog stay in position; you go pick up the bird and bring it back to him and let him smell the bird before casting him on hunting. This is an effective method to use when first breaking your Vizsla to shot by teaching just one thing at a time and not combining shot and retrieve.

With patience and repetition using an appropriate method, you can in a short time have your dog knock you down in giving you the bird. After this critical stage has passed there is seldom any syndrome likely to develop with the retrieve again and you can for the first time really *command* your dog to retrieve anything, anywhere, anytime. There is a big difference between your dog carrying and retrieving for his own pleasure as opposed to being directed to do so by you. There is still that same basic problem of communicating to him exactly what **you** want.

For those who prefer the brute force method of retriever training, it should be used on dogs other than the Vizsla. Some trainers will have success, but it takes experience and the knack of being able to read the right "dog signs" to keep from going too far. Then too, these people will not fool with a dog that they consider untrainable or that develop such problems. They have no false sense of values and will quickly dispose of one dog and search for a better one. For the average owner this is not the way it is.

It is important to remember that retrieving and training your dog to be steady to wing and shot need not be combined. Since the Vizsla is a natural retriever, some trainers have excellent success in breaking their dog for shot and after this training is fixed then allowing the dog to retrieve.

Sometimes it is helpful to let one (or more) dog watch another to build up the jealous and competitive desire in order to get the most attention and praise. Other times this can complicate the problem or have no effect whatsoever.

One important fact should always be remembered. Never **demand** obedience from your dog in the sense that he "ought to understand or ought to know better than to do something," or think that he has any form of reasoning ability for putting one or more facts or situations together to come up with an answer. The use of temper only confuses and cows a Vizsla. The mere fact that one's anger is sensed instantly by his dog is of enough consequence that any further work should be postponed. There comes a time in the development and training that a mild form of physical punishment is effective, but it should be left for those who have

FIELD CH. & AMATEUR FIELD CH. EL-JO'S PIROSKA PAPRIKA
by Dual Ch. Weedy Creek Lobo out of Grey Oaks Antonia
Breeder: Elaine & Joe Saldivar   Owner: Marilyn Fowler
Handler: Harold Wingerter

DUAL CH. BEHI CSECSE GYORS LAB
by Dual & Amtr. Fld. Ch. Victor of Holzworth Farm
out of Fld. Ch. & Amtr. Fld. Ch. Behi Csecse Csiny
Breeder/Owner: Bernard C. & Hilda R. Boggs

nothing to lose and have given up all other training approaches for that situation. When you detect a problem that did not exist before, search back through your training to try and pinpoint the cause.

Just remember that the Vizsla retrieves naturally and loves doing it, but does not instinctively understand demands made upon him. Some Vizsla trainers never have to train for retrieves and cannot understand why some trainers develop problems. However, one cannot plan on being lucky in this regard.

HONORING THE POINT

There is no other dog work more beautiful in the eyes of the dog owner, or observer, than to see one Vizsla freeze on point while sliding to a stop from its hunting speed followed by a brace mate doing the same on a sight honor like he too has his nose full of bird scent. As long as it looks like what has just been described, it is great, and is the way it should be accomplished.

But how does this come about? This can be a subject of considerable controversy but it is a definite requirement in pointing breed field trials. A pointing dog is required to honor when it sees its brace mate on point. It can be placed first though without having an honor as long as an honest opportunity did not present itself. A command by its handler to honor could cause it not to be placed first.

For the most part honoring, or backing, is a trained attribute for the pointing dog. Some trainers are for it and others against it as a requirement for winning. Earlier in this book the statement was made, *"Control your dog!"* This is a pretty good example of that and a very important one. That is quite simply what the honor means, but many will argue that the Vizsla is born with this instinct, although there is not enough evidence to indicate that it falls in the same category as the pointing or retrieving instinct, among others, with the Vizsla.

Whatever the owner or trainer believes is the source of this characteristic, is unimportant, for he still has some training to do in order to perfect and crystallize it in his dog and have him work in a positive way. When breeding he should consider this trait as evidence regardless of his beliefs. The Vizsla that honors naturally, or appears to, when he is trained to be steady at shot will do all of his work better and the owner and trainer is fortunate. Others are not so fortunate and in order to develop the honor by training requires knowledge and experience. Most every other phase of training can be done alone, but this one requires the use of other dogs that are both staunch on point, steady to wing and shot and honor on sight.

218

DUAL & AMTR. FLD. CH. VALHI'S LIBERTY VALANCE
by Dual & Amtr. Fld. Ch. Sir Lancelot out of Ch. Bratt's FK Satin Valentine
Breeder: Pat & Tom Kepler   Owner: Jean & William Lutz

FLD. CH. REBEL ROUSER WINNESHIEK MAC
by Dual Ch. Rebel Rouser Duke out of Rebel Rouser Penny
Breeder: H. F. Rozanek   Owner: Kelly Donham, 1974-79
                                                  Charles Colby

Since the first printing, the American Kennel Club has changed its rules which required a dog to honor its brace-mate in order for the judges to place dogs first and second. That rule caused many problems and was recognized as not being beneficial to the field trial sport. The rules for pointing dogs are reviewed by this organization periodically and changed as deemed appropriate to improve the sport.

The new rule change did not eliminate the requirement for a dog to honor its brace mate, but it did remove most all of the harmful artificial elements associated with the execution of the old rule.

A dog must honor its brace mate when encountering it on point. A handler must not cause his dog to avoid an encounter without beng severely penalized.

Some handlers have difficulty training for the honor, because they have difficulty finding another dog to work with. Some handlers have cut out the profile of a pointing dog from cardboard and used that successfully.

A handler should never enter a field trial with a newly (green) broke dog, if he cannot control his dog under most conditions that he is likely to encounter.

In bird field stakes where time is called on point, the non-pointing dog must be stopped until the brace mate has completed a retrieve or released when the bird is not killed. It is not necessary that the non-pointing dog honor, if he did not see the pointing dog. He should be stopped, but the handler would be wise to have his dog look in the direction of the pointing dog first, and then stop him if he does not honor for no penalty.

Training your Vizsla to honor should be the last part of his training after everything else is firmly fixed. Allowing a dog to honor if he will is all right, but it is not a good idea to do this while a dog is in other phases of training. It should be avoided as well as situations that should require it.

Usually one good feature is lost or diminished when a new one is trained for or intensified. It is a delicate system of balances to get every desirable trait intensified and perfected. The training routine will vary for each dog of the Vizsla breed, and the astute trainer will make allowances for this.

Training to honor is accomplished in a number of ways. Early in the dog's work, even at a derby age, the trainer can make him stop with the "Whoa" command when his dog back casts toward him. He can then make his dog stand and stay until he gets to him, then pet and praise him and cast him on. Then whoa the Vizsla each time the training session is over.

After your dog is steady to wing and shot and the time has finally come to teach the honor, you will need an understanding and helpful friend with a dog as previously described. It helps to have one like that yourself. Set

DUAL CH. & AMATEUR FIELD CH. BROOK'S WILLIE WHOMPUM
by Dual Ch. & Amtr. Fld. Ch. & Can., Mex., & Int. Ch. Sir Lancelot
out of Dual Ch. & Amtr. Fld. Ch. Brook's Amber Mist
Breeder/Owner: Ann & Anthony Lucas
V. C. of A. National Field Champion, 1976
V. C. of A. National Amateur Field Champion, 1978
V. C. of A. National Amateur Field Champion, 1979

FIELD CH. & AMATEUR FIELD CH. HYE TANYA
by Ch. Twin Acres Cassador Selle   out of Bireline's Ginger Heir of Brok
Breeder: D. Bireline   Owner: Sarkis Paparigian
V. C. of A. Amateur Field Champion, 1980

up a situation where the helping dog is permitted to find and point the bird at a distance from your dog. You can either use a lead or short check cord, or if you have trained your dog to stop, command it to, but stop your dog only after he has seen the other dog. Go to him and hold by the collar and praise him and talk to him while the bird is worked. Some trainers prefer to take the dog under training within six feet or so of the pointing dog where he can smell the bird to do this. The honoring dog is better off never to smell the bird of its bracemate. That is not an honor, but rather another point. It is far better to keep the honoring dog upwind and facing the pointing dog. The distance should be whatever is the maximum that the honoring dog can see the pointing dog. As the training progresses the dog should be taken off the lead or the command stopped. Simply stated, the training for honor relative to the trainer is done the same way as breaking for shot except there is no bird marking problem for the dog to become involved in. The dog, instead of pointing a bird, is pointing its brace mate or a situation. Once trained, situations in training and competition happen that require stern correction and discipline for the trained dog on the honor as well as breaking to shot. The trained Vizsla is extremely mannerly, but it is not a machine. Perfection comes only with time, patience and experience but even then it cannot be counted on for a given day of competition.

HOW TO HANDLE YOUR VIZSLA
AND WIN IN A FIELD TRIAL

Now that your dog has completed all the work required to make it steady to shot and honors its brace mate (and can no longer compete in the derby stake), you need to know how you can best compete against the more experienced amateurs and professional handlers. For those who are field trialing for the first time with a finished dog, or with a puppy or derby age Vizsla, you should have a reasonable idea of what is required to win or place in actual competition. But first go to field trials and ride or walk a lot of braces.

There is always the usual anxiety and nervousness with a handler for the first time. This is normal, but the popular misconception that the handler cannot touch his dog or ask questions on certain matters affecting his run should be forgotten by everyone involved in trials licensed by the American Kennels Club. This concern does not exist in trials held under the rules of the American Field where touching, handling and disciplining one's dog is normal. True, the handler is *not* to train or correct his dog in a physical way while under judgment in American Kennel Club trials, but, this does not mean that the handler cannot "touch" his dog or talk to the judges.

DUAL CH. & AMATEUR FLD.CH. ROTHAN'S ROZSDA KISANYA, C.D.
by Ch. Szekeres' Kelet Szel out of Ch. Csinos V Hunt, C.D.X.
Breeder: Shirley & Dr. Paul Rothan   Owner: Shirley Rothan & Hilda Boggs

FIELD CH. RANDY BEE
by Fld. Ch. & Amtr. Fld. Ch. Randy Duke out of Debreceny Waterford Keso
Breeder: Sarah & Terence McCracken   Owner: Joseph Manning

The handler should feel no restraint or obligation, without having to request permission from a judge, to help his dog get free of any entanglement in a fence or barbwire, physically take him away from a poisonous snake, call him off of a skunk or porcupine, or stop his dog and examine him if in obvious pain from thorns, cactus or sand burrs, or if overheated and in need of water, to take whatever steps necessary to insure the safety of his dog without being thrown out of contention. It has happened and will continue, but it is wrong. Perhaps some judges feel it is important that they be asked for permission. These situations have absolutely nothing to do with the performance and manners of the dog being judged. The purpose of trials is not to kill a dog or see how much physical suffering one can endure. Neither should the handler feel that he cannot praise and give his dog a friendly pat when taking a bird from him upon retrieving.

Rules are necessary and proper, but the interpretation of them through education helps insure that they will be understood and applied equally well by all participants and judges.

Many owners, handlers and judges form their own interpretations of the rules and remain rigid and inflexible in their application. This is harmful if they are competing or judging, for nobody really knows what he should do from one trial to the next, or how to train his dog for competition.

Having competed in other Continental breed trials and an occasional Pointer and Setter trial for several years (perhaps best described as apprentice training with no recognized way of graduating), I have observed and learned a few of the practices used for dog training (in trials) and the art of winning in field trials. The reason that I have confidence that knowledge will help another handler win, is that most every time out my brace mate either won or placed, or I did, so I developed a real good idea of what was needed to win. I also made a special point of studying every facet of the sport at these trials. It should be understood by the readers that these practices and suggestions are just a few of the many that the handler needs to know in order to complete effectively once his Vizsla is trained for a particular level of competition.

Figure 10-1 is a diagram and sketch combined to orient the reader on a single course trial with a bird field.

Point A is the starting place for each and every brace. It is here that the two handlers position their dogs relatively close to each other for whatever the reason and give their dogs the "Stand," "Stay," or some other command and the dogs are expected to remain, puppy and derby stakes the exception, until the two judges tell the handlers to cast off their dogs.

The field trial marshal and judges remain together during the entire course, just behind the two handlers who, in some stakes may ride horseback if this provision is stated in the field trial premium. The handler

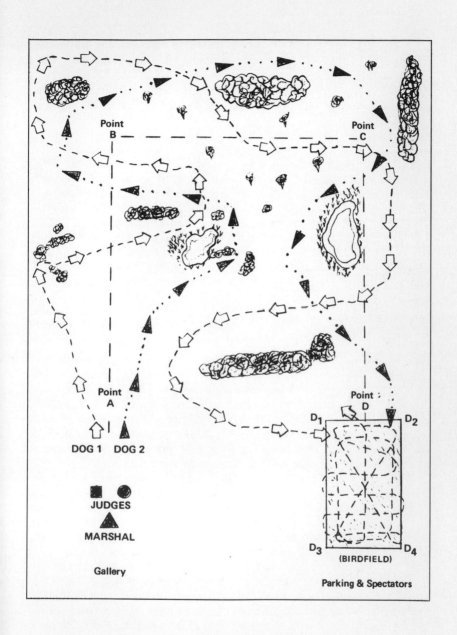

Point B

Point C

Point A

Point D

D₁ — D₂

DOG 1 DOG 2

D₃ — D₄

JUDGES

MARSHAL

(BIRDFIELD)

Gallery

Parking & Spectators

FIGURE 10-1
FIELD TRIAL COURSE

225

can only leave the line of travel designated by the marshal (or judges) when his dog is seen on point or he is scouted and found on point. The gallery follows behind the judges and marshal and can walk or ride horseback but must stay back such that they do not interfere with the competition in any way. They may call "standing dog" if they see one they believe is on point.

Between the Points A and B, there is a straight line approximately three-quarters of a mile long that the handlers, judges, marshal and gallery follow. The line from Points B to C is a distance of one half mile or less that provides a transition area to turn the dogs to go back in the opposite direction along a line from Point C to Point D to the bird field marked D, with boundaries D_1, D_2, D_3, and D_4 usually designated with marker flags. This is the place that the bird planters place birds for the dogs to find. The gunners join their handler and follow him at all times while he hunts the bird field for the shooting of birds he produces in front of his dog.

The total time it takes to travel the two and one-half miles is 22 minutes if there are no delays because of bird work on the course. The speed of the handler ranges from a fast to a brisk walk or as fast as five miles per hour at times. While the judges will try to work with the handler who walks slower than this, it is indicative of the condition expected of the handler. The best foot handlers keep in top condition. The other choice is for the out of condition handler to train his dog to handle from horse and only enter those stakes that permit it. Eight minutes are allowed in the bird field in retrieving stakes for a total time of 30 minutes for each brace. When time is called on point in the bird field this can consume much additional time. An average of 45 minutes is required under good conditions from one brace to the next. (Continuous or contiguous course trials involve a series of courses from 30 minutes or more for each brace using various testing procedures on birds.)

While the judges are still in the bird field, the next brace goes to the starting line, Point A, and waits for the preceding brace to finish up.

The procedure for starting a brace is for each handler to set up his dog and walk to the front or side and wait for the judges' signal to cast off. Each dog should cast off at a fast speed (like a race) to some *specific* objective in the distance and settle into his hunting pattern. On going out from cast off neither dog should loop back, visit each other or start a fight. Socializing causes the judges to believe right away that the dog is not aware of the business at hand, is poorly trained, will not hunt independently and is more interested in other things than hunting. Other factors enter in, usually involving the other handler, that can cause peculiar behavior on the part of *your* dog.

Sometimes the other handler will rough up his dog by hand and voice while setting him up, or holler or bellow like a mating bull moose at the

226

DUAL CH. REDEF'S HELLZA POPPIN
by Fld. Ch. & Amtr. Fld. Ch. Randy Duke
out of Fld. Ch. & Amtr. Fld. Ch. Behi's Piri Csiny

Breeder: Jerry & Carol Feder   Owner: Dr. Paul & Shirley Rothan

DUAL & AMTR. FLD. CH. BEHI'S JERI REDEF
by Fld. Ch. & Amtr. Fld. Ch. Randy Duke
out of Fld. Ch. & Amtr. Fld. Ch. Behi's Piri Csiny

Breeder: Jerry & Carol Feder   Owner: Bernard C. & Hilda R. Boggs

moment you cast your dog off. Some handlers make no effort to control their dog to keep him from interfering. (A dog having a recent sickness or medication can cause the other dog to socialize or interfere when he never would before and the dog about to be offended seems to sense this is going to happen.) Bitches in season can be run under certain conditions as set by the field trial committee, and specified in the premium list for each stake. The only restriction is that males cannot be run over the same course until the next day. With single course trials, this means that bitches in season cannot be run until the last braces of the last stake. In a two day trial, the last stake is opened by some few clubs. There is definite discrimination against bitches which is unjustified in field trials thus giving an unfair advantage to males. Males are credited with far greater breeding achievements than females and that is false and misleading. Somehow we seem to be caught up with the male ego even when it comes to dogs.

The idea that each handler is effectively taking his dog out with another "hunter and his dog" in field trials to hunt separately and independently in the same field does not always work in practice. In such situations, one dog might want to postpone the "hunt" for another day, or go about it without much heart in his work. Sometimes female dogs in the stake are blamed. A Vizsla that does this has not had the proper training and control, or has been involved in too much hanky-panky, and is at that moment soured out on field trials. If not for these reasons, then he may develop a mental block about his handler hollering, or the other handler, or with the brace mate's interference and not do his work properly on that day.

The Vizsla normally controls so easily that excessive and loud hollering all along the course is wasted energy on the part of the handler, but oftentimes he believes he is compelled to handle this way for a number of reasons. Sometimes the judge tells him to move his dog forward or his dog handles to the other handlers voice and he tries to combat the situation. This practice also alerts anything on the course that a "circus" is coming through and the birds and other animals move out of the way usually, which in effect "helps" the dogs. If there are no birds within their hunting range on the back course there is less of an opportunity for a serious breach of manners or performance.

Another distracting habit of some handlers that badly affects the other handler is the use of commands such as "Whoa," and "Come," among others when they have deliberately taught their dogs these commands to cast farther out.

Some handlers carry training devices in sight, or that can be heard, and in their pockets for purposes of intimidation or deceit even though these

FLD. CH. JODI OF CZUKI BARAT
by Can. & Am. Fld. Ch. Ripp Barat out of Czuki O' Lake Catherine
Breeder: Richard M. Olsen   Owner: Lewis F. Simon
VCA Hall of Fame, 1978

DUAL CH. WEEDY CREEK LOBO
by Weedy Creek Skol out of Weedy Creek Merya
Breeder: Jane Graff   Owner: Harold R. Wingerter
VCA Hall of Fame, 1979

may or may not be effective, some see that the use of their whistle distracts the other dog and uses it accordingly.

Another point to know is that the handler's pace should be set without consideration of the sex or general health and size of the other handler, for as a team the dog and his handler must combine to give a purposeful performance. It must be neither too slow or too fast, and under no circumstance should one handler stop on the course if the other dog is making game, unless it is to obtain an honor. No special effort should be made by handlers or judges to accomplish this at the detriment of the non-pointing dog. The practice of bringing a dog back to honor proves nothing, but if done often enough it will cause both dog and handler problems. This is true only in a single course trial with a bird field. The handler whose dog is on out hunting should proceed on without interfering, and ignore the other dog just as if he was out hunting alone. One judge will continue on with him and other judge will stay back. The twenty-two minute back course time is dependent on the forward dog and not the dog and handler that are stopped whether it is for working a bird or some other reason.

In such stakes it is possible for one handler to be finished in the bird field and time called before the bracemate gets there. As long as the delay produced a bird, the basic criteria for that dog has been met. But, if the delay was for some other reason, the handler should make every effort to get to the bird field before time expires.

The handler whose dog establishes point and then intimidates his dog by running to get there and also uses excessive voice commands to be sure his dog stays, is working a dog still in need of training and experience or vice versa. If your dog has not shown to the front or side for a period of time (you are allowed five minutes in a 30 minute stake) and you know this is not normal, then it is proper for you to request permission from the judges to have a scout look for your dog, but you do not leave the normal course unless your dog is seen or found on point. Then one judge will follow you while you work your dog. It is important in these situations that your dog is found on point, otherwise a better decision for you would have been to continue on, or call your dog so he did show. It helps to know your dog's habits well enough to be correct in your decisions.

It indicates good manners and sportsmanship on the part of either handler to do nothing that would interfere with the other handler or his dog. As mentioned earlier, the pace should be set without consideration of the individual handlers, but they should show consideration toward each other by displaying a helpful manner and work to keep the pace even. This is true whether the handler is on foot or horseback, and the "running gear" should be removed from a handler using a horse who overruns the foot handler.

FLD. CH. WEEDY CREEK DUTCHES
by Weedy Creek Skol out of Shirbob's Honey Dew
Breeder: Jane Graff   Owner: Hank Rozanek
VCA Hall of Fame, 1980

FIELD CHAMPION FUTAKI LENKE
by Ch. Ceasar out of Futaki Lincsi
Breeder: Bela Hadik   Owner: Chauncey M. Smith, Jr.

231

Handlers should walk side by side and several paces apart and each should speed up or slow down accordingly without having to be cautioned by the marshal or judges.

Even the most experienced Vizsla owner can fail to recognize his own dog from another one while hunting or in competition, so it is important to keep this in mind. It could mean that a handler might need to correct the other handler, the judge, or himself at times so as to keep the dogs identified. Even the usage of different colored collars does not always prevent a mix-up. Such things have happened between a Vizsla and a different breed running in the same stake. It is much easier however to make a mistake between two Vizslas and it happens to the best of judges. For the most part such mix-ups are unintentional. Judges remember handlers easier than two look-alike dogs or they can be marking the wrong page, so it behooves the handler to be sure that both good and bad performances are associated with him and his own dog. This should not be done in any way that causes the judges to be distracted from their work. It is the alert judge who catches the field trial placements being given to the wrong dog and this happens too.

While on the back course both dogs, while out of view, go on point and a decision must be made later by the judges as to whether one of the dogs is guilty of stealing point or if both were working the bird and pointed at or near the same time. Judges can only judge what they see. The handler may have a better idea of what really took place since he knows his dog, but even he cannot know for sure what took place. However, the judges must make a decision, and as a handler you should know what their decision is before you continue on. Usually they will credit the dogs with a divided find, but one handler must work the bird.

Another important point where such a situation as this exists, or a natural honor, is that both handlers should consider all the factors before casting either dog on. A dog is trained to go on when commanded if it is his point, whereas the honoring dog normally knows that he is to wait. It often happens that the other handler's signal may send your dog. The handler who flushes a bird should first allow the other handler to get into a position where he can maintain positive control over his dog. Such manners benefit both handlers and their dogs. A stop to flush that involves two dogs represents a different situation. In both situations neither dog should become involved in a delayed chase.

While on course from Points B to C a "course wise," or "trial wise" dog will often cast directly into the bird field without hunting the course and the judges may eliminate him because of this. It is subjective judgment oftentimes on the part of the judge, but the handler again knows whether or not his dog is prone to do this. It is up to him to try and stop his dog from going to the bird field too soon. Getting your dog into the bird field first has definite advantages, but normally it will not change the outcome of the stake. Some handlers seem to think that this is a matter of life or death.

Most handlers know that one unproductive usually does not over-shadow an otherwise good total performance. It is not unusual to see some handlers with dogs that *point* on some innoculous command; this can be used effectively during hot weather when the dog could use a breather. This occurs mostly in the bird field as it has no particular advantage on the back course where the dog is not required to stop as he usually is in the bird field. Some handlers even get lucky enough to find a bird planted in the area which may surprise the dog more than it does the handler. After watching the bird planters for awhile it is not too hard to guess at a place to call point by commanding the dog obtusely, then kick around hoping to stumble onto one. If no bird is found then the dog is charged only with an unproductive.

In a slightly different situation at one trial on a bird field callback, a Vizsla and a Weimaraner were both working game and both pointed at exactly the same time while working toward one another some 150 feet apart. The Vizsla's handler thought that his dog honored and handled him accordingly. When the Weimaraner's bird was shot, the Vizsla started to fetch but stopped, and this dog had never had a breach of manners ever prior to this. The Vizsla then acted bewildered. When the Weimaraner finished out and was cast on he continued toward the Vizsla and hardly had the Vizsla's handler cast his dog on than the Weimaraner established point on the bird that the Vizsla had first pointed. As a spectator, I saw that the dogs were both making game and also saw the Vizsla's head turn slightly to establish his point. As the Vizsla handler, I would like to believe that I would have handled that situation properly. **The most important rule is never take your eyes off your dog during the entire stake.** As a judge, that same observation would cause me to give the benefit to the Vizsla and tell the handler to work its bird after the Weimaraner had finished his retrieve.

While in the bird field, the handler with the honoring dog must be alert to everything that is going on. Sometimes birds fly or run in the most unpredictable ways, and oftentimes a handler teaches his dog to allow birds to run under his dog on point and will not allow him to move or touch the bird. If a handler wants to test the honoring dog it can be done very easily if his dog is close enough to the other dog; many handlers will at times deliberately cause the other dog to fault itself in these situations if he is then in contention.

Sometimes the same test comes when a poor gunner shoots and misses or makes a poor hit. The handler should normally not send his dog for a retrieve on a crippled bird or doubtful bird unless ordered to do so by the judges. Neither should he become upset if for some reason none of the birds his dog worked were shot in a retrieving stake, for if his overall work was that good he will be called back for a kill and retrieve later on.

Each handler is faced with the prospect of being braced with either a untrained dog or one that on that particular brace is set off by some happening and forgets all of his training. This causes problems for the trained dog he is braced with, when it brings out the trained dog's jealousy or the trained dog is deliberately interfered with for a long time as opposed to just once or twice.

Good sportsmanship dictates that the offending dog's handler pick up his dog and leave the course under certain circumstances. Before doing so, a request must be made to the judges for the pick-up. Once it is obvious that your dog is out of competition and that he has or will physically interfere with the performance of his brace mate, you should get direct control immediately. On the back course from Points A to D, it is possible in many situations to effectively do this without physically picking up your dog, but not so while you are in the bird field. Rationalization of its performance in order to complete the course and get a chance at the birds in the bird field is wrong. Each handler, upon entering the stake, did in effect claim that his dog was *properly* trained for the competition, and is entitled to only compete within the rules and guidelines set down for that stake. He should not leave the decision to the judges to *order* his dog picked up for such a serious breach as *direct* uncontrollable interference with the brace mate, whether it is on the starting line or in the bird field.

The offending dog's handler should realize that it is wrong to allow his dog to get into this type situation where getting by without being corrected only encourages him the next time under the same type circumstances. Even more harm can occur to the offended dog, for it is not a matter of being able to "hack it" for either dog. It is much easier for any Vizsla to form bad habits than it is for the trainer to correct them or to train for positive habits. Anybody can put down a dog in the field trial that is *allowed* to learn to pick fights with another one.

But be cautious in making that decision to pick up your dog, for it is not unusual for a handler to assume that his dog has made a serious mistake when at that point the judges have him in contention for a placement. Talk to the judges first as the handler often sees what the judge does not or considers something his dog does a serious breach whereas the judges do not.

On the final stretch toward the bird field your dog should hunt to it all the way. Once he enters the bird field you will have to keep him inside of Points D1, D2, D3 and D4 for the designated time. The dog will usually, or should, enter the bird field before his handler, and if he knows

234

his business well enough, a point will be made before you get there. If not, then you must concentrate on keeping your Vizsla hunting in an area away from his brace mate as much as possible and completely cover the bird field according to the lines shown for the Area D.

It is not unusual for the judges to instruct the handler on how he is to send his dog for a retrieve, such as waiting to be instructed to send his dog. Whether you wait until the bird hits the ground, three seconds, or ten seconds later is a personal choice most of the time (three seconds is about optimum). You should handle your dog and the judge should evaluate the performance accordingly, but some judges are sensitive about their *personal* (discretionary) requirements and unless you want to lose, it does not seem judicious to go against their wishes. In the absence of instructions, you should handle your dog completely oblivious of the judges being there.

With all the distractions, it behooves the handler to never delay a command for fetch past the very minimum. In addition, he should try to kick up the bird (kick it hard enough to cause the bird to fly in the direction he kicks) so that his dog can accurately mark the flight and fall without changing positions. This is extremely important even though a dog is allowed a reasonable move for marking. The style in making the retrieve does not seem to matter for usually excessive hunting to find the bird, mouthing, hard mouthing, dropping the bird and extra commands from the handler counts but very little against the dog unless another dog has an otherwise equal performance. The Vizsla should go for the retrieve quickly and deliver directly to hand hardly stopping except to get a good hold on the bird. Anything less than this indicates incomplete training or problems in his training. One retrieve is adequate to win, and many handlers who know that their work is good and their bird handling is clean, hope upon hope that their dog does not find another bird.

In addition to all these factors, the most unpredictable one is called "the luck of the draw." The position of your brace in the stake relative to the weather, time of day, scenting conditions, local wild birds on the course and other game on the course can cause a dog to win or lose on any given day. Sometimes the scenting conditions for that particular brace are terrible and all dogs go birdless for a time. With the first brace of the day, sometimes the birds are so thick and the dogs have so many finds or flushes that they get high and go "bird crazy" and "cut their throats." Ideally none of these factors should change a Vizsla's performance, but then the other conditions at field trials are not ideal either. A field trial dog is *dumb* when he fails to learn that the horse and dog excretions along a line from Points A to D accumulate more with each passing brace and that a big reward is in a small plot of ground near the cars and people. The wiser dog soon learns where to find birds in a hurry and oftentimes will not follow the stenchy line, but will go directly to the bird field from cast off. Some do nothing else but follow the stenchy line.

If your dog leaves the starting line for the bird field, you should bring him back around, or if he finds a bird in the bird field work it out, and then get him back on course in a minimum of time and catch up to the other handler if at all possible. Such bird work has been counted as a back course find and the dog has gone around the course and won the stake.

The most important thing to remember is that your dog knows how to find birds better than you. He knows sterile ground and it is easy to see this by noting the difference in his ground searching pattern between the back course and bird field. Do not lose your temper for your dog senses it immediately. Control your dog positively when the occasion demands. Do not panic. Never take your eyes off your dog and always be able to see his brace mate. Train to win, compete to win, and help improve the sport while doing it. Above all else, remember that your dog is not a machine, nor is anyone else's dog. Nobody knows what the competition is before the trial or until after all the dogs in a stake have run. Never argue with the judge on his placements, but if you are concerned then talk to the Field Trial Chairman. Above all do not be a sore loser.

JUDGING QUALITIES

Once your Vizsla is trained (developed as is the case for puppy and derby ages) and steady to wing and shot for the gun dog or all-age stakes, the field trial handler must know and understand the art of judging in order to be successful. This knowledge also makes him a better winner or loser. Judging is learned by studying the performance requirements for the stake, training dogs for competition, watching many different dogs (including other breeds) perform under judgment and how they are placed, and first hand handling experience under several different judges.

A common judging procedure follows a pattern where the first two dogs are either put first and second or deemed not worthy of a placement. At some point in the running each judge will have four dogs that he considers worthy of placement either with or without discussion between themselves. Later on better performances might shift the order and drop one or more out. Sometimes a discussion between the two judges will raise one or more of the dogs. Both men can see and understand more if they do discuss things between themselves as the stake progresses.

Objective standards for judging are difficult to agree on and most judges base their decisions on experience, subjective elements, or negative factors such as: "One strike and you are out!" Judging is mostly negative — meaning that a judge may look for the slightest infraction from his viewpoint to put a dog out of the stake. Many judging factors are known and

TABLE 10-1

SPEED OF VIZSLA VERSUS BACK COURSE RATINGS

RATING	RATIO	DOG TRAVELS
	Distance or Speed (Dog/Handler)	
Poor	1/1	In horse tracks.
Fair	2/1	S type pattern.
		Straight lines with occasional short casts.
Good	3/1	Snake pattern.
		Same distance to either side, but side casts are wide.
Excellent	4/1	Long casts and forward.
		Same distance to either side with long side casts and always forward.
Outstanding	5/1	Very long casts and hits all forward objectives as well as those to the side.
		Distance forward increases while making very wide side casts.
		Covers all the ground and hits all objectives at extreme speed and always far to the front.

are used unconsciously by those judging, but some judges do use a printed form involving check-off factors as well as written notes. Documentation of each individual dog's performance is not ordinarily available to the handler but judges are willing to discuss their findings with each handler who asks. Each handler should make a practice of watching all the dogs in his stake so that he can be in a position to know how his performance compared with the others. In effect he too judges the stake. Unless this is done it serves little purpose to ask the judge why his dog did not place or what it did wrong.

Subjectivity is an element in judging that should be held to a very minimum. It should not be confused with "judgment" as such. As an example, suppose that two dogs scored the same, whatever rating system or method was used on an objective basis, but one dog actually was more pleasing to watch. Most judges would say that style was the criteria that should be used in selecting the best dog of the two. This is a form of subjectivity and some judges do not have such a good "eye" for this factor and will reject it as a basis for selection.

The most important part of field trial judging is the dog's work on the back course portion of the stake under judgment. At some point both judges decide that the dog is "go," or "no go," based on their observations and judgment, and any excellence after a "no go" decision is made in the bird field does not change that decision. The placements are made on the back course and confirmed in the bird field — or lost.

What then makes a good back course run, hunt or race? Both "run" and "race" are commonly used and generally mean that the dog had looked for no objectives or had no pattern. It means a fast turn around the course following horse tracks from previous braces and definitely does not describe hunting. Yet the judge does not want to watch the Vizsla, for example, hunt the course in a slow methodical manner so a running hunt would be a better description of what is expected in gun dog stakes. In the all-age stake it should be a running race all the way hitting the far away objectives.

Back course evaluations are: outstanding; excellent; good; fair; and, poor. The average handler walks about three miles per hour at field trials when under judgment. If he handles from a horse, he will travel as fast as five miles per hour. In a continuous course stake where the handler is on horseback and the dog runs by the clock for the specified time, the speed is not a factor relative to the total distance traveled as in the single course trial. The single course trial is usually in a horseshoe pattern and is a *fixed* distance. It is based on the *average* time it takes for a handler to walk the twenty-two or thirty minutes.

A horseback handler moving at five miles per hour would need to have his dog hunt the course at a speed of twenty-five miles per hour forward

The customs and equipment and procedures do vary from place to place since the requirements of the field trial do have to accommodate the site conditions encountered. In almost all cases there is some "special" equipment required beyond the needs of a "typical" hunter. These three photos were taken at a Florida field trial.

and to either side to be judged outstanding. Conversely, he could walk at one mile per hour and his dog would only need to work at five miles per hour for the same rating, but this is too slow for the fast stepping Vizsla and the rating speed should not be less than two miles per hour for the handler in field trial competition.

Therefore, based on the author's experience and judging criteria, Table 10-1 gives values or the speed of the dog or distance he travels relative to the handler versus the back course rating with examples for reference. The description will easily fit gun dog patterns and range or all-age patterns and range. The handler should know his Vizsla and recognize whether or not he fits the gun dog pattern and range or all-age pattern and range before entering the stake. Many owners enter both kinds and hope that the one pattern of their dog will suffice for both. For some handlers changing his Vizsla from gun dog to all-age is as simple as walking in one and riding and handling from horseback for the other. Proper selection of grounds for the two stakes is also a factor with some dogs. Heavy cover and close objectives will not permit a dog to run all-age.

The judging sheet of Figure 10-2, presents a condensed listing of judging factors that can be useful in evaluating your own dog and also in judging. As a handler, you should make an effort to judge your own dog.

Whether you think the judge is right or wrong (good or bad) in his work, you should always consider how difficult it must be to ride a horse from daylight to dark for one or two days in all types of weather conditions before openly criticizing him. Trials cannot be conducted without judges and unnecessary abuse and poor treatment by the handlers serves no useful purpose. If you have done your training properly and work at field trialing your turn will come. You too have to be able to judge your own dog's performance correctly in spite of how well you know your own dog. The judge sees your dog only the time down in that stake and judges only what he sees. The handler usually has a tendency of seeing things not readily apparent to the judges. The handler often makes the same mistake he criticizes the judges for since he judges his dog more critically – to a higher standard than the competition will be – than he should and gets aggravated which in turns causes him to over handle his dog.

FIGURE 10-2

FIELD TRIAL JUDGING SHEET

STAKE_____

BRACE_____DOG NO._____DOG'S NAME_____

RATING FACTORS	RATING	REMARKS
CAST OFF		
RANGE		
APPLICATION		
INDEPENDENCE IN HUNTING		
OBJECTIVES WORKED		
OVERALL BACK COURSE		
MANNERS WITH BRACE MATE		
RESPONSE TO HANDLER		
STYLE		
BACKING		NO._____
BACK COURSE BIRD WORK		NO._____
BIRD FIELD BIRD WORK		NO._____
MANNERS ON GAME		
QUALITY OF RETRIEVES		

NOTE: Number rating will *not* be used to decide placements.

RATING: 1 - Poor
           2 - Fair
           3 - Good
           4 - Excellent
           5 - Outstanding

PLACEMENT_____JUDGE_____

POSITIVE AND NEGATIVE JUDGING FACTORS

The judging form of Figure 10-2 does not cover all the positive and negative factors that a judge may look for. While it is impossible to get agreement from one to another, these are some which will serve to guide you as a handler or judge:

POSITIVE

Steady on the line
Good response to handler
Checks to handler properly
Stylish dog
Cast to objective on breakaway
Hunts fast
Intelligent quartering
Busy
Happy
Searches out all objectives
Good casts with purpose
Attractive running
Increases running speed with time
Intense on point
Stylish on point
Snappy movement
Uses wind effectively
Automatically relocates game
Roads moving bird effectively
Knows birdy cover
Locates game accurately

Relocates quickly

NEGATIVE

Not steady on the line
Poor response to handler
No cast to objective
Interfered with bracemate
Ignored handler
Stubborn to commands
Handler hacks dog
Stops and waits for signals
Blinks
Gun shy or sensitive
Lacks intensity on point
Lack of desire in run
Intentionally bumped bird
Sluggish
Hunts when sent to relocate
Hunts when sent to retrieve
Slow pace
Potters
Too close to handler
Tires
Handler does not call point for judges' attention or other handler
Flags on point

POSITIVE

Backs bracemate on sight

Finds birds
Marks birds accurately
Backed bracemate on caution
Proper stop to flush
Steady to wing
Steady to shot
Retrieves on command
Relocates on command
Hunts independently

Bold and aggressive

NEGATIVE

Softens point when handler approaches
Cuts behind
Ground trails
Delayed chase
Located game poorly
Fails to find birds
Poor or no mark on bird
Refuses to back
Backed on command
Chases bird (except puppy and derby age)
Broke position on point
Stole point
Caught bird
Not steady to shot
Did not retrieve dead bird
Poor retrieve
Chews or ate bird
Went to gallery, car of left course
Cut course to bird field
Head trails
Fought with bracemate
Depends on handler
Uncontrolled break
Controlled break

HUNTING A FIELD TRIAL DOG

Some trainers and owners do not hunt a dog that they train for field trial winning. Others see no reason not to, and claim that they would not own a (field trial) Vizsla unless they hunted with him. As time and experience warrants these opinions change and it is true that many field trialers never hunt.

There is one important consideration that needs to be made. That is a dog should be worked on wild game if he is to gain experience and knowledge to develop confidence on his own, to develop a keen interest and to have the desire to seek out the right places for game. This can usually be done before the time that he is broken steady to shot. Under the artificial conditions of field trials it is difficult to stay in contention for wins or placements while allowing your dog to use his own judgment completely. In most of the trials it seems that the handler trains his dog just so he can drive him around the course in front of the horses, keep a minimum of bird contact on the back course, and then have just one find.

On the other hand, a one dog owner who likes both sports of hunting and field trialing can do both with the same Vizsla. But it behooves him to be aware of many differing circumstances and adjust his behavior accordingly while hunting. It is so easy for his dog to unlearn as opposed to directed learning that is initiated by the trainer. If the situation is such the dog learns all the things he needs to know naturally through his own good experiences then all the better, but this would be rather unusual. All other disadvantages considered, it helps to hunt a field trial dog in order to delay or confuse his becoming wise too soon to the repetitive artificial conditions. It helps the handler to field trial his dog because he learns how to train for greater perfection and enjoyment.

It would be wrong to say that a field trial Vizsla makes a better hunter. To begin with, hunting with a bird dog usually involves being with other hunters who will shoot game as soon as it flushes wild and will not normally consider the dog in the process. As a result the dog gets too eager and will forget his manners even if he has been well trained and fully broken. A good meat dog should certainly start on his way as soon as the bird is hit for the job of finding or tracking is so much easier and he will be more effective in finding shot birds. The hunter works hard to find the game in the first place, even when using a good Vizsla, and he certainly does not want to lose his bird. The longer he waits to send his dog after the air washing process of flight, the less are his chances of finding a cripple; unless his dog is a good foot tracker which is not desirable in field trialing.

244

The idea is to train your Vizsla for whatever suits your purposes and enjoy that sport to the maximum. Everyone will have a slightly different idea about this, but it is better that you and your Vizsla be happy in what you are doing than any other consideration. A number of Vizslas used in both sports will break when a bird is shot while hunting but will not break under the same conditions in a field trial — they seem to learn the difference and adjust accordingly.

The photos above and below show that water retrieving is, for many Vizsla owners, an off season pursuit that helps keep their dogs in shape over the summer months. The AKC does not require water proficiency be demonstrated for Vizslas, even though the breed was conceived as an all-round worker in the field.

CHAPTER 11

Water Training And Water Trials

IS THE VIZSLA A TRUE RETRIEVER?

A water retriever is a specialist. None of the pointing breeds can claim to be in the same class with water retrieving breeds. But it is claimed that the Vizsla is the only *natural* pointer-retriever in the pointing breeds. This is not to say that the other pointing breeds do not actively work in the water or water trials. All the German breeds do. Neither does it imply that the Vizsla (smooth and wirehaired) is the only one of this group that retrieves shot game under every condition. Some dogs in any breed can be taught to do that. The basic meaning of this claim is that Vizslas have the capacity to specialize in the same class and to the same degree as the retriever breeds.

Many Vizslas seem to be incapable of walking without carrying objects in their mouths. Some have extremely good eyesight and most all are extremely intelligent with excellent memories. These are certainly necessary qualifications for the retriever class but the Vizsla's coat would eliminate him from serious consideration for general usage.

247

Apacs, one of the first Wirehaired Vizslas imported to North America, is in his summer coat, when photographed by Harvey Basler.

The Vizsla cannot compete against the retriever breeds, as it is not eligible for American Kennel Club retriever competition but fun water trials are held for the Vizsla by local specialty clubs. Water (field) trials are held by the pointing breeds under sanction of the American Kennel Club. These tests usually do not involve the highly skilled performances required for the retriever trials, although they could. This is not the Vizsla's best specialty supposedly and most Vizsla owners lean more toward hunting upland game. Generally hunters most interested in ducks and geese own one of the retriever breeds.

Raba, owned by Al Stevens, takes his pleasure in a formal pond which is permanently inhabited by goldfish. At the time of the photo he was concentrating on a fish.

248

It is unlikely that the Vizsla will get the chance to undergo the rigorous training and experience from a retriever trainer for the purpose of proving or disproving his ability as a true retriever.

The Vizsla is as much at home swimming in water as a fish. He does not mind the cold water and readily retrieves downed ducks, geese or any other bird that is shot down in the water.

He will swim for hours at a time, just for his own pleasure, and will only occasionally touch bottom or stop swimming. It is not unusual to see one swim under the water, and he will put his head under for as long as a minute or more to look for anything of possible interest. Mostly, he likes

One pup is boldly playing in the pond while a less brave soul plays along the shore. First entries are frequently comical, but once in and used to the water, the Vizsla is very much at home.

Vizslas enjoy playing with the humans in the water. Games, retrieving, splashing, etc. are the common thing.

Even dogs that like water usually don't like splashed or sprayed water, but then there's Csinos V. Hunt. Here Nancy Boggs gives her a turn at the hose.

Using her shadow to help her see through the water, Trixie, one of the author's dogs, "hunts" for a fish to grab.

to chase water bugs, dragonflies, fish, butterflies or catch tadpoles. He enjoys playing with anything else in the water as long as he can make a game of it all. The Vizsla will also move gravel or rocks in shallow water much like a raccoon uses its paws, and he will put his mouth on the bottom in an effort to pick something up.

One Vizsla I owned would point bluegills and bass by the hour, always seeming on the verge of pouncing on one. It was a tremendous temptation as the bluegills would swim in and out around her legs while she was so still. Some of my Vizslas have caught bluegills and brought them in. This Vizsla would swim underwater for several feet at a time chasing a water snake while not quite able to catch it.

Another Vizsla would swim around the pond catching one and two year-old bullfrog tadpoles at a time. Then she would swim to the edge of the pond and drop them in at the water's edge and go for more.

My Vizslas cannot be let outside the house during the summer without running and lunging into the pond and they usually stay in until forced to leave. We cannot go swimming ourselves without letting them go too. They join in the fun and never quit swimming.

Ch. Csinos V Hunt, C.D.X., owned by Dr. Paul and Shirley Rothan fought a water hose stream by the hour. She would also fight the water splashed at her by swimmers.

Whenever one of my Vizslas swims to anyone in the family, it means holding him for a time. Generally we will cradle him on his back and hold him with both arms.

Vizslas love to ride in boats, canoes and rafts and will jump out or off to investigate something and return to be pulled back aboard.

There does not seem to be any problem with the dog's coat after swimming every day all summer long and a Vizsla under normal circumstances just does not drown even when still a puppy. The real danger to one comes from power boats or thin ice.

One Christmas day when the pond had just the edges frozen one of our puppies was let out to exercise and a few minutes later I looked over on the far side of the pond and saw him struggling in a hopeless effort to get back onto the ice. My wife ran one direction and I the other. She got to him first and laid down on the ice and was just able to reach far enough to pull him in. The puppy was near exhaustion and barely able to move, but had never given up. Although the puppy was near frozen and exhausted and had a lower than normal body temperature, he suffered no apparent permanent damage and lived to swim in the icy water again.

It seems like there is always *one* puppy in each litter that hits the water with all the gusto there is and this always causes problems in winter when he goes onto the ice or if there is no ice.

A Vizsla easily learns to enter the water with a jumping leap in his anxiety to get to a dummy or bird in the least amount of time. Some will do this without much previous training or encouragement, and some just do so naturally.

Where the need exists to train a Vizsla to water, one of the most effective methods is to take the fishing pole and bird wing used in yard work and start the dog chasing it on land near the water and then move the wing into the water. Another method is to put on your swimming suit and go out into the water and cause him to come to you. Go out farther each time. Some trainers take a dog out from the bank and let him loose to swim back to shore.

A Vizsla learns to swim very quickly—sometimes the first time in the water. He is slow to panic and has the utmost confidence when in the water with his owner.

The Vizsla will adapt to the method of hunting you use. They can be trained to ride quietly until needed for the retrieve.

WATER TRIALS

Vizsla water trials can and should involve the family. Stakes are only limited to the wishes and imagination of those responsible for the trial with novice puppy of differing ages, puppy, derby, gun dog, all-age, children and powder puff stakes with varying qualifications for the dogs and handlers. Dead pigeons are most often used and are thrown by hand from the bank and/or boat and then a blank pistol is fired except for the very young puppies. Both land and water retrieves may be required. The trials are very informal and are easy enough for most anyone to learn how to compete successfully. Sometimes a Vizsla will do well without any previous training as long as he has learned to swim—and some have even done so without previous swimming experience.

Most Vizsla owners just use their dogs for water work during the summer months in water trials, or are content to just go down by the creek, pond or lake and toss sticks for retrieving.

Water retrieving training is the most effective method for teaching land retrieves. It is much easier to catch or stop your Vizsla as he returns to the bank.

For some of the Continental breeds, water retrieve qualification is an American Kennel Club requirement for the Field Champion title. At present it is not required for Vizslas.

WATER TRIAL STAKES

Since the pointing breeds do not compete as retrievers, the specialty clubs are free to establish any type stake they wish and set their own rules

252

under sanction by the American Kennel Club but no champion points can be awarded. The regular American Kennel Club stakes for retriever breeds are: Derby; Qualifying; Open All-Age; Amateur All-Age; and, Limited All-Age. The pointing breeds could use these same stakes with the same rules but usually have: Novice Puppy; Puppy; Derby; Amateur Gun Dog or All-Age; Advanced Gun Dog or All-Age; Finished Gun Dog or All-Age; Powder Puff; Children's and others. Each stake can be made as simple or complicated and difficult as necessary to achieve the purpose intended.

The finished retrieving Vizsla in water trials should heel mannerly to and from the starting line. Most owners who use their Vizsla in field trials stand their dog (sitting the dog is normal) for the bird and shot, and then gives the fetch command when the judges are satisfied with his steadiness. It is highly desirable that the Vizsla leaps with gusto into the water, swim into or beyond the decoys but directly to the bird, pick it up gently, and return directly to its handler and stand (or sit) until the bird is taken from his mouth. On blind retrieves on land and water the dog should, after being sent to the area of the fall, use his nose for the final location, or directed until it is sight located.

While a Vizsla does not have the body mass and the double coat of the retrieving breeds, he does not lack for confidence in the water or enthusiasium for getting there. Spectacular entries are not unusual for Vizslas which have been around water enough to get used to it.

Vizslas seem to have no qualms about putting their heads under water. While watching fish, it is not uncommon to see them put their head under the water to break the reflection or to grab the fish.

Given a little encouragement virtually all Vizslas will enter the water boldly after their first exposure or two and they have their confidence. Forcing this will certainly not get it for you and be sure that the area in which you allow the dog to enter the pond is clear of underwater obstructions so the dog will not have a bad experience during early work.

The Vizsla is a curious dog. Even exposed to water late in life, he cannot ignore it. Likely though you will have to be easier getting him in and confident — and it might take a little longer.

A bold entry is a thing of beauty. It takes some work to ultimately be able to get two Vizslas to leave a dock as these are. There is no sign of "water-shyness" in this photo.

PUPPY STAKE

Puppy competition is divided according to age. The novice puppy is 3 to 6 months and 6 to 9 months with the Open Puppy stake 6 to 15 months of age. The water test consists of either one or two single retrieves thrown from land at distances suitable to the age divisions but not over 80 feet. Novice puppies are not shot over and the Open Puppy may or may not be depending on what the club wants to do. A time may be specified in which the puppy has to enter the water and also for the retrieve once it has entered the water. It should be held on the starting line by his handler. A retrieve to hand is not required.

DERBY STAKE

This stake is for dogs 6 to 24 months of age. While it is not expected that the dog heel to and from the line or stand steady on the line, there is every reason to expect quality performance in every other aspect of the test, and the dog should deliver the bird directly to hand. While some clubs do not require that the derby dog deliver directly to hand, the judges should give credit to dogs that do.

The test usually involves two single retrieves. One is thrown from the bank for the dog about 20 to 40 yards, and the other is thrown from a boat for a swim of 40 to 60 yards. A shot should be fired to get his attention as the bird is tossed. Usually one minute is allowed for entry into the water and five minutes for picking up the bird, but these times are used seldom since good performances do not take near that long.

AMATEUR, QUALIFYING, ADVANCED AND FINISHED

These are all relatively the same stakes. A division can be made to give every contestant an equal chance with differences of training and experience considered. And these stakes can be used as qualifying stakes for a more advanced stake. These stakes are for dogs of any age, but usually are over six months of age. The tests vary between types of retrieves, such as single using no decoys with the bird thrown from the banks and/or from the boat or with decoys, a single and double with and without decoys and blind retrieves. Swimming distances can be set up to eighty yards. The stakes can involve differences in training and manners on the line, retrieving, and not having placed in that stake previously or in higher level stakes. Retrieves may be allowed in an area within a radius of six feet from the starting position. The handler may or may not be allowed to throw objects to direct his dog. The dog may be required to hold his bird until the judges instruct the handler to take it. These four stakes are usually Gun Dog, and if all are used at one trial the requirements for each successive one are more stringent. Time to enter the water and pick up the bird may be required, but usually is not needed.

ALL-AGE

This stake if for dogs over six months of age. It demands a finished and polished performance from the dog. It should require that all dogs entered have won some type of qualifying stake. The test should be difficult involving single and double retrieves through decoys with the handler and dog both working in and out of the blind. Sight retrieves of over 80 yards

Water trials in this country for Vizslas are catching on fast. They are usually held between late spring and early fall since field trial activity then is at a minimum. Here handler and his dog wait "at the line" from which the dog will be sent to retrieve the birds.

may be required. An additional requirement may be making a swim across the water to a bird dropped on the opposite shore and land retrieves by sight and by direction from the handler for birds not marked by his dog. Retrieving distances should be long enough that the dog must show intelligence and the use of all his senses in locating and retrieving. The dog should be required to heel off lead to and from the starting line and the handler may not touch or otherwise position his dog with his hands during the entire test. An absolute minimum of commands should be used in getting the dog to stand steady on line, sending, directing or on the retrieve. The dog should swim in a straight line back, not drop the bird, preferably not shake off water before delivery, and quickly take his position in front of the handler and hold his bird until it is taken, usually on direction of the judges. Hardmouthing should result in disqualification whenever it occurs.

WATER TRIAL JUDGING SHEET

STAKE_____

DOG NO. _____ DOG'S NAME_____

	JUDGING FACTORS	1st Bird	2nd Bird	3rd Bird	REMARKS
1	STAND OR SIT ON LINE				
2	ENTRY INTO WATER				
3	SWIM OUT TO BIRD				
4	MARK OF BIRD				
5	PICK-UP OF BIRD				
6	SWIM BACK WITH BIRD				
7	RETRIEVE TO HANDLER				
8	HEEL TO AND FROM LINE				
	TOTAL SCORE				

PLACEMENT_____ JUDGE_____

_____ Held on line
_____ Steady on line
_____ Not steady on line
_____ Controlled break
_____ Leaped into water
_____ Walked into water
_____ Bothered by decoys
_____ Failed to locate bird
_____ Retrieved to hand
_____ Retrieved decoy
_____ Did not complete retrieve
_____ Dropped bird
_____ Chewed bird
_____ Extra commands used
_____ Took too long to enter water

SCORING: 0 — Disqualified
           1 — Poor
           2 — Fair
           3 — Good
           4 — Excellent
           5 — Outstanding

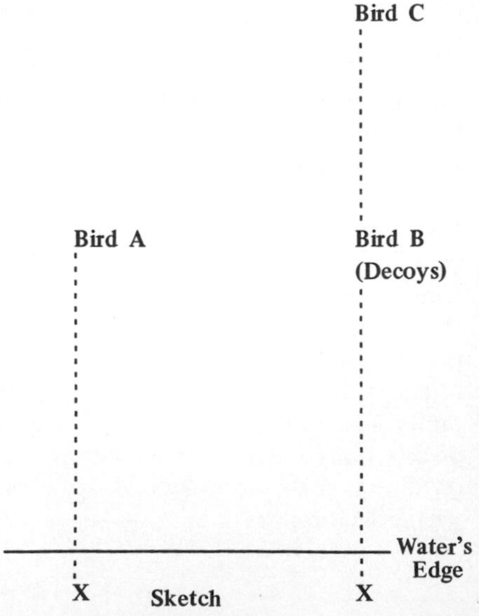

NOTE: Dogs may be placed on score alone.

Bird C

Bird A

Bird B
(Decoys)

Water's Edge

X   Sketch   X

In advanced retrieving, one must work through decoys.   This phase of training is really not difficult, yet many dogs fail in trials at this point. Use decoys in training and when the dog starts to pick one up, yell, "no." If he persists in retrieving it, don't take it and send him back for the bird. He will soon get the idea that you want the one real bird out there.

POWDER PUFF AND CHILDREN'S STAKES

These two stakes usually comprise relatively simple tests to demonstrate the skill of the handler in working the dog. They usually signify limited or no experience and are intended to introduce the women and children to this type of competition with the Vizsla. The experience of the dog is supposed to not be a judging consideration. The stakes involve dogs

259

entered usually in the other stakes and are run at the end of the trial. Usually only single retrieves are required.

WATER TRIAL JUDGING

Water trial judging is more objective than field trials and is very much like obedience judging. The form for judging, Figure 11-1, has been used and found satisfactory in most stakes. Sometimes the dogs perform so nearly alike that no memory will suffice and usually run-offs are required to pick a winner.

There are eight objective judging factors used on the judging form, and all may or may not be used in the rating. The judges can keep in mind all the subjective factors such as: memory, intelligence, nose, courage, perseverance, style, control and time. The two judges could, if they tied in their rating, discuss the subjective factors and possibly agree on which dog was the better one.

On the right hand side of the form is a sketch where the judge can mark the path of each dog to and from the fall which is helpful in remembering specific dogs and their performance.

A check list of good and bad factors is below the rating form and serves only to remind the judge of a specific action of the dog.

The scoring is the same as for the form presented in the field trial chapter: outstanding; excellent; good; fair; and, poor; then one additional one, disqualified. Disqualified is used whenever the dog does not enter the water, does not find the bird, retrieves a decoy, hardmouths or chews the bird or does not retrieve the bird.

The judge should try to create an environment where both the handler and his dog feel that he is helping them do a good job and both judges should insist that the handler handle his dog without instructions once the handler signifies he is ready to commence. Handlers are usually nervous on the line and judges can help the handler overcome some of this.

Vizsla judging should be on dead birds so that the dog will not get pecked in the eye and perhaps ruin him for this type of work, or cause him to kill and hardmouth the bird. The judges should not permit "training" by the handler where he throws objects or tosses his dog into the water during the time he is on the line.

CHAPTER 12

Breeding

PURPOSE OF BREEDINGS

The purpose of breeding is to create new individuals of a species. In this case creating more Vizslas. In nature there is a selection of mates that insures that the weak, sickly or dumb will not perpetuate. They simply do not reach the age where they can reproduce.

Breeders must select mates and they use their experience, knowledge and intelligence to insure that each mating will produce sound Vizslas.

Beyond that, breeders seek to create *better* Vizslas with each mating. For most, it is not enough to "hold" existing quality; there is a strong desire to breed a better Vizsla. This is good.

With most "young" breeds, there is a period of development where virtually all breeding is a crossing of bloodlines to get (hopefully) better qualities while holding good qualities. In time breeders near perfection (true perfection is likely not possible) and it is at this time that close inbreeding is used to stabilize the good that has been developed.

261

This perfection goes for quantity as well as quality. One seeks not just to have one super individual in a litter of idiots. One hopes ultimately to have whole litters of outstanding Vizslas.

The breeder is haunted by the question, "Is true evaluation proving such quality and development even possible?" If it is, it is certain to be an expensive proposition.

For some Vizsla breeders their efforts are just a source of enjoyment, satisfaction and a sense of personal fulfillment (hobby), and to others it is just a method of trying to make a dollar (business). Both kinds are concerned directly with breed improvement and it is probably true that every breeder does contribute to the evolutionary changes in his breed as long as his breedings are pure.

The definition of a pure-bred dog breed is a dog population selectively inbred for a large number of generations past to reveal a distinctive genetic composition manifesting itself with a distinctive combination of physical traits in appearance and behavior as well as in mental makeup. Man determines the number of distinct dog breeds — not nature — for his desired purpose and use. He also determines the strains and lines within his particular breed.

Mrs. Jane Tallman said that she can tell a Vizsla's sire — dam — grandsire and granddam — great grandsire and great granddam and so on when she has seen and known those dogs previously. She believes that this characteristic for recognition is unique in this breed (of look alikes) and it is also confirmed by other breeders making this same claim. Mrs. Tallman said that she raised Boxers and no such identification of genetic family characteristics within that breed was evident.

BACKGROUND OF VIZSLA BREEDINGS

In each dog breed there is what is termed the "sport" and the "fancy." Without going back to define the actual origin and meaning of these two words it is enough to know now they mean one represents and supports the hunting aspects while the other represents the show interests. Also, some breeders have a strong interest in both. These are the dual-minded breeders who use their brood bitches and studs after having proven them in both field and show competition.

The Vizsla has been subject to indiscriminate breedings that nearly wiped it out before. He is pure once again because of the dedication of certain breeders during his most critical periods and any owner in the United States is now privileged to set up his own breeding program.

This Vizsla is due to whelp any day. Other than a slight change in conformation, note that she is an example of good health.

Whelping over and situated in a clean dry whelping box, pups get their first meal.

Considering the practices in the breed's past history, very few people, before the Vizsla was brought into the United States, were fortunate enough to become involved in Vizsla breeding. It was controlled by a registering authority which decided the relative worth of each proposed breeding and approved or disapproved it.

From the few Vizslas used to re-establish the breed after World War II in Europe, and the ones used to establish the breed here later, a great amount of close inbreeding was necessary just to provide Vizslas in quantity, then line breeding later became a more desirable and practical method. But line breeding can be a form of inbreeding although it may not fix faults as firmly.

It probably can be said that after all the breedings done by is owners since Frank Tallman received *Sari* and later *Rex* to start the Vizsla movement here, that the effects of close inbreeding are still a problem in some breedings. Whether this has been responsible for the lack of uniformity of physical appearance is difficult to know. It may be aggravated by differences in breeding philosophy between the field and show type breeders.

Dr. Osborn, a veterinarian and expert breeder, was the largest importer of the Vizsla. He had the "von Schloss Loosdorf" and "Dravavology" from Austria; "Bor," "Duks," "Lila," "Pik" and "Dijana from Yugoslavia; "Ficko" and "Szikra" from Hungary; and, "Olca," "Selle," "Mavidio," "Kubis," "Hana," "Povazia," "Karpat" and "Zabokreky" from Czechoslovakia. He first registered with the original listing in the Field Dog Stud Book in 1953. Dr. Osborn maintained high standards and was looked upon as producing consistently superior Vizslas by those who bought from him.

Charles Hunt and his first wife, Melissa, of Illinois were a close second to Dr. Osborn in importing and breeding Vizslas. After his second marriage to Joan she showed many of their Vizslas. Many of their imports came from England because of his second wife's close association and experience in working for the English government. She finished some of her dogs (one was the second Champion) for show champion titles. She is still active with horses, Vizslas and other dogs as Huntlea Farm in Tennessee.

Frank Engstrom of Minnesota, one of the first breeders and importers, was one of the biggest Vizsla breeders without specialization in its usage such as field or show.

Names of small breeders, who are interested in showing their Vizslas, are mentioned earlier in this book and some of the ones named also breed for field and hunting purposes.

The Vizsla breeder who breeds primarily to produce more Vizslas for hunting purposes is relatively unknown unless he advertises in a national

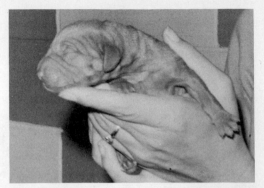
Vizsla puppy at birth is barely a handful and basically helpless

publication. To say that this person is improving the breed by this singular activity would be as presumptuous as saying that the ones breeding for show are not.

Actually the Vizsla breed has relatively few breeders at this time and many are in the one litter, one or two litters per year or every other year category so that the impact of established breeders is practically non-existent.

The breeders who qualify as breeding true to type are those who breed for the dual dog. This could include those breeding and field trialing where the end result of their breeding of field trial winners would be judged as improving the breed, but does not because they too place improper emphasis on just one or a small number of important characteristics of the breed.

These people change from year to year, although some remain active over a period of years, with some dropping out and new ones becoming prominent for a few years. These owners believe that they offer the true type Vizsla when they do breed or use their Vizslas at stud. Very few establish a progressive or a scientific breeding program or develop a strain within the breed. For this reason it would be of no particular value to name field trial Vizsla owners, except in picture captions, and call them breeders because of other variables that do not exist for the part-time breeders of Vizslas exposed only to show competition.

For reference purposes it is appropriate to name past and present breeders who exceed the mentioned litter category such as: Weedy Creek Kennels owned by M. D. (Bud) and Jane Graff of Nebraska; Futaki Kennels owned by C. M. Smith, Jr. of New York; Rozanek Kennels owned by Hand Rozanek of Nebraska; Mile High Kennels owned by J. R. Holcomb of Colorado; Justhill Kennels owned by Leonard and Kathy Hartl; Shirbob Kennels owned by Robert S. and Shirley Foster of Washington; and, the Burjan Kennels owned by Denes and Joyce Burjan of New Jersey.

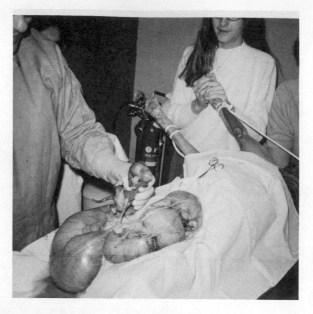

Veterinarian performs Caesarean section on Vizsla. Above he removed the first pup. Below the first pup gets a rubdown to stimulate his breathing as the second is removed from the exposed uterus.

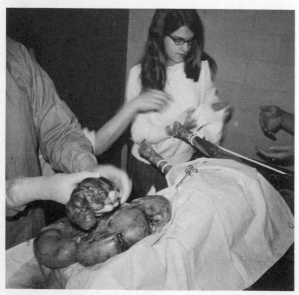

Pup which doesn't respond to rub down is pinched at the nape of the neck to make him cry. These few photos do not tell how this is done but serve to point out that it is possible to save a litter if it is determined the bitch will have a problem.

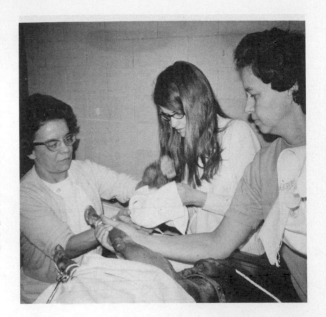

After Caesarean operation puppies and mother settle to relax and recover.

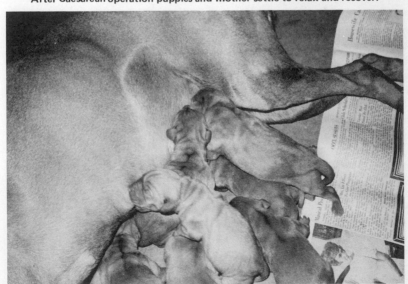

If a person is interested in getting into the art of breeding Vizslas, he should acquire some knowledge about the subject of genetics and breeding practices, but he need not be an expert to do a good job. Then first and foremost a study should be made of as many different dogs and their pedigrees as he can in the breed to decide what strains or types best suit his preferences. The potential breeder ought to know everything that is possible to learn about those dogs either before or during his breeding avocation. Basically, a breeder can become involved as a kennel business with the sole intent of making a profit or as a hobby just to demonstrate how much of his acquired knowledge and experience contributed to his breedings. There is no substitute for getting to shows, obedience and field trials and studying the different Vizslas.

There are no special books written on breeding of the Vizslas, and none are needed, for many books have been written by expert breeders from various backgrounds and professions. They are easy to read and understand for anyone interested enough in scientific breeding. These principles apply equally well to the Vizsla breed. Although many genetic traits and characteristics are visible in relation to prior ancestors it takes experience and study of these books to understand the potential benefit of a scientific breeding program.

VALUE OF PEDIGREES

The pedigree can be either beneficial or detrimental to the prospective breeder depending on his knowledge of genetics (breeding practices) and of the individual Vizslas named in the pedigrees. In this book there are dogs pictured that represent four or more generations. It is difficult to evaluate good or bad points from pictures, but there are several salient features and characteristics than can be seen by the trained Vizsla breeder. This holds for all dogs pictured and generally the proportions of height to length may be distorted and caution should be taken before making assumptions that the picture is a true visual representation of that Vizsla.

The majority of names used in the breed are of Hungarian extraction and are normally used only in registration practices. No two names alike of living dogs are permitted in American Kennel Club registration, but that same dog can have a different registered name in the American Field registry.

There is the tendency for all breeders to slant and distort written and oral portrayals of their dogs, which is both good and bad, but normal and maybe desirable.

Personally knowing all the dogs involved in related pedigrees gives the best assurance of proper judgment and selection. Possibly the best method

TABLE 12-1

ANCESTRY AND GENERATIONS

Generation	0	1	2	3	4	5	6	7	8	9	10
Ancestors*	1	2	4	8	16	32	64	128	256	512	1024

| Individual Dog | Parents | Grandparents | Great Grandparents | Great Great Grandparents | Great Great Great Grandparents | Great Great Great Great Grandparents | Great Great Great Great Great Grandparents | Great Great Great Great Great Great Grandparents | Great Great Great Great Great Great Great Grandparents | Great Great Great Great Great Great Great Great Grandparents |

*NOTE: The number of ancestors in the pedigree can be determined by the following equation:

$$A = 2^n \quad \text{(Where n is the generation of interest.)}$$

EXAMPLE: 6th Generation. $A = 2 \times 2 \times 2 \times 2 \times 2 \times 2 = 64$ dogs

TO FIND THE FRACTION OF CONTRIBUTION OF EACH DOG DIVIDE THAT NUMBER INTO 1.

EXAMPLE: $F = 1/A = 1/64$

is to know two or more dogs listed in linebred pedigrees below the great grandsires and great granddams. Neither of these study methods is used to best advantage. The final choice for breeding will still relate to an individual's personal preference and experience level including the proximity and ease of access to a stud.

Experienced breeders learn that litter brothers and sisters in the same and subsequent litters with the same sire and dam have different combinations of genes and that the odds of two having like characteristics are nearly impossible. It may prove that mating to one male in the litter will result in a poor combination of genes but the mating to a litter brother will be an outstanding mating. This fact in itself can negate individual pedigrees. He may learn that nothing is gained in breeding to a Best In Show or Dual Champion Vizsla stud because these titles do not tell if such a dog is prepotent or will help achieve the balance the breeder is after.

Finally, there is little need to look past the fourth generation (great great grandparents) for good or bad points in dogs intended to be used for breeding purposes except to verify that each dog from the older generations were actually used and trained in some form of competition. This does not apply for those working to eliminate hip dysplasia as there is still no evidence that fourth generation Vizslas having all normal parents do not continue to transmit this disease. This criteria applies to physical looks and trainability primarily. Trainability must be demonstrated in every generation. For the Vizsla to be used for breeding, we prefer that his ability be demonstrated in field trials and hunting to insure that the breed's superior qualities are being perpetuated.

BREEDING FOR TRAINABILITY

Most dog trainers who have several years of experience learn that for their particular breed or breeds they must make a number of adaptations to insure consistent success. Whether this develops from a trial and error process combined with long experience, is of little concern to the average one-dog (at a time) owner.

Thanks to various researchers much of this type guesswork has been eliminated. A puppy must have human contact and also association with dogs to develop as a social well-adjusted animal for the use of his master. It has been scientifically proven that *49 days* is the time that the puppy should be taken from his mother and placed with his owner.

Probably the best known experiments directed toward the critical time and learning of the puppy were conducted by the late C. J. Pfaffenberger of Guide Dogs for the Blind, San Rafael, California. He showed the

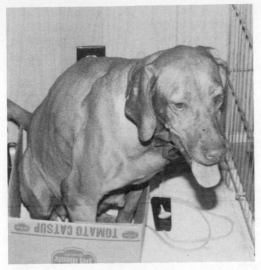

Mother, in her search for a suitable nest, can select interesting places. It is well to anticipate this need and provide a whelping area well before the time is near.

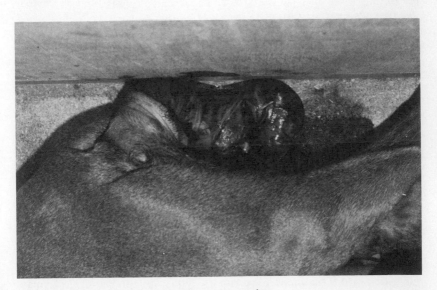

Another puppy arrives.

importance of the kennel dog syndrome from his experiments. This appears in puppies removed from the kennel for the first time at four to six months of age where they show lack of confidence and excessive shyness. Due to his work with German Shepherds the success rate in training these dogs for the use of blind people improved tremendously.

John Fuller, while working at the Jackson Laboratory, Bar Harbor, Maine showed what the "isolation syndrome" was. It handicapped a puppy's learning ability. This work was continued by John Scott and others and they showed that the early part of a learning experience is also critical for determining motivation and that it was extremely difficult to re-motivate a puppy that failed repeatedly. A puppy which has early success will continue to be successful in his training experiences.

This sounds good, but what does it mean? Does it mean that a kennel puppy is good? Does it mean that puppies should not be raised in the kennel? Does it mean that you should not buy a puppy that has had no previous human contact? Does it mean that you should not buy a puppy that has had no dog contact?

Researchers normally do not translate their studies in a manner that the ordinary dog owners understand. The research results mean that when the puppy's eyes are closed he does not learn. As soon as they open he begins to learn at an alarming rate. He must have association at this time with his littermates, followed soon if possible with older dogs, but under the supervision of his mother initially. During this time human contact is not so essential until the sixth week, but is still helpful. At seven weeks of age, each puppy should be separated from the litter by placing it with his new owner. If this is not done by the end of three months, the puppy will develop undesirable behavior (syndromes) in some manner or other and after four to six months is usually not fit to be placed with a new owner.

How then can the Vizsla breeder assure that his puppies that are not sold before the three month period will develop normally? It means that some person must take the puppies from the kennel individually and work with them in a number of ways. It means that it is best to place them in separate kennel runs and continue their human associations by removing them from this environment every day and working with each one separately for a half-hour or more at a time.

No, it does not mean that you cannot take a puppy seven weeks of age home with you and put it into his own kennel and not be as successful as one taken into your home. Apparently you can, for the key is human contact and some form of training several times a week.

Some experienced trainers restrict the new puppy's association and training to themselves because better and more positive control is possible.

Temporary separation from a familiar owner can reinforce emotional attachments. For this, among other reasons, each one of our dogs has no

272

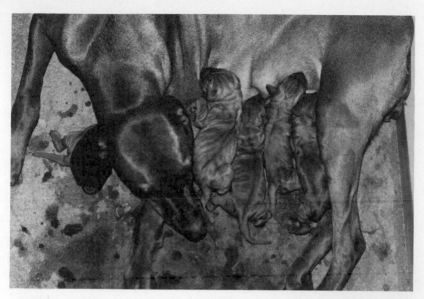

Contented mother, Zindi rests after the birth of her litter sired by Donar. Photo was taken in the Netherlands in 1978.

Champion Jezza rests contentedly with her new son.

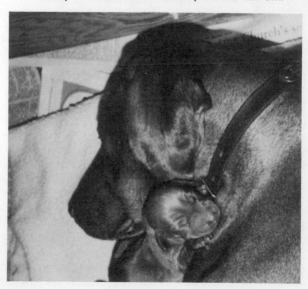

less than two people in our family attending to their daily needs including the training. This does cause some problems, but it prevents more serious ones and that is worth the difference. This work enables any dog to make a transition to a new owner without emotional difficulty at any age.

REGISTRATION AND ETHICS IN SELLING

Many people obviously enjoy any young animal and it is a refreshing and rewarding experience to own one from time to time — or better yet to breed a bitch and raise the litter. The truth is that it is *easier* to buy a puppy from an experienced breeder than to raise a litter. Vizsla litters average six to eight and twelve is not unusual. The normal practice in the United States is to raise all of the litter as opposed to most European methods.

Breeding and raising Vizslas properly is expensive and difficult at times. The use of a male for stud entails some knowledge and experience along with having the responsibility for the bitch while she is being bred.

Before buying a Vizsla, check the background and practices of the breeder offering puppies for sale. This can be done in a number of ways. Write to the Vizsla Club of America, talk to owners, ask the breeder about his guarantee, check advertising and personal claims, check dog publications and the *Pure-bred Dog-American Kennel Gazette* for owner success in the various fields of activity, and then go see the puppies. Why make such a fuss over selection of a Vizsla? No reason, except you ought to be aware that you may have his company for over a decade and for you to put up with a dog that long you should have the best available.

Most amateur Vizsla breeders breed for their own personal enjoyment and satisfaction. Some work to improve the breed. These breeders are usually seen at dog shows, obedience trials and field trails. Their puppy price is higher than the breeder who sells several breeds and always has puppies to sell and is never seen in competition. Sometimes these Vizslas can be as unpredictable as mongrel breedings. Labeling a breeder "puppy factory" is a subject which is somewhat touchy and is subject to individual interpretation or first hand knowledge of a breeder's operation. There seems to be some sort of stigma among pure bred dog breeders against these "puppy factories," as they are called, based on the fear that mass production of Vizslas for sale to the general public is wrong and "sinful." The old adage that "you get what you pay for" certainly holds true in the dog business. But like everything else — price alone is not adequate criteria for selection.

Good breeders build a record, stand behind it, and constantly try to improve upon it. Buy from this type breeder and he will always be

The four males and three females in this photo are the first Wirehaired Vizslas (Versatile Uplanders) born in North America, By Palmajori Apacs out of Sarmelleki Rebeka, the pups were whelped May 30, 1972 and are owned by Wes Basler of Manitoba, Canada. Photo by H. Basler June 7, 1972.

interested in how your Vizsla develops, and especially when used in competition. If you have problems, he will be helpful.

The worst thing that can happen to the Vizsla breed is for it to become a popular dog, which in turn causes every owner to become the "backyard breeder" and every established breeder a "puppy factory."

The breeder who offers a complete money back guarantee can scare off potential buyers. There may be a number of reasons for this, but it is probably due to the fact they do not want to get involved in a long term arrangement, or prefer to be ignorant thus avoiding responsibility in ownership. This fact can easily be established by telling a prospective buyer, or owner requesting stud service, that you are interested in working with dogs that have been cleared by x-ray technology of hip dysplasia. It is judicious not to refer to hip dysplasia as a disease. This usually means that the breeder or stud dog owner has lost either a sale or stud service. But the truth is that nearly 30 per cent of all Vizslas whelped previous to this time had this disease or genetic affliction. The breeder should be prepared with an answer when asked by a potential buyer about practices related to genetic faults in his Vizslas for the public is being educated by every breed organization on this problem. With continued research and selective breeding, a solution will be found.

Learn the standard for the Vizsla breed, use it only as a guide to find out what the breeder knows and practices, and insist on some guarantee on quality and health where you place the most importance, then buy. The price you pay should be related to how good a specimen you get and what you intend to use it for. Obviously, it would be foolish to pay $150 to $300 for a puppy just to use it as a companion when you can buy one for less than $150. For this purpose forget all about guarantees and personal involvement — buy that pup and never correspond with the breeder again. The actual difference in price may not be quality so much as the effort of the breeder to produce and insure quality which can be found in most any singular breedings. The difference is that there is no proven potential for perpetuating quality.

THE COST OF BREEDING TO REPLACE OR ADD A VIZSLA

Each Vizsla owner will face the time when he must think about replacing his aging Vizsla, or of acquiring another one. For those wishing to replace the aging dog, or one lost in an accident, the normal belief is that none could ever fill the void or take the place of the one just lost.

Each Vizsla is distinctively different and each one will likely fill the basic need and void for the owner having just lost one. Those people who have owned other breeds cannot believe that a dog having such consistency in temperament could exist. Each Vizsla exudes with the individual owner a feeling that is very difficult to describe, but it is there with each compatible owner.

Some owners feel that their bitch is not "complete" unless she whelps a litter of pups. There is no known basis for this except for being put in the class of "old wives tales." Once the decision is made to breed though, other factors must be considered. It is difficult to adjust to the false pregnancies after each season for the bitch which is a common occurence. Breeding will not stop this. While it is nothing to be concerned about, the owner should be aware that the bitch will try to build a nest sometime between 30 and 70 days after her season. That nest might be his best cushion or mattress.

The usual Vizsla stud service is $150 - $300, and some stud owners will allow return service in the event of a miss the first breeding. Usually the breeding involves transportation and boarding costs to get the bitch to the selected stud dog.

Some potential breeders make no advance plans, they just wait until the last minute and put the female with a male and hope they mate. If they do mate the date for the bitch to whelp is usually unknown. Based on breeding on the twelveth day after the first show of blood the gestation period is sixty-three days.

Some who breed their bitch will leave her strictly on her own. Some are lucky and others are not. No particular value, under these conditions, can be placed on the bitch and sometimes one will die during or a few weeks after whelp. If she and her puppies do survive, then she is *some* dog and a great mother — just like in real life mother nature does not allow the weak to live and the strong must carry on the species. This is a good method of culling, but not very practical; yet this can be the most profitable method of breeding. Most reputable breeders do better than this, but it does cost them more money.

A single trip to the veterinarian for the novice breeder can save his bitch from dying during or after whelp. There are many causes for a bitch having problems that can be corrected through Caesarean delivery costing $125 - $150 plus an emergency call fee. One can observe the bitch during her seasons to tell if she has an inadequately developed vulva, but it is more difficult to tell if her vagina is not properly developed or that she has problems with her uterus. Sometimes the operation is necessary when a blockage occurs wherein the bitch is perfectly normal. A hysterectomy in some bitches may be warranted with Caesarean delivery. Unless it is required to save her life it should be postponed so she can nurse her puppies.

Breeding of pure-bred Vizslas should not be considered casually. The usual breeder's out of pocket costs for a litter are as follows:

1.	Check and worm bitch before breeding	$15-20
2.	X-ray for hip dysplasia before breeding and submit to OFA or Vizsla Club of America	$45-50
3.	Stud fee	$150-300
4.	Shipping fees and board	$60-120
5.	Whelping box (material)	$30
6.	Two sets of whelping box bottom of commercial carpet	$25
7.	Veterinarian fee during pregnancy	$10
		plus extra to palpate
8.	Hormone shot to stimulate delivery	$7-10
9.	Pit shot after whelp to expel placentas	$7-10
10.	Welded wire pen (material)	$60
11.	Advertising	$200
12.	Telephone	$30

13. Tails docked and dewclaws removed at three
    days after birth for eight puppies $35-45 (8 pups)
14. Antibiotics for Vizsla rash $12-18
15. Temporary distemper shots $60-65 (8 pups)
16. Antibiotics for uterus infection $25-25
17. Cremation of dead puppy $10-15
18. Puppy worming $8-10
19. Food expense at end of seven weeks $70

Total out of pocket expenses at the end of seven weeks
for litter $860-1085
Expense for each puppy: (8 total) $107-135

Puppies not sold after seven weeks create additional out of pocket expense, or when the breeder wishes to hold all the litter for evaluation when nearly grown.

20. Food for nine months (8 puppies) $675-1000
21. Permanent immunization against distemper
    hepatitis and leptospirosis $160-240
22. X-ray and cost of analysis $280-320
23. Rabies shots $80-120

Total out of pocket expenses from seven weeks
to nine months $1195-1680
Additional expense for each puppy: $150-210
(Note: No veterinary expense has been considered for illness, surgery or additional worming.)

Costs to each breeder will vary based on local rates and he will also have some miscellaneous expenses not listed. This listing of costs is only intended as a guide. Amortizing the bitch and other capital expenses as a business operation would add to the selling price of each puppy. Some costs may not be necessary but it is apparent that the selling price must be more than the breeder's cost.

This cost analysis represents what one-time breeders will end up paying. It does not matter whether the bitch and stud dogs are title holders or not. Good reputable Vizsla breeders will have the extra expense of proving their dogs in some form of competition.

Raising puppies can be a pleasure, but it is a bad thing to breed and not be able to sell the litter and have to dispose of the unwanted puppies some way other than selling them. Each novice breeder must face the prospect of his friends being his only buyers, or being the ones he gives the puppies to.

278

The treatment and discussion concerning the cost of breeding for a replacement Vizsla, as opposed to buying from another breeder, is not for the purpose of discouraging the owner and potential breeder, but more to demonstrate that this undertaking is not without sacrifice of time and money. Not many owners can, in such a short time, spend up to $1000 outside of their normal budget, especially when they expect to realize a quick return from puppy sales. There is much less involvement and cost in out of pocket money by buying from another breeder.

Once the litter is whelped, the owner is to begin his role as a salesman — like it or not, capable or not. That ability is not profitable and the salesman must turn to the advertising mediums — national and local. This will involve prompt answering of inquiries. If you spend time answering each inquiry personally and extolling on the virtues of your litter and trying to explain just what a Vizsla is, you will soon tire. If you take pictures and send them along with pedigrees you will find this becomes expensive for they are seldom returned. You are time and money ahead to make up whatever information you plan on giving out and have it reproduced at a small fixed price per copy which will be less expensive.

Just before the puppies are seven weeks of age, the local newspapers and other larger city newspapers should be used for classified advertising. This requires the owner to make himself available to the telephone during certain hours as well as arranging times when prospective buyers can come and look. Some calls come from what seem to be sincere people who are genuinely interested in a Vizsla. Some make appointments during your prime time in the evening hours causing you to cancel other plans. Then they fail to show up, or do not show the common courtesy of cancelling the appointment. Many calls and letters are from people looking for something free or are just curious. Being able to predict what to say at the right time is the mark of a good salesman, and that most people are not — with all due credit to the enthused breeder for his dogs.

Face the facts. It is virtually impossible to sell a relatively rare or unpublicized dog breed. The person who does buy, asks very little and sometimes does not even ask the price. He has made up his mind that he wants a Vizsla and sometimes he knows when and from whom he will buy it. It generally holds that someone else sold him on the breed a long time ago and the opportune time for him to buy is right. For this reason it is good for the breeder interested in regular or occasional breeding of litters to keep his name or kennel before the potential buying public all the time, whether by competitive activities or advertising.

Therefore, it follows that the one-time breeder may spend more money than he actually intended and then have more dogs than he can possibly keep or sell. Some one-time breeders are lucky the first time and do sell the number that was whelped, but it is a risky gamble.

A potential sale means nothing unless money changes hands in the form of a deposit or sale. There is never a sale until the full price is paid to the breeder. The breeder should not hold or promise a puppy without a deposit from the buyer.

THE MATING PROCESS

A dog should not be used at stud until he has been checked for and found clear of canine brucellosis and canine hip dysplasia. Each bitch should also be tested. They should both have had recent vaccinations for parvovirus, other required vaccinations and the bitch checked for worms.

Bitches should not be bred on two successive seasons (estrus) unless the first litter was smaller than normal. Never breed three seasons in succession.

The stud owner must be aware of his responsibility to protect the bitch while in his care to insure that she is not lost, stolen, hurt or bred to the wrong male or more than one.

Bitches come in season at different intervals for their first time and they will vary afterwards. None should be bred until after their second season or before two years of age. A male should not be used at stud until he has matured, although this is not as critical as for the bitch.

Your veterinarian can take a vaginal or cervical smear for a culture around the fifth day to begin the process to determine fertility. It is rare that a bitch is fertile before the fifth day.

The female season lasts about three weeks with ovulation occurring somewhere in the mid-period of 11 to 13 days.

Some owners may want to delay estrus in order to compete in field trials, and this decision should not be made without full knowledge of the potential consequences. Consult with your veterinarian and give him full details of the reason you want the delay or postponement. There may be some risk in using products developed to delay estrus.

Select the dog or bitch you use in breeding for conformation, temperament, size, trainability, health, performance and anything else important to your breeding plans. Avoid breeding to titled dogs for no other reason than their titles. That may help sell puppies, but nothing else may be gained.

The actual mating can be simple or difficult. Everyone has their own special techniques other than letting nature work for them. Mating usually goes better when using an experienced stud dog with a virgin bitch, or an experienced bitch with a virgin male. The bitch is ready for copulation whenever she stands and flags her tail while making romantic overtures. It may require another day or so before she will let the male mount. Once a tie is made, the male, after a short time, will dismount and turn to the rear. Both dogs will then face in opposite directions. The tie may last anywhere from five minutes to an hour. When all else fails, artificial insemination procedures can be used by the veterinarin.

Sometime between the 22nd and 29th day, your veterinarian can palpate the uterus and feel pea-like lumps when the bitch is pregnant. It is more difficult for him to do after that time. The owner can usually detect signs at about 35 days by her size and/or enlarged or pink color to the nipples.

Pregnant bitches should not have their activities restricted until very late in the pregnancy. They can be field trialed as late as the 55th day without danger under normal conditions.

A bitch can whelp as early as the 57th day and as late as the 68th day without complications. It is best to consult your veterinarian after the 64th day. It may be necessary for your bitch to undergo a Caesarean operation.

Shortly before the bitch's temperature drops, she will make a nest of something. It is important that she does so where you want, rather than in the clothes closet or on the bed. Provide a whelping box for her a week or two before she whelps to accustom her to it. Provide newspapers or something similar for nesting material.

The bitch will make her nest, become restless, and experience a drop in temperature before she goes into labor. Her temperature will drop below 100 degrees and her head will feel cold to the touch 24 hours prior to whelping followed by an increase to over 100 degrees one or two hours before whelping.

Regardless of anyone else's advice, be present at the time your bitch whelps. Provide yourself with a thermometer, a dozen bath towels and paper towels, garbage bags, alcohol, dull scissors, a hemostat to clamp the cord (tie if desired) and a baby scale. The room temperature should be

Most canine mothers are solitary and really prefer to be left alone by all. So it is unusual when a Vizsla mother permits another bitch to enter the whelping box and help clean pups.

from 92-97 degrees Fahrenheit for the puppies. It is easier to use a heat lamp or a cardboard box with a heating pad in the bottom covered with a cloth material.

After laboring for a period of time, the first puppy comes out in a complete transparent package. The puppy will emerge before the placenta and you must quickly remove this from the birth canal. Sometimes the amniotic sac is broken before the puppy emerges or with the sac remaining inside with the navel cord still attached to the sac. There are methods that the placenta can be removed with the puppy.

Pick up the puppy and afterbirth and place in a towel. Break the amniotic sac at the puppy's head, pinch the neck skin and shake vigorously until it cries. Once it is breathing normally, dry it off and then crush-cut the navel cord one inch from the body. It may be necessary to force the nasal fluids out by holding the puppy facing away from you and slinging it with a wrist action. Record the time of delivery, the amount of white on the puppy, sex and weight. Check for birth defects. Continue to weigh each puppy every day until weaned. There should be no weight loss unless something is wrong.

The navel cord dries up and drops off in two or three days. The bitch should not be allowed to bite off the navel cord whenever you are attending the delivery.

Puppies do not have normal body temperatures until the fourth week. They depend on artificial heat and humidity to stay healthy and grow properly. A bitch will cull a cold puppy. Puppies twitch and jerk in their sleep when normal and healthy.

Each new-born puppy needs the first milk (colostrum) for immunity and as an aid to bowel functioning. Allow the mother to nurse each puppy as soon as they have been cleaned and dried. Return the puppies to the holding box each time she delivers another puppy. The entire process should last on an average of five hours. As soon as she has finished delivering, take her outside to relieve herself. See that she has plenty of water.

Lactating bitches need to eat much more than normal to remain healthy and keep the puppies well fed. A large litter should be closely monitored.

After delivery, take the bitch to the veterinarian for shots of antibiotics and Pitocin to prevent infection and to help contract the uterus to expel whatever is left after parturition. Bitches can develop peritonitis a few days after whelping a litter for failure to expel a dead puppy and die as a result.

After the puppies have nursed for a few days, pay careful attention to the breast area. Nipples that are not nursed may have mastitis. They

282

will become hard and inflamed. This udder infection can kill puppies and the mother if not checked in time.

Tails should be docked and the dew claws removed from two to four days after birth.

The bitch will have a vaginal discharge that is a dark bloody color for several days. If it should last too long, the veterinarian should be consulted and the bitch checked for an infection.

The breeder can relax for 18 days or so while the bitch takes total care of her puppies. Once solid puppy food is fed, the bitch will leave the stools. During this time period, the puppies eyes and ears are closed for the first 10 days to two weeks and they just eat and sleep. Never scold the bitch for cleaning up the stools and urine as it is instinctive and normal.

Weaning can occur as early as three weeks and as late as six. Puppies toenails should be trimmed regularly to protect the mother from pain and infection. After weaning, the udder will cake naturally and return to normal in a short time without any kind of treatment.

The time between when the bitch weans her puppies (with your help) and seven weeks of age, means a lot of attention by the breeder depending on facilities. Puppies need fed at least four times a day, or they can be placed on a self-feeder. Moistened food will provide some of their liquid requirements and make it easier to eat. They should be given plenty of fresh water. Should loose stools develop, remove the water and provide it for a short time between feeding and stop wetting down the food. When no change in stools is noted after one day, consult with your veterinarian.

At seven weeks of age, the puppies are ready for their new owners. Good breeders stand behind their breedings and assist the new owners in any way needed.

Before you decide to become a breeder, you should study the subjects of breedings and whelping and observe a whelping when possible.

PUPPY GROWTH

Puppies should grow at a constant rate. Deviation from a straight line weight increase depends on the supply to each one at feeding time. Some puppies are able to eat more than others, but this seems to average out. The size of a litter affects the average rate of growth.

Size at birth has little bearing on daily growth rate although the smaller the puppy, the longer it will take to reach a given weight. Weight at birth seems to have little or no affect on weight at full growth.

The graph shows the results of four litters during their first four weeks. Litter A had only one puppy and it grew at the maximum possible rate for it did not have to compete for milk. When fully grown this female weighed 46 pounds. Litters B and C had eight puppies each, and litter

D had seven puppies. The daily excursion for Litter B was two to six ounces, litter C two to four ounces and Litter D five to 16. The first born in Litter D weighed nine ounces and grew at one to two ounces each day. The largest puppy weighed 14 ounces and grew at a rate of two to three ounces each day. Litter D grew at a faster rate than the litters with eight puppies. At maturity there were no large or small dogs in any of the litters. An average rate of growth for a litter of eight would probably be near one and a half ounces per day.

The purpose of weighing each puppy every day is to monitor weight as an indication of poor health in one or all of the litter. An indication of the quality of the bitch's milk could possibly be determined by the total average growth of the litter.

REGISTRATION

The breeder should send for a litter registration application prior to breeding. The owner of the sire completes section A on the date of the mating. The owner of the bitch (breeder) completes section B on date of birth of the litter. Only when ownership has changed while the dam was in whelp should section C be completed. After completing the form, the breeder should submit it to the American Kennel Club along with the required registration fee.

The American Kennel Club will return a packet with a form for each puppy. At the time of sale, the breeder notes the sex, color, and completes section A on the reverse side. The owner completes section B and submits it to the American Kennel Club along with the required registration fee. A litter registration number is assigned and this number may be used to enter the dog in competition until a single registration number is received.

Any Vizsla registered in the American Kennel Club is eligible for registration in the American Field Stud Book, but not vice versa in many cases.

The breeder should provide a pedigree form for the new puppy owner and explain the litter registration form in detail.

Selection of a name can be a problem for some new owners. The American Kennel Club registers the dog's name for life and it cannot be changed. Some breeders register the individual puppies and sell them with a transfer form to new owners. Sometimes conditions, other than the initial purchase price, are negotiated when purchasing a puppy. A new owner buys the right to name his puppy. He must obtain consent to use a registered kennel name.

VIZSLA LITTER GROWTH RATES

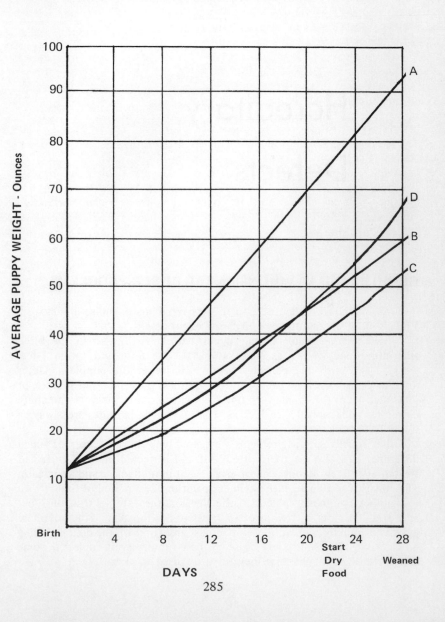

AVERAGE PUPPY WEIGHT - Ounces

DAYS

Birth 4 8 12 16 20 Start Dry Food 24 28 Weaned

CHAPTER 13

Hereditary
Defects

GENETIC AND ENVIRONMENTAL BREED PROBLEMS

Two common problems related to the overall health and soundness of a Vizsla's physical condition are birth and environment.

Environmental problems can occur before birth wherein the bitch transmits round worms, as one example, to the fetus and within a few weeks after birth the parasites become active in the puppies. Other internal parasites can be caused by mosquitoes, flies and other sources, or reinfested from the kennel surroundings. This requires the owner to apply corrective and control measures as well and these parasites are always a threat to the dog.

Other equally serious problems are caused by airborne viruses, of which distemper can also be transported. If not detected early enough and treated effectively it will result in permanent brain damage and also death. This disease can ruin an entire kennel operation for a period of time.

Another common problem in the Vizsla is the external (button type) and eyelid tumors, as well as other types under the skin. Some of these grow very rapidly and will develop almost anywhere on the dog, including on the toes. The course and cause of these tumors is still subject to some debate, but it is possible that they too are caused by viruses.

In a different category is the once dreaded problem of red mange where the bitch can infect all of her puppies at birth. Very few Vizsla owners will get by without being troubled by one or more of these type problems, and there are other problems of lesser significance.

A few of the more prevalent, not in order, are monorchidism (only one testicle descended in the scrotum), cryptorchidism (no testicles in the scrotum) and hip dysplasia. The monorchid dog should be neutered and the cryptorchid dog is considered to be sterile. The Vizsla with hip dysplasia should not be bred, nor should a monorchid be bred as these faults are genetic in nature and would continue to be transmitted.

HEREDITARY PROBLEMS

Hereditary defects in dog breeds increase with their popularity. The Vizsla is a candidate because of its lovable, friendly and intelligent nature.

Unsubstantiated statements are often made that a breed's problems are caused through ignorance of novice breeders. They may be ignorant of the breed standard in many cases, but it is a fact that those breeders who have been associated with the breed for many years have not demonstrated improvement or even status quo in some cases. The lack of agreement on a uniform standard in the different countries causes some problems in a breeder defining the proper visualization of the breed. Breeders are also very secretive concerning problems they encounter in their breedings.

There was an extensive controlled mating and radiograph evaluation program on Vizslas conducted at the University of Minnesota in the late 1960's that lasted for seven years for the study of hip dysplasia. The Vizsla stock was donated by Dr. Osborn and involved nine dogs from nine separate litters. These nine dogs were responsible for the breeding colony of 208 Vizslas used in the study.

Nancy M. Heinold, D.V.M. researched the hereditary defects known to exist in the Vizsla breed for this chapter. The Vizsla breed does not have too many, but early recognition and attempts to correct those that are present will help correct and improve the breed.

HIP DYSPLASIA

Vizsla owners are aware of the importance in controlling hip dysplasia in their breeding program. This is the only known hereditary defect that its breeders are trying to control or eliminate.

Hip dysplasia is the poor, or improper bone, formation in the hips — acetabulum and femur joint. It is also present in a lesser degree in the front shoulders. The seriousness of the disease in the hips is measured in degrees for radiologist and veterinarian communication from one to four, with four being the most severe.

The dysplasia gene is bi-sexual, dominant, has incomplete penetration of varying severity and is either unilateral or bilateral. It is possible to approach 100 percent incidence of hip dysplasia in a given breed if not controlled on a continuous basis in the individual's own stock. The total Vizsla population shows statistical evidence of it being in the 30 per cent range.

Recent research by the University of Kansas and others show that canine hip dysplasia is a *dominant hereditary* factor and is a *neuromuscular disease* as opposed to the earlier belief that it was a bone/ligament disease. The actual diseased mechanism causing the hip dysplasia is the small pectineus muscle on the inner surface of the thigh. This muscle stops growing between the tenth and 121st day of age due to a lesion in the spinal cord in the loin area. This causes a constant upward force against the acetabular rim by the head of the femur producing the shallow acetabular socket that is seen by x-ray technology.

The Orthopedic Foundation for Animals (OFA) was established for the purpose of studying radiographs and providing a concensus report for individuals submitting radiographic films. A number is assigned for dogs without hip dysplasia.

Only dogs 24 months of age or older at the time of radiography qualify for an OFA number. The primary reason is that studies show that the rate of onset of the disease varies from a few months to 36 months. At 24 months, 92.5 percent of those in a Vizsla colony study program having hip dysplasia were diagnosed. At 36 months of age 97.5 percent were identified. The rate of progression of radiographic signs of hip dysplasia is relatively slow which makes the problem of early recognition very difficult or impossible.

"Hip dysplasia is a condition in which subluxation of the femoral head leads to abnormal wear with erosion of the joint cartilage, thickening of the joint capsule and formation of periarticular osteophytes in early adulthood. The shape of the hip joint undergoes changes, the acetabulum become more shallow than normal, and the femoral head flattened. Subluxation may be caused by joint laxity or insufficient support of the femoral head by the acetabular roof," according to Sten-Erik Olsson, VMD, MD and Hakan Kasstrom, DVM.

There is no agreement among researchers if it is a neuromuscular disease, a bone-ligament disease or something else. The degree of subluxation (joint looseness) varies from a small amount to total luxation. Osteoarthritis is progressive with age and is associated with this disease. Looseness of the joints precedes the wearing and proliferative response.

A normal dog can appear dysplastic when positioned improperly. If the radiograph shows slight subluxation or shallow acetabulum, it might

288

be advisable to x-ray again with better positioning. The patellas must be rolled in and the pelvis must be perfectly straight with the legs pulled back. The radiograph should show the patellas centered on the femurs. Improper positioning alters the depth of the hip joint.

Palpation of the young puppy can reveal hip dysplasia at a very early age. Those not palpating abnormal should be x-rayed at one year of age for a final evaluation. This method has not been proven worthwhile since it is an art and a difficult one to learn. Another technique claimed to be effective is fulcrum (palpate) x-ray at one year or older. The Vizsla Club of America's method operated by the University of Minnesota assured almost 100 per cent confidence by requiring two x-rays — one at a year or more of age and another one of the same Vizsla at 30 months. This method had obvious disadvantages to a breeder interested in breeding before this age. The amount of prior saturation of gene banks involving this disease would continue to result in litters with almost 100 per cent dysplastic puppies to the minimum level which cannot be determined. The time involved to completely eliminate the dysplasia gene from the brood stock is unknown when the breeder conscientiously works at the problem using only normal Vizslas. Litters having a very high percentage are very unusual in the Vizsla breed.

The only positive method to identify hip dysplasia is through radiographic analysis. An owner may suspect the problem, if he has a trained eye for the symptoms. Lameness can occur after strenuous exercise. Sometimes a waddling gait or bunny-hopping where the hind legs do not move independently might be an indication. A dog may have difficulty moving the hip joints and overextend the hock joints or walk from the stifles down. Hip dysplasia will eventually result in atrophy of the hind leg muscle mass with an accompanying buildup of the front shoulder muscles. I recently observed a pointing dog from another breed with rear muscles completely atrophied and were no longer used for support. He had learned to walk and balance on his front legs. Dogs having severe hip dysplasia will sometimes lay down in the same plane as they walk and are unable to rise without help. They will sit in the most comfortable position to alleviate pain and have difficulty rising to a standing position.

I know more than one Vizsla diagnosed radiographically for hip dysplasia and were neutered. They remained active and never showed any of the symptoms associated with the disease. Two of these dogs would be classed as over active all their lives. Could mistakes have been made by the veterinarians? Ask to look at the radiograph and get a second reading and opinion before neutering your dog.

Management of a dysplastic dog entails rest, very little exercise, comfortable quarters and good footing. Consult your veterinarian for pain management.

Proper positioning for OFA evaluation is very important so the accompanying procedures should be followed by your veterinarian.

The average breeder can best benefit himself by knowing that hip dysplasia is intensified by lack of recognition of its existence and by close inbreeding or line breeding as these two methods intensify both good and bad characteristics.

After reading this do not panic and believe that out breeding is the cure, just stick to your breeding plan and include the current approved methods for determining the disease in each and every Vizsla you sell or breed. Research will improve knowledge of this disease and the methods of detecting it so that it will cost less to the breeder and eventually help eliminate it from the total breed population.

JAWS

An undershot or overshot jaw is not always easy to recognize by novice breeders. The overshot jaw results in the lower jaw being shorter than the upper jaw. The undershot bite has the lower jaw longer than the upper jaw. The overshot jaw has been observed. One entire litter with overshot jaws was donated to Pilot Dogs, Columbus, Ohio and neutered.

Owners should not be concerned about this problem in their Vizsla until after the puppy teeth have been replaced by the permanent teeth and the jaws have quit growing. Puppies should be checked before being sold as this defect can often be detected at a few weeks of age.

HEMOPHILIA A

A reported disease in Vizslas, Hemophilia A is an X chromosome recessive trait. Males are most often affected with the disease and the females are the carriers. A breeder in California alerted me to this problem in 1970 in that area.

The severity varies depending on the degree of Factor VIII deficiency with severe cases causing death in puppyhood. Mild cases can survive the tail docking and dew claw removal processes which is usually done at four days.

Common signs are joint hemmorhage with lameness, lumps that appear suddenly on the body and bloody stools or urine. When vaccinated with live virus (similar to a viral infection) these affect the number and function of blood platelets for ten to 14 days afterwards. Platelets are needed for clotting as well as other factors, and the hemophiliac may bleed during the vaccination. Frequency of bleeding from dog to dog can occur once a year or month. A carrier can be detected by showing a reduced Factor VIII-C which is 50 to 60 percent of normal.

INSTRUCTIONS FOR OFA X-RAY PROCEDURES

Age Requirements: Only dogs that are at least 24 months of age or older at the time of radiography can quality for a breed O.F.A. number. The hip joint status of younger dogs will be evaluated, but a consensus report only will be issued. The dog's registration certificate or copy of this information should be available at the time of radiography.

Restraint: Dogs should not be fed on the day of radiography. General anesthesia is preferred for good hip joint evaluation. Sedation or tranquilization can also be used to obtain good positioning in easily managed dogs.

Film Size: For the large and giant breeds of dogs, 14" x 17" film size is recommended. Smaller film sizes may be used for smaller breeds if the area between the sacrum and the stifles can be included.

Film Identification: Permanent film identification in the film itself is required in order for radiographs to be certified. Lead letters, and I.D. camera, or radio opaque tapes can be used to identify film (a) with the name of the hospital or veterinarian, date taken, name of owner, registered name or number of dog, breed and age of dog or (b) with the hospital's or veterinarian's identification number or case number. In the latter case, the radiograph must be accompanied by an affidavit referring to such film by its said identification number and stating the information with respect hereto required in (a) above. If the above information is illegible or missing, the O.F.A. cannot accept the film for certification.

Positioning: Dorsal recumbency; with the rear legs extended and parallel to each other. This standard ventrodorsal view is the basis for evaluation of hip joint status with respect to hip dysplasia. Care should be exercised to be sure the pelvis is not tilted.

Exposure: Good contact is desirable (high MAs, low KVp). Grid technique is recommended for all large dogs.

Radiation Safety: Proper collimation and protection of attendants is the responsibility of the veterinarian. Gonadal shielding is recommended for male dogs.

Application For O.F.A. Film Evaluation: The owner or agent should complete and sign the O.F.A. application card. This information is best obtained directly from the dog's certificate of registration. Application cards are available upon request from the O.F.A. The radiograph, signed card, and a check for $12.50 for the service fee should be mailed together to: Orthopedic Foundation for Animals, Universty of Missouri-Columbia, Columbia, MO 65201.

VON WILLEBRAND'S DISEASE (VWD)

This is another hereditary blood disorder discovered in Vizslas. These cases are isolated when compared to such problems as exist in Doberman Pinschers. The Ohio State University College of Veterinary Medicine assumes that all Doberman Pinschers will bleed excessively during surgery and alters the anesthesia plan to prevent complications. In the Doberman Pinscher it varies with different geographical areas from five to 40 percent.

VWD is an autosomal incompletely dominant trait and occurs in both sexes. There is variable expression within a family or litter. It has low Factor VIII-C as does Hemophilia A. Differentiation between these two diseases requires specialized clotting tests along with a pedigree study. Von Willebrand's Disease is not sex-linked as with Hemophilia A. It has other abnormalities such as prolonged bleeding time, specific defect of platelet retention and agglutination, and low or abnormal Factor VIII-RA. VWD has a tendency to be less severe clinically than Hemophilia A. Spontaneous bleeding episodes are not normally experienced, but minor surgery for cosmetic or elective procedures can result in serious or fatal bleeding.

At birth, signs may be excessive and result in fatal bleeding from umbilicus. It may be a serious problem with tail docking or dew claw removal. Recurrent bloody diarrhea induced by stress; chronic low-grade bloody inflamed external ears; prolonged bleeding in estrus and after whelping; small surface hematomas; occasional bloody urine; recurrent shifting lameness with radiographic changes similar to eosinophilic panosteitis; abortions; stillborn pups or those that fade and die early in life; and, excessive bleeding when the toenails are cut too short or from an injury. Since this disease is less severe than Hemophilia A, affected dogs survive to reproduce.

ENTROPION

Congenital entropion has been confirmed in a Vizsla by an opthalmologist in mid-Ohio, and this problem is known to exist in other geographical areas. A dog's orbits (bony sockets) appear too large for its eyes. Lower lids appear loose and are rolled under causing the hair to rub the corneas. This causes intense pain as evidenced by excessive tears and abnormal blinking.

Entropion in the Vizsla is unlike that observed in other breeds. It is similar to that found in Weimaraners and Doberman Pinschers where the orbit is too large for the eye. This is caused by a hereditary skull defect. Affected dogs should be surgically corrected and neutered.

SKULL DEFECTS

Vizslas in certain breeding lines develop enlarged frontal bones above the eyes. The mode of inheritance has not been determined although it behaves similar to a recessive gene. The bones directly above the eyes are greatly enlarged and protrude above the level of the skull. Vizslas have other skull defects one of which is non-parallel planes that form the top of the muzzle and the top of the skull as viewed from the side.

In breedings where skull defects occur, it behaves somewhat like hip dysplasia where penetration is incomplete. One or more generations may be skipped. This defect was also observed while I was in Budapest, Hungary in 1977.

TAIL DEFECTS

Tail deformities have been observed in Vizsla litters. The tail will be a stub or crooked. Crooked tails can be caused accidently by the birth process and not be related to a congenital defect. Dogs born with a stub tail should be neutered as this is a hereditary defect. New mutations are not welcome whether it be stub tails (brachyury) or long silky hair.

Brittanys and a few other breeds have one gene which dictates the presence of a short tail and is desirable. Conscientious breeders of Vizslas will prevent a puppy with a stub tail from being used for breeding so that his problem will not spread.

EPILEPSY

Idiopathic epilepsy is present in some Vizsla lines. Several dogs with this problem have been traced to one male. Its cause is unknown, but the seizure is caused by an electrical misfiring of the brain.

The owner of a dog having seizures should be aware that not all seizures are caused by epilepsy. Neither should an owner rationalize that epileptic seizures are the result of a head injury. The dog should be tested in order that other diseases or injury processes may be ruled out.

A seizure is usually preceeded by an aura in which the dog realizes that something unusual is about to occur. He may act nervous, get close to his owner, or there may be no noticeable change. Dogs having seizures will usually start to twitch and fall to the ground shaking with its body stiff. The victims breathe heavily, salivate excessively, and may appear to be choking. Legs often move rapidly in a bicycling manner. The eyes become blank, the pupils enlarge, and often the eyes will roll back and expose the whites. Sometimes their bladders and bowels will empty. Several minutes may pass before body movements slow down, soften and the motions stop. When the seizure is over, dogs appear not to see and will get up and stagger and are very weak. Physical responses gradually return to normal.

Dogs having seizures more than once a month should be placed on medication. If not controlled, the frequency can increase until the dog reaches status "epilepticus" which is life threatening.

Epileptic dogs should be neutered.

DEMODEX MANGE

Generalized demodex is hereditary. It is caused from a defect in the immune system, and the body cannot control the demodex mites which normally appear in the hair follicles.

Localized demodex has also been observed in Vizslas. Puppies under stress may have small areas of hair loss which can be treated. This may not be a hereditary problem.

Localized hair loss around the eyes is a form of demodex mange and is hereditary. Affected dogs have a bald appearance around the eye from the lack of hair at the edges of the eyelids. It may extend outward several millimeters.

This problem appears in several Vizsla lines and appears to have originated from the far west. It is not known if this mange initiated from the environment, stress or allergic reaction.

More knowledge is needed in order that breeders can effect a cure, or change their breeding practices. It could affect the entire population in time unless some control measures are initiated.

SKIN TUMORS

This problem occurs in all breeds with no greater frequency in the Vizsla. Skin tumors grow quite rapidly as a rule, are reddened and become hairless. Malignancy is more prevalent in older dogs.

Histiocytomas exhibit the same behavior, but are benign and occur only on young dogs. These tumors should be removed.

Lipomas are a fatty, soft, slow growing tumor under the skin. They can get very large, but are benign. These can be removed at the owner's convenience whenever his dog is under anesthesia for some other reason.

Warts need be removed only if they occur in some area on the dog where they are caused to bleed.

Small dark tumors are evident on the eyelids of Vizslas. These look like a mole and are usually benign. If they cause no discomfort to the dog, they need not be removed.

Sebaceous cysts are lumps in the skin that open, drain, close and repeat the cycle. They should be removed when this persists.

OTHER HEREDITARY DEFECTS

Cryptorchidism: This is a hereditary defect. Its mode of inheritance is believed due to a single autosomal sex limited recessive gene. Studies on dogs are inconclusive. Cryptorchids dogs may be fertile but usually the body heat in retained testicles kills the sperm. Monorchid dogs are most always fertile, but affected dogs should not be bred. Puppies can sometimes draw in one or both testicles and they may not both descend into the scrotum for nearly six months. When it is necessary to castrate, the retained testicles should be removed to prevent cancer later on.

Defective Toes: The frequency of this defect is low. The problem is assumed to be one of inheritance.

Temperament: Those Vizslas with poor temperament believed caused from a hereditary factor should be neutered. Bad temperament can be environmentally produced and these dogs should not be removed from a breeding program just for that behavior.

Conformation: Both good and bad structural characteristics are produced from the entire gene pool of mated dogs. It is a complicated process with most breeders making their selections of mates by reasons only known to themselves. Selection by phenotype is typical with pedigree studies unable to relate to genotype of mates being used. Breeding for the perfect Vizsla must be done using both characteristics and ruthlessly bypassing undesirable qualities that are seen or known to exist in a dog or its pedigree.

CHAPTER 14

Specialty
Breed
Clubs

NATIONAL SPECIALTY BREED CLUB

The new Vizsla owner usually wants to know more about his dog and also wants to communicate with other Vizsla owners. Books, magazines and specialty dog clubs such as the Vizsla Club of America serve this need. The first Vizsla book (paper back) became available early in 1969 entitled, *How To Raise And Train A Vizsla,* by Ernest H. Hart.

The Vizsla Club of America represents the Vizsla on a national scale and was incorporated in the State of Missouri in 1953 with Frank J. Tallman from Kansas City as the first club president. At that time the club was called "The Magyar Vizsla Club of America, Inc." Later in 1960, it was changed to "The Vizsla Club of America, Inc." when recognition for the breed was granted by the American Kennel Club. This club made its first efforts toward filing a formal application for "Member" status in 1969. This was a specific milestone stated by the original founders of the club in its Articles of Incorporation.

Articles of Incorporation were filed for record in Jackson County, Missouri, June 22, 1953, Book 4713, page 659. While these original Articles of Incorporation are still in effect, a new Constitution and By-Laws was developed around it and accepted by the American Kennel Club in 1965. The Constitution and By-Laws was changed and approved again in 1971 in line with the application and approved for "Member" status with the American Kennel Club.

The Vizsla Club of America through a volunteer Editor has published *The Vizsla News* since 1953 generally on a monthly and semi-monthly basis to serve the breed and its members.

A strong and effective national specialty breed club is essential to the growth and public acceptance of the Vizsla breed. Each owner may not be interested in belonging, but most owners benefit from its existence.

Vizsla owners come from all walks of life and have little if anything else in common other than Vizsla ownership but in many cases it is enough to strike up many close and enduring friendships. The national club serves this function for those who attend the specialty shows and field trials held by it. It provides Vizsla owners the opportunity to come together from all over the United States, Canada and Mexico to compare directly their efforts and successes. The most important fact to remember is that each owner believes that: *His dog is always just a little bit better than all the others.*

Owner education through a national effort to teach the way for maximum enjoyment and satisfaction from their Vizsla ownership, development of precepts based on the Articles of Incorporation and the Constitution and By-Laws, success and failure of other owners, and the overall advancement and improvement within the breed, is best performed by a PARENT breed club. The Vizsla Club of America through its officers, board of directors and members work at these efforts.

This work is accomplished from the money received from annual dues, events and donations and through all the volunteer help provided by its officers, board of directors and individual members assigned to committees. Good effective workers are always in demand and represent the most important asset of the organization.

The PARENT club has a responsibility to each member. It must insure that new members meet the membership rules as prescribed, must enforce all club rules equitably and fairly in matters involving its operations and any disputes arising among its members, and provide the leadership, assistance and education for its members to enjoy Vizsla activities.

No two members of the club want the same thing from their Vizsla. The management, through the Board of Directors, must recognize and respect this fact and orient educational programs to cause all the members to think and work constructively.

297

A portion of the gallery riding the Vizsla National at Ohio, Illinois. National events provide the opportunity for breeders and fanciers to see some of the best Vizslas side by side. This helps everyone evaluate the breed more effectively.

A parent club concept is a business and should always be recognized as an operation into perpetuity. It is capable of being a small or a large business by the size of its membership and the work done on a non-profit basis. Its size will always be reflected by the ranking of the Vizsla breed in the American Kennel Club registration of dogs and how effective it meets the needs of the owners as a parent club.

LOCAL SPECIALTY CLUBS

The Vizsla breed also has a group of energetic and active owners in local specialty clubs in the United States who are pushing each other to make the Vizsla a better bird dog. They are actively forming new clubs and fulfilling the requirements of the American Kennel Club to hold point giving field trials and dog shows primarily.

Local specialty clubs are in: Arizona (1), California (5), Colorado (1), Connecticut (1), Illinois (1), Iowa (2), Maryland (1), Michigan (1), Nebraska (1), Central New England (1), New Jersey (1), New York (1), Ohio (2) and Washington (1). These clubs have American Kennel Club approval to conduct licensed events. Other clubs are in the process of completing the AKC requirements in different states.

These Vizsla groups are dynamic. The owners are forceful in their effort to bring their breed into the forefront and limelight honestly and based on the merits of their Vizslas. They are a fast growing group while some of the other specialty bird dog breeds are just doing well to hold what they

Above mounted judges wait for the handlers to get in position with their dogs for casting off. To the right official guns wait until their talents are called upon.

At left, the tailgate camaraderie is in full swing. National events also provide for fun and visiting friends.

Above dog passes close to gallery as they proceed along the course of the field trial. Dogs do not belong in the gallery and when they do end up there, it can be a problem if the horses aren't "trial broke" and used to dogs.

At left, Paul Sabo adjust stirrips of his trial horse, Smokey, for the author's daughter, Nancy.

299

have. The present owners of Continental bird dog breeds are not switching to the Vizsla. Most of the present Vizsla field trialers became first interested in this sport when they bought a Vizsla.

Many of the local specialty Vizsla clubs open their field trial stakes to the other pointing breeds which is an option under the American Kennel Club rules. Some have started to restrict stakes in their trials. These clubs have done this to encourage, develop and also retain Vizsla field trialers, or beginners, who might lack confidence in competing directly against the more developed breeds and more experienced handlers.

A drop-off in Vizsla entries can be noted after point trials (licensed) are begun by Vizsla specialty clubs where all or most all stakes are open to the other pointing breeds. Some specialty clubs believe that it cannot afford to gamble on losing money by closing to the other breeds. Oftentimes the desire for a club to make money, for no valid reason, alienates its own members. Such specialty clubs eventually exist only in name and a treasury that does not benefit the local breed owners. Such local specialty clubs hurt the Vizsla movement in this way.

A Vizsla owner who wishes to start a specialty club in his local area, or another one in the same state, can contact the parent club, other local clubs or write directly to the American Kennel Club for help. A sample constitution and by-laws for a local specialty club can be obtained from the American Kennel Club and once a tentative locally descriptive name, constitution and 20 to 30 member addresses exist, the club secretary can request consideration for making application for sanctioned matches and field trials. Specific material must then be collected for each area relative to the members experiences in prior American Kennel Club competition and litter registrations. After holding a minimum acceptable number of matches and/or trials, and other minimum requirements, it is possible for the specialty club to make application to hold either point shows or field trials or both. The exact requirements often vary depending on a club's progress and service to the breed locally.

Above Hilda Boggs and Dr. Paul Holzworth prepare to cast off in the Amateur Gun Dog Stake at the Spring Nationals held at Colorado Springs in 1969.

At the same event Shirley Rothan, Hilda Boggs and Jane Graff (from l. to r. facing camera) compare notes on the last brace.

Al Sulesky waits for marshal to call for the next brace of which he is half.

Vizsla Specialty Clubs

PARENT SPECIALTY CLUB
Vizsla Club of America, Inc.

LOCAL SPECIALTY CLUBS
Central California Vizsla Club
Conestoga Vizsla Club
Connecticut Valley Vizsla Club
Hawkeye Vizsla Club
Lone Cypress Vizsla Club of the Monterey Peninsula, Inc.
Miami Valley Vizsla Club, Inc.
Nebraska Vizsla Club
Puget Sound Vizsla Club
Rio Salado Vizsla Club, Inc.
South Coast Vizsla Club
Vizsla Club of Central New England
Vizsla Club of Colorado, Inc.
Vizsla Club of Eastern Iowa
Vizsla Club of Greater Cleveland
Vizsla Club of Greater New York
Vizsla Club of Illinois
Vizsla Club of Western Michigan
Vizsla Club of Northern California
Vizsla Club of Northern New Jersey
Vizsla Club of Southern California, Inc.

CHAPTER 15

Vizslas

In Other Countries

There are Vizslas in relatively small numbers in many countries throughout the world. Canada, Great Britian, Holland, Hungary, Germany, Austria, Czechoslovakia and France have specialty clubs to promote the breed. Other countries could have specialty clubs for the breed since that information is difficult to obtain.

Owners in the English speaking countries have sought out copies of The Vizsla, although the first edition was written primarily for owners in the United States.

This book has been bought by owners in Australia, Canada, Great Britian, Hungary, Italy, Mexico, Netherlands, Scotland, South Africa, Switzerland and West Germany.

Many European, African, South American countries, and Mexico, belong to the Federation Cynologique Internationale (FCI) with headquarters in Belgium, and use that organization's Vizsla standards and rules for dog show and field competition.

CANADA

History

The Canadian Kennel Club does not provide a means to check the facts, or to obtain useable historical information on the breed. It publishes Dogs in Canada.

Most information on the breed has been researched from the newsletters published by the Vizsla Club of Canada, The Vizsla Society of Canada, *The Vizsla Voice* and *The Vizsla News and Views.*

The Vizsla Club of Canada was formed in 1963 but the national concept failed due to the scarcity of Vizslas there and the great distances involved in keeping a national organization functioning. It published *Vizsla Views.*

The Vizsla Society of Canada was formed in 1976 and was later changed to the Vizsla Society of Ontario. It publishes the *Vizsla Voice*.

The Vizsla Club of Western Canada was formed in 1972 in Alberta. It publishes *Vizsla News and Views.*

Ed McCoy, Hamilton, Ontario, owned a male Vizsla in 1953 and helped establish the breed on the Niagara Peninsula. He was instrumental in promoting bird dog field trials in Ontario.

Early imports of Vizslas into Canada came from Czechoslovakia and Austria. Mr. A. G. Gerle of Montreal imported a male and female from Czechoslovakia in the fall of 1957. It was through his efforts that the Vizsla was recognized by the Canadian Kennel Club in 1958. Mr. Gerle won field trials with Csikcsicsoi Ari-Nora, an import from Budapest, in all-breed competition.

Dr. & Mrs. Albert William Bela Kemenes-Kettner founded the Bakony Kennels around the end of the 1950's with dogs from Mr. Gerle, imports from Hungary and with puppies they exchanged with the Hunt Kennels in the United States.

The late Dr. P. A. Wright started the Napkelte Kennels in 1961 with Janora's Pawlane Suntan which he purchased from John Janora, Buffalo, New York. Since that time he has imported several Vizslas from Hungary and the United States. He was active as a field trial judge.

Wes Basler started Gamefinder Kennels in Winnipeg, Manitoba in the mid-1960's with Vizslas from Frank Engstrom's Kennels in Minnesota. He later acquired and bred Wirehaired Vizslas, the first in North America. That breed was officially recognized by the Canadian Kennel Club in 1979.

There were other no less important breeders in Canada during this time period who were instrumental in establishing the breed which now totals approximately 3,000.

Field Trials

The Canadian Kennel Club rules and procedures for field trials are very similar to those of the American Kennel Club, but there are also marked

BARSONY HOBBIT VADASZ, C.D.X.
by Ch. Arany Duffy Pajti, C.D. out of Kyska Romina, C.D.
Breeder; C. Rae Purvis   Owner: Jayne & Howard Coneybeare

CANADIAN CH. NAPKELTEI BAJOS OPAL, C.D.
by Cariad's Tallissen von Wold out of Napkeltei Judit v Hunt
Breeder: Dr. P. A. Wright   Owner: Ingeborg S. Horvath

differences. In addition, the Canadian Kennel Club has provisions for Field Dog (FD) and Field Dog Excellent (FDX) titles.

The Field Trial Champion title requires 10 points of which only two points can be used from puppy and two points from derby stakes, and three points must come from senior unrestricted stakes —— that is from one gun dog or all age stake open to all pointing breeds. This one provision alone limits Vizsla field champions. A field champion title cannot be earned from specialty club trials closed to other breeds as in the United States. Vizslas can beat other breeds when properly trained. I know of only one field champion that has not won or placed against all the other breeds in the United States.

The schedule of points for field trial champion title in Canada is similar to the schedule set for the amateur field trial champion title by the American Kennel Club. Performance standards are very nearly alike. Canadian dogs can effectively compete and win in the United States and vice versa.

Canadian dogs can enter puppy stakes until they are 18 months old. They can enter derby stakes until they are 27 months old.

Provisions are made for championship stakes such as: National Championship, Regional Championship, Provincial Championship, and others as may be determined.

The first Vizsla national field trial was held in Carighdu, Alberta, September 26-27, 1964.

The first field trial held in Fenwick, Ontario under Canadian Kennel Club approval was in 1965 with 27 entries.

Field trials are not nearly as numerous as in the United States. None of the Canadian field champions are alive. The first one was Ch. Rigo von Klein owned by Eugene Klein, Vancouver, British Columbia followed by American Field Champion Ripp Barat and American Field Champion Ripp Barat's Rippy. This represents the sum total of all Canadian Field Champions.

Vizslas have been much more successful in earning the recently established Field Dog and Field Dog Excellent titles as compared to the other breeds. Ch. Cin Cillis Yeona owned by Ray Rowan, Ontario, was the first dog in Canada to earn the Field Dog title with scores of 99, 94½ and 89. She also earned a Prize I in the North American Versatile Hunting Dog Association's Natural Ability Test. Mr. Rowan's Vizsla, Ch. Cin Cillis Sasha is the first dog of any breed to have won the Field Dog Excellent title, and the first Vizsla in Canada to earn a prize rating in the N.A.V.H.D.A.'s Utility Field Test.

Most of the dogs qualifying for the Field Dog and Field Dog Excellent titles open to all pointing breeds have been Vizslas since these titles were first offered in 1976.

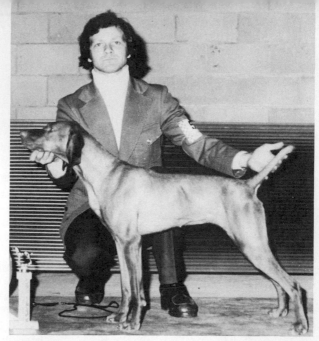

CANADIAN CH. CIN CILLIS YEONA, F.D.
by Am. & Can. Ch. Napkeltei Talisman out of Can. Ch. Cindi Cin Cilli
Breeder: Sue Dimmell   Owner: Ray Rowan
N.A.V.H.D.A. Prize I

CANADIAN CH. ARANY DUFFY PAJTI
by Can. Ch. Bakony Betyar Franci out of Can. Ch. Devecseri Bozsi
Breeder: T. P. Chamney   Owner: June & Jim Spencer

The actual testing is done under conditions and performance standards similar to those for the field trial champion titles. The training is very similar to that required to win at regular field trials.

Field Dog competition is run for 15-30 minutes one dog at a time and judged on eight categories from 10-20 points each. The Field Dog Excellent Test requires that the dog be steady to flush and shot, back and make a water retrieve. This test lasts for 30 minutes and dogs may be run in braces or alone.

Each dog is scored according to its own performance similar to obedience with a maximum score of 100 points and a passing score of 75 points. Three passing scores are needed for each title.

Canadians are active in the North American Versatile Hunting Dog Association's Natural Ability Trials and Utility Trials which are open to all versatile pointing breeds. This non-profit organization's purpose is to foster, improve, promote and protect the versatile hunting dog breeds in North America by sponsoring field trials for the versatile breeds and truly test their versatility. Dogs are scored individually.

Each year several field trials are run under the minimum requirements of the American Field, Chicago, Illinois. The dogs competing in these trials are mostly English Setters and Pointers.

Both the N.A.V.H.D.A. and Vizsla Society of Ontario now hold trials under the rules of the National Shoot To Retrieve Association with headquarters at Indianapolis, Indiana. This organization is composed of regionals and sanctions trials which award championship points. Dogs are braced together for approximately 30 minutes with birds being shot by either the handler or his gunner. The gunner flushes birds. Points are awarded for obedience, ground race, one back, points and retrieves. The dog having the most points and retrieves wins and needs not be steady to flush or shot.

Dog Shows

The Canadian Kennel Club rules and procedures for dog shows are very similar to those of the American Kennel Club. There are also some very important differences. The most important one is that the exhibitor **must** compete for every award for which he is eligible unless excused by the official veterinarian or show superintendent. Thus, a dog must compete in every class entered and if he wins breed, must compete in group, and if he wins group, must compete in best in show or lose whatever ribbon, prizes or other awards won up to the time he failed to show.

The classes offered are Junior Puppy Class, Senior Puppy Class, Canadian-Bred Class, Bred by Exhibitor Class, Open Class and Specials Only. There are also unofficial classes and stakes.

CANADIAN CH. CIN CILLIS SASHA, F.D., F.D.X., C.D.
by Am & Can. Ch. Napkeltei Talisman out of Can. Ch. Cindi Cin Cilli
Breeder: Sue Dimmell   Owner: Ray Rowan
N.A.V.H.D.A. Prize II (NA), Prize III (UFT)

CANADIAN CH. BARSONY SHILO VADASZ
by Can. Ch. Arany Duffy Pajti out of Kyska Romina, C.D.
Breeder: C. Rae Purvis   Owner: June & Jim Spencer

From the puppy classes evolves a Best Puppy (Breed), Puppy Group and Best Puppy in Show which can get complicated since a puppy can also win Best of Breed, lose in Group, but win in Puppy Group and win Best Puppy in Show. There are obviously other combinations that must be understood.

Placements are made in each class and the class winners compete for Winners Male, Reserve Winners Male, Winners Female, Reserve Winners Female, Best of Breed, Best of Opposite Sex, Best of Winners and Best Puppy in Breed (follows selection of Best of Winners).

Points may be won at breed, group or best in show levels. A maximum of ten points is needed for the champion title. Unlike the American Kennel Club, no major points are needed, but the 10 points must have been won under three different judges at three different shows. One other dog must be beaten each time, so it is possible to earn the title by beating the same dog at 10 shows. Points allocated range from one to a maximum of five points where 13 or more dogs are in competition.

Dogs registered by the American Kennel Club must pay one dollar listing fee to compete. Before a champion title is awarded, the owner must obtain either a registered noseprint or tatoo and then obtain a Canadian Kennel Club registration. A dog must not be entered in "Specials Only Class" until such registration is obtained.

Vizslas have a height disqualification in its standard, and cannot be given the champion title until it reaches one year of age and is officially measured.

The Canadian Kennel Club has provisions for a Championship Show, Limited Breeds Show, Specialty Championship Show, Field Trial Conformation Show, Sanction Match and Booster Show.

The Booster Show is popular and is held in conjunction with a regular Championship Show. The first Vizsla Booster was in 1964. Displays and demonstrations are provided by breed clubs for educational purposes and it is usually a social affair too. This is very similar to the specialty show offered by a Vizsla club in the United States at an all-breed show.

In 1958, the Canadian Kennel Club recognized the smooth coat Vizsla with the first Vizslas being shown at the Ladies Kennel Club in Montreal. The first Canadian-owned Vizsla to win Group first was Aprod Prucsok of Bakony Kennels Limited in 1963. The first Canadian show champion was Ch. Agres Z Povazia owned by Mr. A. G. Gerle.

In 1967, Canadian and American Ch. Count Jonish Mignotte, owned by Elizabeth Mignotte, Exeter, Ontario won Best of Breed at the Vizsla Club of America Specialty at the Chagrin Kennel Club all-breed show in Ohio.

Three Vizslas from the kennels of Angela Boys, Canterbury, England are (l. to r.) Galfrid Fergus, Mocsarkereso Vac of Galfrid and Galfrid Vilmos. Photo by Jessett.

Obedience

The Canadian Kennel Club offers the same obedience classes as the American Kennel Club with minor exceptions. An Obedience Trial Champion title is attained by earning all three titles: Companion Dog (C.D.), Companion Dog Excellent (C.D.X.), and Utility Dog (U.D.). Then the prefix "O.T.Ch." can be used before the dog's name.

The first Canadian obedience title (C.D.) was earned in 1961 by Marge Meminger, Erie, Pennsylvania with Ch. Kedves V. Hunt.

Rules and Regulations

Pamphlets for Field Trial Rules and Regulations for Pointing Breeds, Regulations and Standards for Obedience Trials and Dog Show Rules can be obtained by writing to The Canadian Kennel Club, 2150 Bloor Street West, Toronto, Ontario M6S 4V7.

GREAT BRITIAN

History

Vizslas have been in England for as long as they have been in the United States. In 1974, there were between 600-800 Vizslas there and several were exhibited regularly in dog shows.

Many of these were descended from Erneszt, Agnes (imported in 1951), Adalyn von Hunt, (U.S. import 1956), Tardosi Gyongi (Hungarian import 1959), and Sibriktelepi Tigi (Hungarian import 1962). Joram de la Creste was imported from France in 1963 and was supposedly smuggled out of Yugoslavia. He was used at stud and eventully ended up at the Saline Kennels in Scotland. His poor temperament or bad training was responsible for his short life and he is held responsible for some of the temperament problems in English Vizslas. English Vizsla owners have recognized some of the problems in the breed, and have worked hard to correct them.

The Hungarian Vizsla Club was founded in 1968 and later divided to form the Hungarian Vizsla Society in the early 1970's. These two clubs are entirely separate with both holding field trials, but neither one has run its own show.

In Great Britian only the puppies can be registered. A separate stud book is for registering dogs after winning their first Challenge Certificate (Championship). A dog's name can be changed once, and a breeder can add his own kennel name.

Field Trials

A show champion can become a "Champion" by being placed in a field trial or run for a Qualifying Certificate. This is obtained on a field trial

Galfrid Gaspar, by Matai Lurko out of Sari of Galfrid (Hungarian Import), is owned by Angela Boys, Canterbury, England. Photo by Jessett.

Show Ch. Chantilly Jester, by Szeppataki Csaba out of Saffron Flora, is posed by breeder/owner, Mrs. Heather McCabe, after he won Best of Breed at Leeds in 1978. Photo by Garwood.

day by convincing the judges that the dog running by itself can hunt, point, swim and retrieve tenderly. A field trial title is earned by winning two trials that are open to all the hunting, pointing and retrieving breeds or by winning one championship stake.

Field trials are held on native game (birds and furred animals) and are run over different courses or beats.

Vizslas are run under the same requirements of a pointer-retriever in the German Shorthaired Pointer and Weimaraner trials and are run singly. There are pairs or brace trials where the two dogs must compliment each other quartering and hunting involving other hunting dogs.

Field trial dogs are required to quarter ground in search of game, point game, be steady to flush and shot and retrieve tenderly on command. A water test is also held where a Puppy or Novice Stake has the dog retrieving from, or across, water that has had a bird shot in the air. In all other stakes, the dogs must make a blind retrieve from across water, re-enter the water with the bird with no shot fired.

A dog must quarter the ground in front of a line of two to four walking guns, with the handler being slightly ahead of the guns, or even with them. The judges indicate the limit of the dog's range and he must be turned by whistle or other signals at the limit of that range. Dogs are expected to be under control at all times. They should walk to heel on command, drop to whistle or hand signal, quarter on signal, drop when either ground game moves, game flies or a shot is fired. The handler must indicate to the judges when his dog is on point. A minimum of noise by whistle or voice is expected.

Judges look for the dog that covers its ground well, retrieves tenderly to hand, is totally steady and properly marks a falling bird.

Field trial requirements are much more stringent and the running pattern is more formal than for trials held in the United States. The dogs in Great Britian are expected to perform according to the rules without exception. Performance and trainability makes the winning dog.

We cannot make a fair comparison to field dogs in Great Britian and the United States, but we can say their dogs are better trained and the judging is to stricter standards.

Their trials are normally run in one hour heats with two judges watching one dog run by itself. The dog is handled on foot with each dog running an entirely new area on native game. Fighting, gunshyness, failure to perform and hardmouthing can disqualify a dog from further competition.

The All-Purpose Gun Dog, by David Layton, breeder of German Shorthaired Pointers in England is recommended for giving details on field and show competition. Mr. Layton now owns a Wirehaired Vizsla.

Ch. Abbeystag Bruna, by Sh. Ch. Futaki Lazslo out of Sh. Ch. Abbeystag Wolfox Flora, is owned by Sheila and Jim Gray, Shattesbury, England.

Ch. Abbeystag Emilio, by Sh. Ch. Futaki Lazslo out of Abbeystag Wolfox Flavia, was bred and is owned by Jim and Sheila Gray, Shaftesbury, England.

Dog Shows

Crufts is as familiar to most dog owners as Westminster. Many people from the United States attend Crufts and then come back for Westminster.

English dog classes are: Special Yearling (for dogs under two years of age, both sexes); Post Graduate (dogs or bitches not having won a Challenge Certificate, or won more than five first prizes having a given monetary limit); Open Bitch (for bitches of all ages including champions); Open Dog (for dogs of all ages and champions); and, Best of Breed.

The show champion title for gun dog breeds is won by winning three Challenge Certificates under three different judges for either best dog or best bitch at selected championship shows. Champions must compete in the open classes with dogs competing for their Challenge Certificates.

Ch. Oroshaza Zindi of Bohoc from Oroshaza Kennel of Heather McCabe, Scotland, was the youngest bitch at eight months to win a Challenge Certificate.

Sheila and Jim Gray have been successful in both show and field under the Abbeystag Kennel. He imported Futaki Lazslo from the United States for his foundation stud.

All dogs taken to Great Britian and Australia must undergo a six month quarantine. This has somewhat of a stifling effect on importing and showing dogs in these countries by foreign owners.

Angela Boys is an ardent breeder of Vizslas and has made several imports from Hungary,and has attended several Hungarian dog shows. She has worked hard to promote the breed in England and has been very successful in showing her dogs. The Galfrid prefix for her dogs combine British, Hungarian and American bloodlines. She is active in using her Vizslas as working gun dogs.

HOLLAND

History

The Vizsla was first brought into Holland in 1951 to 1952, and the first one was owned by a Mr. Knip of Amsterdam, but his bitch was apparently not bred for the lack of a stud dog.

The first Vizsla club in Holland was formed in 1975, and its newsletter is *Vizsla Varia.*

Pedigrees of Dutch bred Vizslas are likely to contain the names of the following dogs: Dutch Sh. Ch. Gerecsei Elias Eszaias (male imported from Hungary); Pasareti Baki (bitch imported from Hungary); Dutch Sh. Ch. Magas Ezsak Romano (dog, son of the above two); Dutch Sh. Ch. Galfrid Imre (dog imported from England); and, Galfrid Oten (dog imported from England).

Abbeystag Estelle, by Sh. Ch. Futaki Lazslo out of Abbeystag Wolfox Flavia, is owned by Heather McCabe and J. L. Doldersum.

Bohoc Aranka, by Donar v. h. Schauws out of Oroshaza Zindia is shown at 5½ months old. She is an example of Holland breeding.

317

The estimated number of Vizslas in 1980 was between 500 and 1000. Of these there are two imported Wirehaired Vizslas with a litter.

Dogs can only be registered by the breeder (owner of the bitch) and can only get the kennel name of the breeder (if he has one). The pups must be registered before they are six months of age and once registered the name cannot be changed. All pups born from registered parents enter the Dutch Stud Book.

Field Trials

Field trials are held under the rules and regulations of the Federation Cynologique Internationale (FCI) and under the regulations of the National Kennel Clubs.

Only one Vizsla has won an official field trial open to all breeds (a working Challenge Certificate under CAT/CACIT) in international competition. She is Csardas Puszta v.h. Lage Hutten owned and trained by Mr. O.v.d. Horst. There are no dual champions.

Dog Shows

Dog shows are held under the rules and regulations of the Federation Cynologique Internationale (FCI). Approximately eight International Championship Shows are held each year where all breeds can win Challenge Certificates (CAC & CACIB). The International Winner Show held in Amsterdam has approximately 4,700 dogs of all breeds. Holland has also held specialty shows for Vizslas.

HUNGARY

History

Hungary is the place of origin of the Vizsla and its National Dog. Hungary's borders have been greatly reduced, and that which remains is somewhat similar to many places in the United States with a wide range of terrain and climatic conditions. Hunting methods with the Vizslas resulted from an abundance of game on this terrain from which developed its intense desire to hunt game birds and animals. Its gentle and loving nature probably resulted from the home environment and close association with the nobility.

The Vizsla in its original form is believed to have been part of the migration of many thousands of Hungarians from somwhere in Asia in 895 AD to where they settled in the Carpathian Basin peacefully with the Moravian-Slovak tribes already settled there. At that time they used their Vizslas with falcons and nets. They continued development along these methods until the firearm came into use after which they developed into superior searching, pointing and retrieving dogs working to the gun.

Another of Holland's Vizslas is Oroshaza Lyana of Bohoc owned by J. L. Doldersum. In this photo, Lyana is 10 months old.

German Show Ch. Alpha vom Arany Homok, by Bosaenfai Hangos out of Helvecia Dodi (both Hungarian imports), was bred and is owned by Prof. Dr. Med. Gunther Dotzauer.

German Show Ch. & International Ch. Kevei Gazsi (Hungarian import), by Helvecia Bato Csibesz out of Kevei Csibi Fruska, is owned by Prof. Dr. Med. Gunther Dotzauer, Koln, Germany. He was bred by Pauliny Laszlo.

It was in 1879 at the Hannover International Dog Show that official characteristics of pointers were determined. It just so happened that the Hungarian Vizsla met all of these characteristics set down whereas most other breeds had to be trained to point game.

The present day Vizsla is a development of systematic cross-breeding in the 19th century using the limited basic Vizsla breed. Hungarians still breed quality Vizslas under the control of the National Association of Hungarian Dogbreeders (Magyar Ebtenyesztok Orszagos Egyesulete-MEOE). This organization is under the Ministry of Agriculture and Food and maintains the Stud Book Register (Magyar Ebtorzskonyv-MET). This organization controls and organizes all aspects of dog activity such as breeding, boarding kennels, training, sports events, dog shows, registration, etc. It is organized into breed clubs which are operated by a committee chosen from the members.

The Secretary General, currently Miklos Farkashazi, is elected by the general assembly for a four year term and is head of the Association's head office, MOE, Budapest XI, Fadrusz Utca 11/A.

The National Association of Hungarian Dogbreeders is controlled by the general assembly convened yearly by the president of the Association. The participants are the central committee, the board of auditing and disciplinary committee as well as the presidents and representatives of the different clubs and county organizations.

The breed clubs supervise specialist breeding and provide necessary instruction and information to the club members.

The Federation Cynologique Internationale (FCI) was founded in 1911, and the National Association of Hungarian Dogbreeders became a member in 1933. It has dog-breeding association members from 38 countries with its headquarters in Belgium. It provides registration and organizes dog shows, trials and award titles according to uniform regulated principles. The Vizsla standard adopted by this organization was developed for the breed in Hungary.

Dog Shows

Dog shows are organized by the National Association of Hungarian Dogbreeders using their standard and regulations. They are also conducted under the rules and regulations of the Federation Cynologique Internationale (FCI). Under this international organization, a dog must be at least six months old and have a valid pedigree issued by the Association. Foreign exhibitors must have a pedigree accepted by the FCI.

Titles awarded at Hungarian dog shows are: Hungaria Prima Junior, Hungaria Derby Champion, Hungaria Champion, and Laureate Hungaria

Miklos Farkashazi demonstrates obedience exercises with three of his Vizslas for the author while visiting in Hungary.

Champion. Titles awarded at the FCI dog shows are CACIB and Reserve CACIB Champion beauty titles.

Males and females are judged separately in Puppy Class (Kolvok Osztaly), Junior Class (Fiatal Osztaly,) Open Class (Nyilt Osztaly), Working Class (Munka Osztaly), Owner Class (Gyoztes Osztaly), and Derby Class (Derby Osztaly).

Class ribbons when merited are:

> Excellent (Kituno) Solid blue ribbon with medallion
> Very good (Nagyon Jo) Solid red ribbon with medallion
> Good (Jo) Solid yellow ribbon with medallion
> Acceptable or poor ((Megfelelo) Solid green ribbon with Medallion
> Puppy Class solid white ribbon with medallion

Title ribbons and lace are:

> Hungaria Prima Junior blue and white ribbon with medallion
> Hungaria Derby Winner red and white ribbon with medallion
> Budapest Winner CAC red, white and green ribbon with medallion
> Hungaria Winner CAC red, white and green ribbon with medallion
> Hungaria Breed Winner yellow lace (cord) with tassle
> CACIB red, white and green lace (cord) with tassle
> CACIB Reserve red, white, green and silver lace (cord) with tassle

The Federation Cynologique Internationale Budapest dog show September 4, 1977 presented an interesting new experience for my wife and me. We attended the judges dinner at the kennel club one evening and then were invited to the formal opening toast on the day of the show for the judges, officials and dignitaries which was then followed at 9:00 A.M. with the formal opening of the show.

There were approximately 38 rings where judging lasted all day and was concluded with final judging of the various categories, group and best in show followed by a formal closing.

Throughout the day there were many dog activities, other than class breed judging, involving drill teams, guard dog competition and other things to entertain the spectators.

Judging was very informal with the dogs being shown singly from each class. The judge dictated the qualities of the dogs to a steward and a copy of the judge's opinion was given to the handlers. The dogs were not groomed, stacked or gaited as we are accustomed to doing. Some of the dogs were shy and were difficult to touch by the judge. It was not unusual to see a judge stop work and engage in a private conversation with a friend from outside the ring, or a handler take his toddler son into the ring to show his dog.

Each Vizsla competes against itself. Only those dogs in each class receiving a blue ribbon go back into the ring to be judged competitively. Green, white and red ribbons are given the first placed dog in each class.

We observed both good and bad Vizslas in Hungary as we have elsewhere. Their male Vizslas appeared better than those in the United States while the females seemed of equal quality. All had very deep chests. Unfortunately, there were some with the skull deformity. Somehow, I had expected that their controlled breeding might have eliminated that problem.

Even though some of the Vizslas misbehaved in the show ring, they are much more obedient with their owners than I have observed in the United States.

Dogs are owned at every economic level in Hungary, and their owners exercise very close supervision over them. It was very rare to see dogs off lead anywhere, and muzzles are in common use on all breeds,- especially at the show.

Field Trials/Hunting

Hunting Associations are led by the National Association of Hungarian Hunters and its members are eligible to join local associations. Members receive the official publication *Nimrod*. The Association stresses the importance of game protection and management, trains professional hunters and examines and licenses hunters. A non-member cannot hunt and the number of Association members is limited.

The highest authority of state game farms is the Forestry and Wood-Industrial Office of the Ministry of Agriculture and Food, and is also the highest authority for hunting administration. The office regulates closed seasons, controls boundaries of shooting territories and the rent of hunting grounds. Infringement of hunting rights results in expulsion from the Association and loss of the gun license.

Over 80 percent of the hunting ground is leased to hunting associations and the remainder belongs to the state. Individuals cannot rent shoots. Professional hunters must be employed on each shooting territory. The number of association hunters on a hunt is controlled by the size of the shooting territory which permits one hunter for each 100-150 hectares to 250-300 hectares depending on the type of game being hunted.

Most of Hungary has no fences. Some of the territories that are fenced, have towers, and appear to be controlled shooting areas.

Field trials are organized by the National Association of Hungarian Dogbreeders and its breed clubs under their standard and regulations. They may also be held under the rules and regulations of the Federation Cynologique Internationale (FCI) where CACIB and Reserve CACIB champion titles are awarded.

A day's shooting in Hungary can be for duck, hare, pheasant, partridge, fox, deer and wild boar. The Vizsla is expected to retrieve birds, hares

323

and foxes, and track a wounded boar or deer when necessary, or bark treed as the occasion requires. It is a dog for all kinds of hunting.

In field trial competition, Vizslas are required to quarter ground in search of game, point, be steady to flush and shot and retrieve from on land or water. They must also retrieve a fox over an obstacle, bay a deer and follow a simulated injured deer for several miles. They must handle kindly and be under the handler's control at all times.

Bibliography

1. *American Field.* Published weekly by the American Field Publishing Company. Chicago, Illinois. 1953-1981.
2. *American Kennel Club Rules Applying to Registration and Dog Shows.*
   American Kennel Club Rules Applying to Registration and Field Trials.
   American Kennel Club Rules Applying to Registration and Obedience Trials.
   The American Kennel Club, 51 Madison Avenue, New York, New York 10010.
3. Biro, Dr. Lajors Pal and Fest, Jozsef Willer Sandor. *English–Hungarian – Hungarian–English* Dictionary. Brooklyn, New York: K. P. Schick, 1957.
4. Byrd, Rondell. "Sightless See Again," *The Wonderful World of Ohio,* (January 1969).
5. *The Complete Dog Book.* An official publication of the American Kennel Club. Garden City, New York: Garden City Book, 1961.
6. Drage, Geoffrey. *Austria – Hungary.* New York: E. P. Dutton & Co., 1909.
7. Elquhoun, Archibald R. & Ethel. *Whirlpool of Europe.* New York: Dodd, Mead & Co., 1907.
8. Griffin, Jack R. "Midwest," 'One Man's Best Friend,' *Chicago Sun Times.* July 19, 1965.
9. Heady, Ray. "Hunting With Vizslas, Hungarian Pointers, and Their Kansas City Godfather," *The Kansas City Star.* November 14, 1965.
10. "History of the Vizsla" The Canadian Vizsla Club. (Mimeographed).
11. "Hungary," *The Encyclopedia Americana.* (1959 ed.), XIV, 501-508b.
12. Kende, Mihalyi (Mike). Former Secretary of the National Vizsla Club of Hungary. He researched the National Record Office, the National Szechenyi Library in the Agricultural Library, *Nimrod Hunting News* and *Fox Hound.* From this he published a series of articles with translation by Elmer Halden and edited by Mrs. Joan Hunt. These were published in the January, February and March 1965 Vizsla News. He researched two years to get this Vizsla history.
13. Lyon, McDowell, "Gun Dogs from Abroad," *Outdoor Life.* March 1955.
14. Lyon, McDowell. "Multiple Game Dog," *Outdoor Life.* June 1956.
15. The Magyar Vizsla Club of America Articles of Incorporation. 1953.

326

16. Orthopedic News Releases of the Orthopedic Foundation for Animals, Inc.
17. Osborn, I. S., D. V. M. "The Osborn Vizsla." Printed matter.
18. Osborn, I. S., D. V.M. "Congenital Hip Dysplasia and Its Ramifications," and an address "Dysplasia In Vizslas." Published by the Vizsla Club of America. Pamphlet. 1961.
19. *Plainsman Herald.* Denver. November 18, 1965.
20. Tallman, Frank J. "The Hungarian Vizsla," Pamphlet. 1954.
21. Personal correspondence and records from Robert Foster, Mrs. Jane Tallman, Bela Hadik, Chauncey M. Smith, Jr., and Mrs. Joan Hunt.
22. Personal experiences and observations of author from 1961 to 1981.
23. Pfaffenberger, Clarence. *The New Knowledge of Dog Behavior.* New York: Howell Book House, Inc., 1968.
24. *Pure-Bred Dogs–American Kennel Gazette.* Published monthly by the American Kennel Club. 1952-1982 .
25. "The Regal Hun." *Outdoor Nebraska.* January 1964.
26. Scott, John Paul. "A Time To Learn," *Psychology Today.* March 1969.
27. Stetson, Joe. "Sporting Dog of Hungary," *Field & Stream.* November 1954.
28. Stetson, Joe. "Take Your Choice," *Field & Stream.* June 1955.
29. *Springfield News & Sun.* (Ohio). February 3, 1969.
30. Whitney, Leon F., D. V. M. *The Complete Book of Dog Care.* Garden City, New York: Doubleday & Com pany, Inc., MCMLIII.
31. The Vizsla Club of America Constitution & By-Laws. 1965.
32. The Vizsla Club of America Secretary job 1965.
33. *The Vizsla News.* Published by the Vizsla Club of America. Editors: Norma J. Hatfield, Charles Hunt, Jane Graff, B.C. Boggs, Kathy Hartl, Carole Smith, Carolyn Arrasmith, Gail Day and Marge Mehagian. Volume IV-XXVIII.
34. *You and Your Dog.* 4-H Care & Training Project. Ralston Purina Company.
35. *Hungarian Review,* "Hungary's Hunting Conditions, Expo 1971, Budapest (Bulletin IV) pgs. 15-17. 1972 Vol. 1, No. 4.
36. *German Shorthaired Pointer News.* "My Epistle on England." Dianne K. Schumacher. April 1981.
37. Pal Sarkany & Imre Ocsag. *Dogs of Hungary.* Corvina Press. 1977.
38. Private Correspondence with Mr. Jim Gray, England, Angela Boys, England, Leno Doldersum, Holland, Ray Rowan, Canada and Mrs. June Spencer, Canada.
39. *Field.* "Vizsla, an all-rounder." George Wilkinson (England)
40. Regulations and Standards for Obedience Trials (1-1-78). The Canadian Kennel Club.
41. Dog Show Rules (1-1-81). The Canadian Kennel Club
42. Field Trial Rules and Regulations for Pointing Breeds (1-1-77). The Canadian Kennel Club
43. "The Vizsla in Canada" (Article) by Dr. P. A. Wright.
44. "Some Historic Dates and Facts in Canada" (Article) by Dr. P. A. Wright.
45. *The Vizsla Voice.* Published by the Vizsla Society of Ontario. Volume 5.
46. *Vizsla News and Views.* Published by Western Canada Vizsla Club. Volume 7, No. 1 & 4.
47. *Canine Hip Dysplasia.* Proceeding of the Canine Hip Dysplasia Symposium and Workshop held in St. Louis, Missouri, October 19-20, 1972. Sponsored by the Orthopedic Foundation for Animals, Inc.
48. *The Vizsla Field.* Published by Bill Fisher, Maryville, Missouri. September 1980 - February 1981.
49. Dodds, W. Jean, D.V.M. *Selected Hematological Problems of Animals.* Norden News. Pages 14-19.

Appendices

TABLE 1
AMERICAN KENNEL CLUB VIZSLA REGISTRATIONS

YEAR	1961	1962	1963	1964	1965	1966	1967	1968	1969	1970	1971
MONTH PUBLISHED											
January	0	34	33	63	75	69	106	155	118	155	171
February	325	56	38	38	76	76	116	126	136	142	181
March	169	25	39	49	83	110	106	107	137	122	197
April	75	49	44	67	85	79	103	125	138	155	182
May	66	54	42	84	90	115	125	212	147	144	185
June	37	107	52	60	97	118	109	114	148	159	182
July	54	83	62	53	64	84	95	106	116	135	144
August	30	34	33	59	79	90	100	111	134	174	186
September	34	31	58	57	71	124	123	125	133	195	163
October	42	29	54	65	73	90	100	148	126	161	169
November	31	37	53	59	99	124	123	139	137	175	187
December	33	58	51	95	81	130	135	137	207	201	222

NOTE: Actual registration precedes these dates by two months.

TABLE 1 (Continued)
AMERICAN KENNEL CLUB VIZSLA REGISTRATIONS

YEAR MONTH PUBLISHED	1972	1973	1974	1975	1976	1977	1978	1979	1980	1981
January	232	190	207	168	134	149	162	148	143	130
February	193	152	144	186	181	210	139	123	114	149
March	213	215	197	199	190	172	164	212	193	164
April	181	211	194	156	147	161	138	134	160	165
May	206	208	189	159	173	178	182	161	162	168
June	158	180	164	179	131	125	156	141	155	167
July	192	144	174	139	125	128	190	131	123	161
August	184	163	155	126	118	144	146	105	128	169
September	161	181	167	167	131	135	146	147	155	176
October	180	200	153	186	162	181	179	148	127	170
November	176	179	239	173	156	191	132	152	181	164
December	213	201	211	169	175	161	141	149	174	174

NOTE: Actual registration precedes these dates by two months.

331

TABLE 2
AMERICAN KENNEL CLUB YEARLY
REGISTRATION FOR VIZSLAS

YEAR	RANK	REGISTRATIONS	% INCREASE
1960	53	325	New Breed
1961	48	661	+103
1962	51	575	-13.8
1963	52	589	+2.4
1964	49	799	+35.6
1965	49	967	+21.0
1966	46	1255	+29.8
1967	47	1388	+10.6
1968	46	1578	+13.0
1969	47	1720	+9.0
1970	47	1973	+14.4
1971	48	2242	+13.6
1972	48	2206	-1.7
1973	48	2233	+0.01
1974	49	2197	-1.6
1975	48	1968	-10.5
1976	49	1867	-5.2
1977	50	1877	+0.005
1978	50	1845	-1.08
1979	N/A	1736	-6.0
1980	N/A	1837	+5.8

Note: Registration figures are from January 1 to December 31 each year.

AMERICAN KENNEL CLUB
VIZSLA REGISTRATION

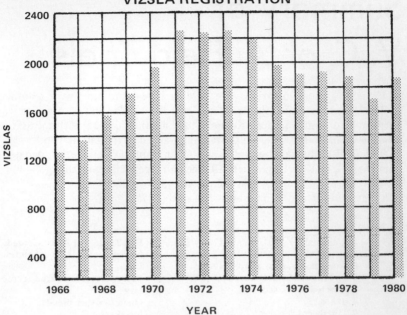

AMERICAN KENNEL CLUB
VIZSLA LITTER REGISTRATION

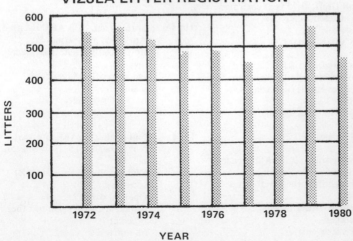

Summary of
V. C. of A. Field Trials

From 1954 to 1960 trials were held each year and most were recorded in *The American Field.* In the fall of 1961 the Vizsla Club of America was permitted to hold American Kennel Club Sanctioned trials with the aim of holding licensed trials. This approval was granted in the fall of 1962.

The field trial stakes recorded are: Open Puppy, Open Derby, Amateur Gun Dog, Open Gun Dog, Open All-Age and Open Limited All-Age.

The first Field Futurity was held in the fall of 1969.

Championship stakes have been run since 1975.

1961 8th Annual fall trial. 1st AKC Sanctioned.
November 4-5, New Sharon, Ia.
Tom Pratt, field trial secretary
Restricted to Vizslas.
4 stakes.
27 Vizsla entries.

1962 Spring trial. 2nd AKC Sanctioned.
May 5-6, Lincoln, Neb.
Bud Graff, field trial chairman
Restricted to Vizslas.
4 stakes.
38 Vizsla entries.

1962 Fall trial. 1st AKC licensed.
November 3-4, New Sharon, Ia.
Charles Hunt, field trial secretary
Open to other breeds.
5 stakes.
44 entries.

1963 Spring trial. 2nd AKC licensed.
May 4-5, New Sharon, Ia.
Joe Bentley, field trial secretary.
Open to other breeds.
6 stakes.
32 Vizsla entries.

1963 Fall Trial. 3rd AKC licensed.
November 9-10, New Sharon, Ia.
Betty Kenly, field trial secretary
Open to other breeds.
6 stakes.
67 Vizsla entries
(The 2nd Sanctioned B Match was held November 10 in conjunction with this trial.)

1964 Spring trial. 4th AKC licensed.
April 4-5, Muscatine, Ia.
Betty Kenly, field trial secretary
Open to other breeds.
6 stakes.
61 Vizsla entries.

1964 Fall trial. 5th AKC licensed.
November 14-15, New Sharon, Ia.
Richard Buhman, field trial secretary
Open to other breeds.
6 stakes. (Two open to other breeds.)
68 entries.

1965   Spring trial. 6th AKC licensed.
May 1-2, Bloomfield, Ia.
Bernard C. Boggs, field trial secretary
Open to other breeds
6 stakes (Two open to other
breeds.)
75 entries. Approximately 67
Vizsla entries.

1965   Fall trial. 7th AKC licensed.
October 9-10, Greenup, Ill.
George Solberg, field trial secretary
Vizslas only.
5 stakes.
91 entries.

1966   Spring trial. 8th AKC licensed.
April 30, May 1, Volo, Ill.
George Solberg, field trial secretary
Vizslas only.
5 stakes.
95 entries.

1966   Fall trial. 9th AKC licensed.
November 12-13, Crab Orchard,
Ill.
Harold Wingerter, field trial sec-
retary
Vizslas only.
5 stakes.
72 entries.

1967   Spring trial. 10th AKC licnesed.
April 22-23, Bloomfield, Ia.
Allan Hahn, field trial secretary
Vizslas only.
5 stakes.
77 entries.

1967   Fall trial. 11th AKC licensed.
October 28-29, Rising City,
Neb.
Richard Reinhardt, field trial
secretary
Vizslas only.
6 stakes.
101 entries.

1968   Spring trial. 12th AKC
licensed.
April 20-21, Kansasville, Wisc.

George Solberg, field trial secretary
Vizslas only.
6 stakes.
63 entries.

1968   Fall trial. 13th AKC licensed.
November 9-10, Harpster, Ohio
Bernard C. Boggs, field trial secretary
Vizslas only.
6 stakes.
115 entries.

1969   Spring trial. 14th AKC licensed
April 26-27, Colorado Springs,
Colo.
Johnny Laucus, field trial secre-
tary
Vizslas only.
6 stakes.
90 entries.

1969   Fall trial. 15th AKC licensed.
October 11-12, Kansasville,
Wis.
George Solberg, field trial secre-
tary
Vizslas only.
5 stakes (Open limited 1 hour.)
104 entries.

1969   Field Futurity. 1st.
October 13, Kansasville, Wis.
Hilda Boggs, futurity chairman
Winner: Redstone's Skol

1970   Spring trial. 16th AKC licensed.
April 4-5, Baldwinsville, N.Y.
Carl Richey, Sr., field trial secretary
Vizslas only.
5 stakes.
95 entries.

1970   Fall trial. 17th AKC licensed.
October 24-25, Raymond, Neb.
Betty Rozanek, field trial secretary
Vizslas only.
5 stakes.
69 entries.

1970   Field Futurity. 2nd
October 23, Raymond, Neb.
Tony Lucas, futurity chairman
Winner: Lobo' Lucky Lad

1971   Spring trial. 18th AKC licensed
April 10-11, Ohio, Ill.
Jim Arrasmith, field trial secretary
Vizslas only.
5 stakes. (Open limited 45 minutes.)
111 entries.

1971   Fall trial. 19th AKC licensed.
October 23-24, Raymond, Neb.
Betty Rozanak, field trial secretary
Vizslas only.
5 stakes.
106 entries.

1971   Field Futurity. 3rd.
October 22, Raymond, Neb.
Roger Paluska, futurity chairman
Winner: Lucky Lobo's Butch Cassidy

1972   Spring trial. 20th AKC licensed
May 6-7, Baldwinsville, N. Y.
Carole Smith, field trial secretary
Vizslas only.
5 stakes. (Open Limited 45 minutes.)
123 entries.

1972   Fall trial. 21st AKC Licensed.
October 28-29, Branched Oaks, Raymond, Nebraska
Betty Rozanek, Field Trial Secretary.
Vizslas Only.
5 Stakes.
114 entries.

1972   Field Futurity, 4th
October 27, Raymond, Neb.
Sylvester Armstead, Futurity Chairman
Winner: Earl's Red Rogue

1973   Spring trial. 22nd AKC licensed.
April 7-8, Crook, Colorado.
Tim Lundy, field trial secretary
Vizslas only.
5 stakes
73 entries.

1973   Fall trial. 23rd AKC licensed.
October 27-28, Clarksville, Maryland.
Tom Kepler, field trial secretary
5 stakes.
98 entries.

1973   Field Futurity, 5th
October 26, Clarksville, Maryld.
Tom Kepler, Futurity Chairman
Winner: Amber Sunshine Cherie

1974   Spring trial. 24th AKC licensed.
April 27-28, Ohio, Illinois.
Dorothy Rosenberg, field trial secretary
5 stakes.
136 entries.

1974   Fall trial. 25th AKC licensed.
October 26-27, Porterville, California.
Marion Fishback, field trial secretary
5 stakes.
83 entries.

1974   Field Futurity, 6th
October 25, Porterville, Cal.
May Carpenter, Futurity Chairman
Winner: Villan Von Nobilis

1975   Spring trial. 26th AKC licensed.
May 3-4, Baldwinsville, New York
Joyce Burjan, field trial secretary
3 stakes.
70 entries.
1st National Championship Stake
(no champion named) (points only)

1975   Fall trial. 27th AKC licensed.
October 25-26, Raymond, Nebraska.
Betty Rozanek, field trial secretary
5 stakes.
107 entries.

1975   Field Futurity, 7th
October 24, Raymond, Neb.
Barth Steere, Futurity Chairman
Winner: Spring Creek Shiloh

6 Spring trial. 28th AKC licensed.
April 16-18, Denver, Colorado.
Tim Lundy, field trial secretary
3 stakes.
45 entries.
2nd National Championship Stake
(points only)

6 Fall trial. 29th AKC licensed.
October 9-10, Medford, New Jersey.
Dr. Bernard E. McGivern,
field trial secretary
5 stakes.
98 entries.

6 Field Futurity, 8th
October 8, Medford, New Jersey
Pat Kepler, Futurity Chairman
Winner: Popple Dungeon Tolgyfa
(Field Futurity Ended)

7 Fall trial. 30th AKC licensed.
Third National Championship Stake.
First National Amateur Championship Stake.
October 21-23, Fort Ord, California
Marion Fishbach, field trial secretary.
4 stakes.
60 entries.

8 Fall trial. 31st AKC licensed.
Fourth National Championship Stake.
Second National Amateur Championship Stake.
November 2-4, Ohio, Illinois.
Linda Busch, field trial secretary
4 stakes.
111 entries.

9 Fall trial. 32nd AKC licensed.
Fifth National Championship Stake.
Third National Amateur Championship Stake.
October 18-20, Clarksburg, New Jersey.
Joyce Burjan, field trial secretary
4 stakes.
94 entries.

9 Fall trial. 33rd AKC licensed.
Sixth National Championship Stake.
Fourth National Amateur Championship Stake.
October 28-30, 1980, Fort Huachuca,
Sierra Vista, Arizona
Maxine Saperstein, field trial secretary
4 stakes.
75 entries.

1981 Fall trial. 34th AKC licensed.
Seventh National Championship Stake.
Fifth National Amateur Championship Stake.
October 26-28, 1981, Branched Oak,
Lincoln, Nebraska
Jane Graff, field trial secretary
4 stakes.
117 entries.

Vizsla Club of America Field Trial Winners

OPEN PUPPY STAKE

Year	Dog's Name	Sire	Dam
1961 F	Osborn's Starfire F	Rakk Selle	Osborn's Miss Kubis
1962 S	Osborn's Cimmeron	Brok Olca	Osborn's Copper Lady
1962 F	Ripp Barat's Rippy M	Ripp Barat	Sissy Selle
1963 S	Jorgen's Lady Olca F		
1963 F	Queen Inga F	Jerry's Red Flash	Lady Von Amana
1964 S	Weedy Creek Dutches F	Weedy Creek Skol	Shirbob's Honey Dew
1964 F	Bullet V Selle M	Len's Duke Selle	Nickla
1965 S	Behi's Csinos Csiny F	Haans V Selle	Futaki Juliska
1965 F	Pirolin M	Futaki Darocz	Wag's Inn Kedish
1966 S	Chip Odysseus M	Jake Jacaranda	Shirbob's Honey Dew
1966 F	Rusty Jay Laucus M	Haans V Selle	(Maggie Troy ex Fritz v Kisner)
1967 S	Windswept Spot M	Futaki Darocz	Konya V Selle
1967 F	Nik V Romarlin M	Ferro V Hunt	Honey Toots
1968 S	Good Upland Jet M	Rozsdas Antal	Pittro's Smart Girl
1968 F	Futaki Lenke F	Ch. Caesar	Futaki Lincsi
1969 S	Bundles Red Dude M	Jodo Red	Ripp Barat's Bundle
1969 F	Rebel Rouser Dutch M	Rebel Rouser Duke	Fld. Ch. Weedy Creek Dutches
1970 S	Lucky Lobo's Relentless M	Dual Ch. Weedy Creek Lobo	Lucky of Czuki Barat
1970 F	Dudley M	Dual Ch. Weedy Creek Lobo	Luckie Dutchess Selle
1971 S	Jodo's Candy King	Field Ch. Jodo Red	Candy Queen
1971 F	Earl's Red Rogue M	Dual Ch. Weedy Creek Lobo	Cricket
1972 S	Earl's Red Rogue M		
1972 F	Teks Joey Dezso Barat M	Ch. Debreceny	Ripp Barats Bundle
1973 S	El-Jo's Ochoa M	Du.Ch. Weedy Creek Lobo	El-Jo's Country Girl
1973 F	Piper's Lord Dudley M	Du.Ch. Rebel Rouser Duke	Ch. Gretl Von Tatabanya
1974 S	Rebel Rouser Bandieto M	Du.Ch. Rebel Rouser Duke	Rebel Rouser Penny
1974 F	Piper's Windy April F	Ch. Arra's Mr. Jake	Du.Ch. & Am.Fld Ch. Amber's Windy Autumn
1975 S	Rebel Rouser Cherokee F	Rebel Rouser Bandieto	Piper's Lady Lucy

Note: S or F after date means **Spring** or **Fall**
F or M after dog's name means **Female** or **Male**

338

1975 F	Rebel Rouser Cherokee F		
1976 S	Rowdy Rebel Windy's Knight M	Du.Ch. Rebel Rouser Duke	Du.Ch. & Am.Fld. Ch. Amber's Windy Autumn
1976 F	Sam's Stormy M	Du.Ch. Sir Amber Sam	Diane
1977 F	Bowcott Jeff of Amber Sam	Du.Ch. Sir Amber Sam	Randy Duke Jutka
1978 F	Futaki Cady F	Fld.Ch. & Am. Ch. Bratt's FK Gippen	Futaki Lenke
1979 F	Randy Boy Piper M	Fld.Ch. & Am. Fld.Ch. Randy Duke	Ch. Gretl Von Tatabanya
1980 F	Voros Tars Nitro Express F	Rebel Rouser Bandieto	Rebel Rouser Dezi
1981 F	Rebel Rouser Best Bet B	Rebel Rouser Bandieto	Rebel Rouser B Nuts

Vizsla Club of America Field Trial Winners

OPEN DERBY STAKE

Year	Dog's Name	Sire	Dam
1961 F	Derekas Rex Selle M	Rex Selle	Osborn's Copper Lady
1962 S	Gyp	Unknown	
1962 F	Futaki Darocz M	Ch. Hunor	Piri
1963 S	Haans V Selle M	Kosa V Selle	Konya V Selle
1963 F	Ripp Barat's Rippy M		
1964 S	Weedy Creek Dutches F		
1964 F	Weedy Creek Dutches F		
1965 S	Weedy Creek Dutches F		
1965 F	Pumpkin Fun Galore M	Shayo Fun Galore	Gemma Fun Galore
1966 S	Jodi of Czuki Barat M	Ripp Barat	Czuki of Lake Catherine
1966 F	Ch. Rustic Fun Galore M	Shayo Fun Galore	Gemma Fun Galore
1967 S	Szekeres' Kis Szereto F	Futaki Darocz	Szekeres' Kezdet
1967 F	Bobo Buck Selle M	Futaki Darocz	Konya V Selle
1968 S	Honey of Holzworth Farm F	Fritz V Loosdorf	Belle of Honey Dew
1968 F	Justhills' Sandy F	Fld. Ch. Jake Jacaranda	Weedy Creek Sasha
1969 S	Withheld		
1969 F	Baron of Czuki Barat M	Ripp Barat	Czuki of Lake Catherine
1970 S	Bundle's Red Dude M		
1970 F	Dudley M		
1971 S	Golden Girl of Highland Hills F	Coon Valley Pal	Matrishka Nessi
1971 F	Bundles' Jodo Red	Fld. Ch. Jodo Red	Ripp Barat's Bundle
1972 S	Earl's Red Rogue M		
1972 F	Bratt's FK Gippen M	Ch. Janos VW Come Lately	Dual Ch. Szekeres' Kis Szereto
1973 S	War Lords Bo M	Jeb Von Flidar	Ginger Queen
1973 F	Sir Amber Sam M	Du.Ch. & Am. Fld.Ch. Sir Lancelot	Du.Ch. & Am. Fld.Ch. Brook's Amber Mist

339

1974 S	Rebel Rouser Bandieto M		
1974 F	Rebel Rouser Bandieto M		
1975 S	Rebel Rouser Cash M	Du.Ch. Rebel Rouser Duke	Rebel Rouser Penny
1975 F	Rebel Rouser Winneshiek Mac	Du.Ch. Rebel Rouser Duke	Rebel Rouser Penny
1976 S	Rebel Rouser Cherokee F		
1976 F	Cline's Olympia Blitz M	Fld.Ch. Earl's Red Rogue	Ch. Arra's Valor Blitz
1977 F	Willie's Bushwak Barney McGee M	Du.Ch. & Am. Fld.Ch. Brook's Willie Whompum	Ch. Timarka's Tsindee of Amber C.D.
1978 F	Rebel Rouser Scout M	Rebel Rouser Bandieto	Ch. Arra's Miss Brandi
1979 F	Sam's Big Red M	Du.Ch. Sir Amber Sam	Randy Duke Jutka
1980 F	Hye Bektor M	Hye Sadana	Hye Jon
1981 F	Voro Tars Nitro Express B	Rebel Rouser Bandieto	Rebel Rouser Dezi

Vizsla Club of America Field Trial Winners

AMATEUR GUN DOG STAKE

Year	Dog's Name	Sire	Dam
1961 F	Ripp Barat M	Brok Olca	Rata z Povazia
1962 S	Ripp Barat		
1962 F	Ripp Barat		
1963 S	Haans V Selle M	(Non-regular stake)	
1963 F	Haans V Selle		
1964 S	Haans V Selle		
1964 F	Hunor M	Nikki's Arco	Shirbob's Folly
1965 S	Haans V Selle		
1965 F	Dual Ch. Futaki Darocz M		
1966 S	Futaki Juliska F	Ch. Hunor	Piri
1966 F	Jake Jacaranda M	Pepper Olca	Shirbob's Honey Dew
1967 S	Jodi of Czuki Barat M		
1967 F	Weedy Creek Dutches F		
1968 S	Pittro's Smart Girl F	Rusty Red	Ridgeland's Olca Selle
1968 F	Weedy Creek Chacha M	Weedy Creek Skol	Weedy Creek Merya
1969 S	Withheld		
1969 F	Bobo Buck Selle M	Dual Ch. Futaki Darocz	Konya V Selle
1970 S	Heidi of Windsweep F	Haans V Selle	Weedy Creek Dutches
1970 F	Ch. Nik V Romarlin M		
1971 S	Amber's Windy Autumn F	Fld. Ch. Jodi of Czuki Barat	Ch. Brook's Amber Mist
1971 F	Fld Ch. & Am. Fld. Ch. Amber's Windy Autumn		
1972 S	Dual Ch. Weedy Creek Lobo M	Weedy Creek Skol	Weedy Creek Merya
1972 F	Dual Ch. Ambers Windy Autumn F		

340

1973 S	Du.Ch. Brook's Amber Mist F		
1973 F	Du.Ch. & Am. Fld.Ch. Sir Lancelot M	Fld.Ch. Hubertus Aprod	Neshanica
1974 S	Du.Ch. & Am.Fld.Ch. Rippy of Webster Woodlands M	Fld.Ch. & Am. Fld.Ch. Jodi of Czuki Barat	Du.Ch. & Am.Fld.Ch. Brook's Amber Mist
1974 F	Fld.Ch. & Am.Fld.Ch. Randy Duke M	Distelfink's First Raitt	Mid-Summer's Fawn
1975 S	Fld.Ch. & Am.Fld.Ch. Jodi's Jump-N-Bing Bang Bucz M	Fld.Ch. & Am.Fld. Ch. Jodi of Czuki Barat	Ch. Jump-N-Jill
1975 F	Fld.Ch. Brook's Willie Whompum M	Du.Ch. & Am. Fld. Ch. Sir Lancelot	Du.Ch. & Am.Fld.Ch. Brook's Amber Mist
1976 S	Fld.Ch. & Am.Fld. Ch. Jodi's Jump-N-Bing Bang Bucz M		
1976 F	Bratt's FK Gippen M	Du.Ch. & Am.Fld. Ch. Janos VW Come Lately	Du.Ch. Szekeres' Kis Szereto

Vizsla Club of America Field Trial Winners

OPEN GUN DOG STAKE

Year	Dog's Name	Sire	Dam
1961 F	Ripp Barat M		
1962 S	No stake held		
1962 F	No stake held		
1963 S	Won by German Shorthaired Pointer		
1963 F	Osborn's Starfire F		
1964 S	Won by German Shorthaired Pointer		
1964 F	Field Champion Brok Selle M	Brok Olca	Baba Selle
1965 S	Futaki Darocz M		
1965 F	Ripp Barat's Rippy M		
1966 S	Futaki Juliska F		
1966 F	Field Champion Ripp Barat's Rippy M		
1967 S	Field Champion Ripp Barat's Rippy		
1967 F	Field Champion Alena V Claus F	Rigo Von Holte ex Koko Alena Olca	
1968 S	Jodi of Czuki Barat M		
1968 F	Weedy Creek Lobo M		
1969 S	Chip Odysseus M	Fld. Ch. Jake Jacaranda	Shirbob's Honey Dew
1969 F	Field Champion Jodi of Czuki Barat M		
1970 S	Bobo Buck Selle M		
1970 F	Amber's Windy Autumn F		
1971 S	Amber's Windy Autumn		
1971 F	Dual Ch. Brook's Amber Mist F	Ridgeland's Copper Gypsy	Ridgeland's Olca Selle

341

1972 S	Dual Ch. Weedy Creek Lobo M		
1972 F	Ripp Barats Bundle F	Toms Benjie	Ripp Barats Priscilla
1973 S	Stake not run.		
1973 F	Stake not run.		
1974 S	Stake not run.		
1974 F	Stake not run.		
1975 S	Stake not run.		
1975 F	Stake not run.		
1976 S	Stake not run.		
1976 F	Stake not run.		

Vizsla Club of America Field Trial Winners
OPEN LIMITED GUN DOG STAKE WINNERS

Year	Dog's Name	Sire	Dam
1973 S	Fld.Ch. & Am.Fld.Ch. Amber's Windy Autumn F		
1973 F	Fld.Ch. Randy Duke M		
1974 S	Fld.Ch. & Am.Fld.Ch. Randy Duke M		
1975 S	Stake not run.		
1975 F	Fld.Ch. & Am.Fld.Ch. Randy Duke M		
1976 S	Stake not run.		
1976 F	Behi Csecse Csiny F	Ch.Szekeres' Kelet Szel	Du.Ch.Behi's Csinos Csiny C.D.

Vizsla Club of America Field Trial Winners

OPEN LIMITED ALL-AGE STAKE

Year	Dog's Name	Sire	Dam
1961 F	No stake		
1962 S	No stake		
1962 F	Ripp Barat M		
1963 S	Ripp Barat		
1963 F	Ripp Barat		
1964 S	Brok Selle M		
1964 F	Haans V Selle M		
1965 S	Ripp Barat		
1965 F	Ripp Barat		
1966 S	Ripp Barat's Rippy M		
1966 F	Field Champion Futaki Juliska F		
1967 S	Ripp Barat		
1967 F	Field Champion Osborn's Starfire F		
1968 S	Jodi of Czuki Barat M		
1968 F	Weedy Creek Lobo M		
1969 S	Withheld		

1969 F	Dual Ch. Weedy Creek Lobo M		
1970 S	Rebel Rouser Duke M	Haans V Selle	Fld. Ch. Weedy Creek Dutches
1970 F	Champion Brook's Amber Mist F Given		
1971 S	Withheld		
1971 F	Field Champion Jodi of Czuki Barat		
1972 S	Withheld		
1972 F	Fld. Ch. Rebel Rouser Duke M		
1973 S	Fld.Ch.Rebel Rouser Duke M		
1973 F	Bratt's FK Gippen M		
1974 S	Withheld		
1974 F	Fld.Ch. & Am.Fld.Ch. Randy Duke M		
1975 S	Stake not run.		
1975 F	Fld.Ch. & Am.Fld.Ch. Randy Duke M		
1976 S	Stake not run.		
1976 F	Withheld		

Vizsla Club of America Field Trial Winners

OPEN ALL-AGE STAKE

Year	Dog's Name	Sire	Dam
1961 F	No stake		
1962 S	Derekas Rex Selle M		
1962 F	Ripp Barat M		
1963 S	Ripp Barat		
1963 F	Haans V Selle M		
1964 S	Ripp Barat M		
1964 F	Won by German Shorthaired Pointer		
1965 S	Won by German Shorthaired Pointer		
1965 F	No stake		
1966 S	No stake		
1966 F	No stake		
1967 S	No stake		
1967 F	Field Champion Jake Jacaranda M		
1968 S	Field Champion Jake Jacaranda		
1968 F	Weedy Creek Lobo M		
1969 S	Withheld		
1969 F	No stake		
1970 S	No stake		
1970 F	No stake		
1971 S	No stake		
1971 F	No stake		
1972 S	No stake		

TRIPLE CHAMPIONS

1981
Dual Ch. Cariad's Kutya Kai Costa U.D.

DUAL CHAMPIONS

1965
Futaki Darocz (D)
    Ch. Hunor ex. Piri

1969
Weedy Creek Lobo (D)
    Weedy Creek Skol ex. Weedy Creek Merya

1970
Bobo Buck Selle (D)
    Dual Ch. Futaki Darocz ex. Konya V Selle
Szekeres' Kis Szereto (B)
    Dual Ch. Futaki Darocz ex. Ch. Szekeres' Kezdet

1971
Brook's Ambert Mist (B)
    Ridgeland's Copper Gypsy ex. Ridgeland's Olca Selle
Behi's Csinos Csiny, C.D.(B)
    Haans V Selle ex. Fld. Ch. Futaki Juliska

1972
Sir Lancelot (D)
    Fld. Ch. Hubertus Aprod ex. Neshanica
Amber's Windy Autum (B)
    Fld. Ch. & Am. Fld. Ch. Jodi of Czuki Barat ex. Dual Ch. & Am.
    Fld. Ch. Brook's Amber Mist

1973
Pirolin (D)
    Dual Ch. Futaki Darocz ex. Wag Inn's Kedish
Chip Odysseus (D)
    Fld. Ch. Jake Jacaranda ex. Shirbob's Honey Dew

1974
Rippi of Webster Woodlands (D)
    Fld. Ch. & Am. Fld. Ch. Jodi of Czuki Barat ex. Dual Ch. & Am.
    Fld. Ch. Brook's Amber Mist
Rebel Rouser Duke (D)
    Haans V Selle ex. Fld.Ch. Weedy Creek Dutches

344

1975

Sir Amber Sam (D)
>   Dual Ch. & Am. Fld. Ch. Sir Lancelot ex. Dual Ch. & Am. Fld. Ch.
>   Brook's Amber Mist

Jodi's Jump-N-Bing Bang Bucz (D)
>   Fld. Ch. & Am. Fld. Ch. Jodi of Czuki Barat ex. Ch. Jump-N-Jill

Csibesz Rotkopf (D)
>   Ch. Debreceny Dezso ex. Ch. Totton's Fenyes Vadasz

1976

Arco's Arco (D)
>   Nikki's Arco ex. Arco's Lady Bird

Rothan's Rozsda Kisanya (B)
>   Ch. Szekeres' Kelet Szel ex. Ch. Csinos V Hunt C.D.X.

Brook's Willie Whompum (D)
>   Dual & Am. Fld. Ch. Sir Lancelot ex. Dual Ch. & Am. Fld. Ch.
>   Brook's Amber Mist

1977

Janos VW Come Lately (D)
>   Ch. Kiraly Z Rokudvar ex. Whit Selle Miske

1978

Cariad's Kutya Kai Costa C.D.X. (D)
>   Ch. Glenn Cottage Loki Barat C.D.X. ex. Ch. Cariad's Gaybine C.D.

Victor of Holzworth Farm (D)
>   Fritz of Connlly-Dale ex. Sally Creek

1979

Mehagian's Peppy Paloma (B)
>   Ch. Sandor Barat ex. Hall's Desert Gypsie

Cline's Olympia Blitz (D)
>   Fld. Ch. Earl's Red Rogue ex. Ch. Arra's Valor Blitz

W.D. Regina (B)
>   Dual Ch. Rebel Rouser Duke ex. Dual Ch. & Am. Fld. Ch. Amber's
>   Windy Autumn

Valhi's Liberty Valance (D)
>   Dual Ch. & Am. Fld. Ch. Sir Lancelot ex. Ch. Bratt's FK Satin
>   Valentine

1980

Behi Csecse Gyors Lab (B)
>   Dual Ch. & Am. Fld. Ch. Victor of Holzworth Farm ex. Fld. Ch. &
>   Am. Fld. Ch. Behi Csecse Csiny

Fieldstone's Hey Duke (D)
>   Dual Ch. Rebel Rouser Duke ex. Dual Ch. & Am. Fld. Ch. Rothan's
>   Rozsda Kisanya C.D.

Bratt's FK Gippen (D)
>   Dual Ch. & Am. Fld. Ch. Janos VW Come Lately ex. Dual Ch.
>   Szekeres' Kis Szereto

345

FIELD CHAMPIONS

1964
Brok Selle (D)
　　Brok Olca ex. Baba Selle

1965
Futaki Darocz (D)
　　Champion Hunor ex. Piri

1966
Ripp Barat's Rippy (D)
　　Fld. Ch. Ripp Barat ex. Sissy Selle
Osborn's Starfire (B)
　　Rakk Selle ex. Osborn's Miss Kubis
Futaki Juliska (B)
　　Ch. Hunor ex. Piri

1967
Ripp Barat (D)
　　Brok Olca ex. Rata Z Povazia
Alena Von Claus (B)
　　Rigo Von Holt ex. Koko Elena Olca
Jake Jacaranda (D)
　　Pepper Olca ex. Shirbob's Honey Dew

1968
Weedy Creek Dutches (B)
　　Weedy Creek Skol ex. Shirbob's Honey Dew
Jodi of Czuki Barat (D)
　　Fld. Ch. Ripp Barat ex. Czuki of Lake Catherine
Bullet V Selle (D)
　　Len's Duke Selle ex. Nickla
Futaki Jocko (D)
　　Haans V Selle ex. Fld. Ch. Futaki Juliska

1969
Weedy Creek Lobo (D)
　　Weedy Creek Skol ex. Weedy Creek Merya
Chip Odysseus (D)
　　Fld. Ch. Jake Jacaranda ex. Shirbob's Honey Dew
Jodo Red (D)
　　John Brok Cribaba ex. Blair's Red Dolly
Hubertus Aprod (D)
　　Edenkert Csibesz ex. Tardosi Pletuka
Rebel Rouser Duke (D)
　　Haans V Selle ex. Fld. Ch. Weedy Creek Dutches

1970
Bobo Buck Selle (D)
　　Dual Ch. Futaki Darocz ex. Konya V. Selle
Szekeres' Kis Szereto (B)
　　Dual Ch. Futaki Darocz ex. Ch. Szekeres' Kezdet

1971
Brook's Amber Mist (B)
  Ridgeland's Copper Gypsy ex. Ridgeland's Olca Selle
Behi's Csinos Csiny C.D. (B)
  Haans V. Selle ex. Fld. Ch. Futaki Juliska
Amber's Windy Autumn (B)
  Fld. Ch. & Am. Fld. Ch. Jodi of Czuki Barat ex. Dual Ch. & Am. Fld. Ch. Brook's Amber Mist
Sir Lancelot (D)
  Fld. Ch. Hubertus Aprod ex. Neshanica

1972
Rebel Rouser Dutch (D)
  Dual Ch. Rebel Rouser Duke ex. Fld. Ch. Weedy Creek Dutches

1973
Pirolin (D)
  Dual Ch. Futaki Darocz ex. Wag Inn's Kedish
Randy Duke (D)
  Distelfink's First Raitt ex. Mid-Summer Fawn

1974
Rippi of Webster Woodlands (D)
  Fld. Ch. & Am. Fld. Ch. Jodi of Czuki Barat ex. Dual Ch. & Am. Fld. Ch. Brook's Amber Mist
Futaki Lenke (B)
  Champion Caesar ex. Futaki Lincsi
Earl's Red Rogue (D)
  Dual Ch. Weedy Creek Lobo ex. Cricket

1975
Marcihazi Buszke (D)
  Terbeleki Csongor ex. Zagyvaparti Elli
Sir Amber Sam (D)
  Dual Ch. & Am. Fld. Ch. Sir Lancelot ex. Dual Ch. & Am. Fld. Ch. Brook's Amber Mist
Brook's Willie Whompum (D)
  Dual Ch. & Am. Fld. Ch. Sir Lancelot ex. Dual Ch. & Am. Fld. Ch. Brook's Amber Mist
Jodi's Jump-N-Bing Bang Bucz (D)
  Fld. Ch. & Am. Fld. Ch. Jodi of Czuki Barat ex. Ch. Jump-N-Jill
Csibesz Rotkopf (D)
  Ch. Debreceny ex. Ch. Totton's Fenyes Vadasz

1976
Behi's Piri Csiny (B)
  Ch. Szekeres' Kelet Szel ex. Dual Ch. Behi's Csinos Csiny C.D.
Rothan's Rozsda Kisanya (B)
  Ch. Szekeres' Kelet Szel ex. Ch. Csinos V. Hunt C.D.X.
Arco's Arco (D)
  Nikki's Arco ex. Arco's Lady Bird
Rebel Rouser Rusty (D)
  Dual Ch. Rebel Rouser Duke ex. Ch. Trigger's Charlotte

1977

Behi Csecse Csiny (B)
　　Ch. Szekeres' Kelet Szel ex. Dual Ch. Behi's Csinos Csiny, C.D.
Bratt's FK Gippen (D)
　　Dual Ch. & Am. Fld. Ch. Janos VW Come Lately ex. Dual Ch. Szekeres'
　　Kis Szereto
Janos VW Come Lately (D)
　　Ch. Kiraly Z Rokudvar ex. Whit Selle Miska
Renbrok's Drucker Schuh (D)
　　Ch. Great Guns Riding High ex. Renie's Amber Gypsy C.D.
Rotkopf's Amber Sparkler (B)
　　Royal Povazia ex. Lady of Lynnhurst
Victor of Holzworth Farm (D)
　　Fritz of Connlly Dale ex. Sally Creek
Doc's Spot (D)
　　Fld. Ch. Hubertus Aprod ex. Sweet Pat
Randy Bee (D)
　　Fld. Ch. & Am. Fld. Ch. Randy Duke ex. Debreceny Waterford Keso

1978

Cariad's Kutya Kai Costa C.D. (D)
　　Ch. Glenn Cottage Loki Barat C.D.X. ex. Ch. Carlad's Gaybine C.D.
El-Jo's Piroska Paprika (B)
　　Dual Ch. Weedy Creek Lobo ex. Grey Oaks Antonia
Mehagian's Peppy Paloma (B)
　　Ch. Sandor Barat ex. Hall's Desert Gypsy
El Cazador's Ripp Van Winkle (D)
　　Ch. Sandor Barat ex. Hall's Desert Gypsy
Rebel Rouser Winneshiek Mac (D)
　　Dual Ch. Rebel Rouser Duke ex. Rebel Rouser Penny
Kataki's Riki Knoh (D)
　　Dual Ch. & Am. Fld. Ch. Rippi of Webster Woodlands ex. Ch. Bratt's FK
　　Kataki

1979

Cline's Olympia Blitz (D)
　　Fld. Ch. Earl's Red Rogue ex. Ch. Arra's Valor Blitz
Windy Duke's Rex (D)
　　Dual Ch. Rebel Rouser Duke ex. Dual Ch. & Am. Fld. Ch. Amber's Windy
　　Autumn
Hye Tanya (B)
　　Twin Acres Cassador Selle ex. Bireline's Ginger Heir of Brok
W. D. Regina (B)
　　Dual Ch. Rebel Rouser Duke ex. Dual Ch. & Am. Fld. Ch. Amber's Windy
　　Autumn
Valhi's Liberty Valance (D)
　　Dual Ch. & Am. Fld. Ch. Sir Lancelot ex. Ch. Bratt's FK Satin Valentine
Willie's Bushwak Barney McGee (D)
　　Dual Ch. & Am. Fld. Ch. Brook's Willie Whompum ex. Ch. Timarka's Tsindee
　　of Amber C.D.
Amber Duke's Dandy (D)
　　Fld. Ch. & Am. Fld. Ch. Randy Duke ex. Dual Ch. & Am. Fld. Ch. Brook's
　　Amber Mist

1980

Rotkopf's Minor Miracle (B)
Dual Ch. & Am. Fld. Ch. Csibesz Rotkopf ex. Fld. Ch. & Am. Fld. Ch. Rotkopf Amber Sparkler

Rowdy Rebel Windy's Knight (D)
Dual Ch. Rebel Rouser Duke ex. Dual Ch. & Am. Fld. Ch. Amber's Windy Autumn

Behi Csecse Gyors Lab (B)
Dual Ch. & Am. Fld. Ch. Victor of Holzworth Farm ex. Fld. Ch. & Am. Fld. Ch. Behi Csecse Csiny

Fieldstone's Hey Duke (D)
Dual Ch. Rebel Rouser Duke ex. Dual Ch. & Am. Fld. Ch. Rothan's Rozsda Kisanya C.D.

Futaki Gippen's Cullen (D)
Dual Ch. & Am. Fld. Ch. Bratt's FK Gippen ex. Fld. Ch. Futaki Lenke

1981

Cody's Dark Star (D)
Ch. Peter's High Velocity ex. Randy's Misty Morn

Rotkopf's Whiz Kid (D)
Dual Ch. Cline's Olympia Blitz ex. Rotkopf's Amber Sparkler

Snl's Cas-See Mez (B)
Rebel Rouser Bandieto ex. Piper's Lady Lucy

Spring Creek Edition (D)
Spring Creek Sunshine ex. Spring Creek Soybean Jesse

Piper's Tecumseh Fox (D)
Ch. Piper's Rex Stout C.D. ex. Rebel Rouser Piper's Cleo

Magma's Samantha Of Voros Tars (B)
Thor's Thunderer ex. Milehi Miss

AMATEUR FIELD CHAMPIONS

1971
Amber's Windy Autumn
Jodi of Czuki Barat

1972
Pirolin

1973
Brook's Amber Mist
Sir Lancelot

1974
Randy Duke
Rippi of Webster Woodlands

1975
Marcihazi Buszke
Jodi's Jump-N-Bing Bang Bucz
Rothan's Rozsda Kisanya C.D.
Holzworth Bit-O-Honey
Dual Ch. Weedy Creek Lobo ex. Honey of Holzworth Farm

1976
Brook's Willie Whompum
Csibesz Rotkopf
Arco's Arco

1977
Bratt's FK Gippen
Behi's Piri Csiny
Rotkopf's Amber Sparkler
Markos Von Debrecen (D)
      Herzog Schloss Loosdorf ex. Ch. Besa Von Debretsin
Janos VW Come Lately
Victor of Holzworth Farm

1978
El-Jo's Piroska Paprika
Mehagian's Peppy Paloma
Randy Bee
Behi Csecse Csiny

1979
Doc's Spot
El Cazador's Ripp Van Winkle

1980
Hye Tanya
Bratt's FK Kataki (B)
      Dual Ch. & Am. Fld. Ch. Janos VW Come Lately ex. Dual Ch. Szekeres'
      Kis Szereto
Futaki Gippen's Cullen
Valhi's Liberty Valance

1981
Ch. Rotkopf's Vand Suzsannah C.D. (B)
      Ch. Rotkopf's Dancing Wheat Seek ex. Ch. Totton's Fenyes Vadasz
Kataki's Riki Knoh (D)
Behi Csecse Gyors Lab (B)
Fieldstone's Hey Duke (D)
Willie's Bushwak Barney McGee (D)

OBEDIENCE TRIAL CHAMPIONS

1981
Cariad's Kutya Kai Costa (D)
      Ch. Glenn Cottage Loki Barat C.D.X. ex. Ch. Cariad's Gaybine C.D.
Gold-In-Hills Janos (D)
      Ch. Timarka's Taco ex. Gold-In-Hills Zsa Zsa

NATIONAL CHAMPIONSHIP STAKE WINNERS

1975 S	No champion named
1976 S	Du.Ch. & Am.Fld.Ch. Brook's Willie Whompum M
1977 F	Fld.Ch. & Am.Fld.Ch. Randy Duke M
1978 F	Fld.Ch. & Am.Fld.Ch. Randy Duke M
1979 F	Du.Ch. & Am.Fld.Ch. Mehagian's Peppy Paloma B
1980 F	Du.Ch. Sir Amber Sam M
1981 F	Du.Ch. & Am.Fld.Ch. Mehagian's Peppy Paloma B

NATIONAL AMATEUR CHAMPIONSHIP STAKE WINNERS

1977 F	Mehagian's Peppy Paloma B	Ch. Sandor Barat	Hall's Desert Gypsy
1978 F	Du.Ch. & Am.Fld.Ch. Brook's Willie Whompum M		
1979 F	Du.Ch. & Am.Fld.Ch. Brook's Willie Whompum M		
1980 F	Fld.Ch. & Am.Fld.Ch. Hye Tanya (B)		
1981 F	Fieldstone's Tip Top Timmy M	Du.Ch. Rebel Rouser Duke	Du.Ch. & Am.Fld.Ch. Rothan's Rozsda Kisanya, C.D.

VIZSLA CLUB OF AMERICA
HALL OF FAME

1978

Dual Ch. Futaki Darocz
(June 9, 1961 - October 11, 1966)
by Ch. Hunor out of Piri
Breeder: Bela Hadik
Owner: Bela Hadik

Fld. Ch. & Amtr. Fld. Ch. Jodi of Czuki Barat
(June 2, 1964 - July 5, 1972)
by Fld. Ch. Ripp Barat out of Czuki of Lake Catherine
Breeder: Richard M. Olson
Owner: Lewis & Sharon Simon

1979

Dual Ch. Behi's Csinos Csiny, C.D.
(February 12, 1964 - November 4, 1976)
by Haans V. Selle out of Fld. Ch. Futaki Juliska
Breeder: Robert & Nancy Perry
Owner: B. C. & Hilda Boggs

Dual Ch. Weedy Creek Lobo
October 3, 1964 - September 17, 1976)
(By Weedy Creek Skol out of Weedy Creek Merya
Breeder: Jane Graff
Owner: Harold Wingerter

1980

Fld. Ch. Weedy Creek Dutches
(May 7, 1963 - November 9, 1976)
by Weedy Creek Skol out of Shirbobs Honey Dew
Breeder: Jane Graff
Owner: H. F. Rozanek

Ch. Csinos V Hunt, C.D.X.
(August 23, 1962 - November 17, 1975)
by Ch. Csisckas of Goncoltanya out of Asta V. Schonweide
Breeder: Charles & Joan Hunt
Owner: Paul & Shirley Rothan

1981

Am. & Can. Fld. Ch. Ripp Barat
(February 2, 1959 - May 29, 1974)
by Brok Olca out of Rata Z. Povazia
Breeder: I. S. Osborn
Owner: Betty Kenly

Dual Ch., Amtr. Fld. Ch., Can. & Mex. Ch. Sir Lancelot
(April 1, 1966 - March 18, 1978)
by Fld. Ch. Hubertus Aprod out of Neshanica
Breeder: William Riley
Owner: Bill Goodman

352

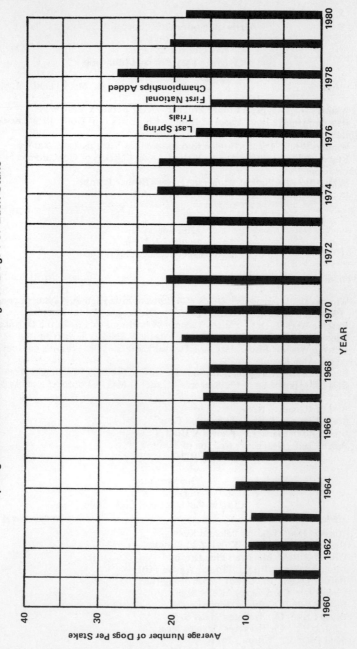

GROWTH OF VIZSLA CLUB OF AMERICA FIELD TRIALS
Spring and Fall Combined Average of Dogs For Each Stake

First National
Championships Added

Last Spring
Trials

Average Number of Dogs Per Stake

40
30
20
10

1960 1962 1964 1966 1968 1970 1972 1974 1976 1978 1980

YEAR

353

Vizsla Club of America Specialty Shows
1st Specialty
August 29, 1965
Chagrin Valley Kennel Club, Ohio

54 entries   Judge: Mr. Kenneth M. McDonald

Winners Dog: Gypsy's Bronze Bomber   Ripp Barat ex Sissy Selle
Reserve Winners Dog: Csopi V. Hunt   Ch. Csisckas of Goncoltanya ex Gellert
Csintalan
Winners Bitch: Diane's Golden Karratz   Janos Vitez ex Lady Burdee
Reserve Winners Bitch: Csinos V Hunt   Ch. Csisckas of Goncoltanya ex Asta V
Schonweide
Best of Breed & Best of Winners: Gypsy's Bronze Bomber
Best of Opposite Sex: Ch. J'ann of Misty Hills

2nd Specialty
August 27, 1966
Chagrin Valley Kennel Club, Ohio

56 entries   Judge: Dr. Richard H. Gaetz

Winners Dog: Arpadhazi Almos   Ch. Piros of Mile High ex Naylor's Feher
    (Awarded to Reserve Winners Dog)   (Not registered in AKC)
Reserve Winners Dog: Fenyes Vadasz   Ch. Hunor ex Ch. Zlatna Devojka V Hunt
Winners Bitch: Behi's Csinos Csiny   Haans V Selle ex Futaki Juliska
Reserve Winners Bitch: Magyar's Tundor Karratz   Ch. Wilson's Pal Joey ex   Ch.
Diane's Golden Karratz
Best of Breed: Ch. Brok Selle Son of a Gun   Brok Olca ex Bodka Hana
Best of Opposite Sex: Ch. Szekeres' Kezdet   Max V Loosdorf ex Miss Olca Kub-
is
Best of Winners: None
Stud Dog: Ch. Brok Selle Son of a Gun
Brood Bitch Class: Ch. Kedves V Hunt, C. D.
Brace Class: Distelfinks Red son of J'ann
            Ch. J'ann of Misty Hills

3rd Specialty
August 27, 1967
Chagrin Valley Kennel Club, Ohio

72 entries   Judge: Cecil Y. Smith

Winners Dog: Bakony Baletoni Keve
Reserve Winners Dog: Kiraly Z Rokudvar
Winners Bitch: Mencye's Pipe Dream
Reserve Winners Bitch: Brook's Amber Mist
Best of Breed: Ch. Count Jonish Mignotte
Field Dog: Ch. Szekeres' Kelet Szel
Field Bitch: Ch. Behi's Csinos Csiny
Brace Class: Ch. Szekeres' Kelet Szel
            Ch. Szekeres' Aranjos Heja
Stud Dog: Ch. Wilson's Pal Joey
Brood Bitch: Ch. Magyar's Tundor Karratz

354

4th Specialty
August 25, 1968
Chagrin Valley Kennel Club, Ohio

61 entries   Judge: Mr. Bernard W. Ziessow

Winners Dog: Old Weird Harold Pike of Duke ex Valines Bulba
Reserve Winners Dog: Klasik Fun Galore Shayo Fun Galore ex Gemma Fun Galore
Winners Bitch: Debreceny Lila Ch. Sandor V. Debretsin ex Ch. Bolen's Geza Bell
Reserve Winners Bitch: Rothan's Rozsda Kisanya Ch. Szekeres' Kelet Szel ex Ch. Csinos V Hunt, C. D.
Field Dog: Ch. Rustic Fun Galore Shayo Fun Galore ex Gemma Fun Galore
Field Bitch: Dual Ch. Szekeres' Kis Szereto Dual Ch. Futaki Darocz ex Ch. Szekeres' Kezdet
Best of Breed: Ch. Debreceny Dezso Herzog Schloss Loosdorf ex Ch. Besa V. Debretsen
Best of Opposite Sex: Ch. Bolen's Geza Bell Fld. Ch. Ripp Barat ex Bolen's Athena
Best of Winners: Old Weird Harold
Brace Class: Karratz Special Edition
             Karratz Amber Edition
Stud Dog: Flick Pheasant Wood
Brood Bitch: Ch. Bolen's Geza Bell

5th Specialty
August 24, 1969
Chagrin Valley Kennel Club, Ohio

57 entries   Judge: Dr. Rex B. Foster

Winners Dog: Cigany Csillag, C. D. Osborn's Norstar ex Lady Rakk
Reserve Winners Dog: Field Champion Weedy Creek Lobo Weedy Creek Skol ex Weedy Creek Merya
Winners Bitch: Timarka's Tsindee of Amber Field Champion Jodi of Czuki Barat ex Ch. Brook's Amber Mist
Reserve Winners Bitch: William's Kapraztato Ch. Rothan's Betyar Gaza ex Fawn
Field Dog: Good Upland Jet Rozsdas Antal ex Pittro's Smart Girl
Field Bitch: Ch. Behi's Csinos Csiny, C.D.   Haans V Selle ex Field Champion Futaki Juliska
Best of Breed & Best of Winners: Timarka's Tsindee of Amber
Best of Opposite Sex: Ch. Szekeres' Kelet Szel Ch. Hunor ex Ch. Szekeres' Kezdet
Brood Bitch: Ch. Brook's Amber Mist

1st Futurity

Judge: Margaret Meminger

Best in Futurity: Magyar's Lady Patricia
Best of Opposite Sex to Best in Futurity: Oury's Alfi Staraza

355

May 31, 1970
Stone City Kennel Club, Illinois

33 in competition   Judge: Cecil J. Schoeneck

Winners Dog: Jodi's Mickey Finn Field Champion Jodi of Czuki Barat ex Ch. Brook's Amber Mist

Reserve Winners Dog: Eds Golden Gypsy of Hanover Ch. Gypsy's Bronze Bomber ex Weedy Creek's Elsie

Winners Bitch: Thora's Hau Talleria Ch. Old Weird Harold ex Ch. Brook's Amber Mist

Reserve Winners Bitch: Bako's Mistique Osborn's Norstar ex Vikingshold Miss Take, C.D.

Field Dog: Ch. Nik V Romarlin Ferro V Hunt ex Honey Toots

Field Bitch: Ch. Miss Nessi Coon Valley Pal ex Matrishka Nessi

Best of Breed: Ch. Brook's Amber Mist Ridgeland's Copper Gypsy ex Ridgeland's Olca Selle

Best of Winners: Thora's Hau Talleria

Best of Opposite Sex: Ch. Old Weird Harold Pike of Duke ex Valines Bulba

Stud Dog: Ch. Old Weird Harold

Brood Bitch: Ch. Brook's Amber Mist

2nd Futurity

Judge: Del Gladowski

Best in Futurity: Joshk's Gypsy Cellar Ch. Old Weird Harold ex Ch. Thora's Hau Tascha

Best of Opposite Sex to Best in Futurity: Thora's Hau Talleria Ch. Old Weird Harold ex Ch. Thora's Hau Tascha

7th Specialty
August 1, 1971
Santa Barbara Kennel Club, California

78 entries   Judge: Mrs. Augustus Riggs

Winners Dog: Debreceny Badger Ch. Debreceny Dezso ex Ch. Debreceny Lila

Reserve Winners Dog: Rustin V. Zomar Lark Ch. Markos von Debrecen ex Ch. Lady Zorina of Nine Oaks

Winners Bitch: Amber Shambles Shamrock Herzog Schloss Loosdorf ex Mitchi Aki Shamrock

Reserve Winners Bitch: Sageacre Dezdemona Ch. Debreceny Dezso ex Ch. Bolen's Geza Bell

Veteran Dog: Ch. Akil Von Debretsin Ch. Sandor von Debretsin ex Csilla von Debretsin

* Field Dog: Ch. Debreceny Dezso Herzog Schloss Loosdorf ex Ch. Besa v. Debretsin

* Field Bitch: Ch. Bolen's Geza Bell Fld. Ch. Ripp Barat ex Bolen's Athena

Best of Breed: Ch. Debreceny Dezso

Best of Winners: Amber Shambles Shamrock

Best of Opposite Sex: Ch. Debreceny Dijana Ch. Fleckes of Sageacre ex Debreceny Jolie May

Brace Class: **Ch. Napkelte Vadasz Dalos   Ch. Janoras Pawlane Suntan ex Ch. Bakony Csikcsicsoi Boske**

Totton's Baron Hiduk   Ch. Napkelte Vadasz Dalos ex Totton's Princess Tutu
Stud Dog: **Ch. Debreceny Dezso**
Brood Bitch: **Ch. Bolen's Geza Bell**

3rd Futurity

Judge: Herman Cox

Best in Futurity: **Debreceny Badger**
Best of Opposite Sex to Best in Futurity: **Totton's Stephania of Torkopf**
Ch. Debreceny Dezso ex Totton's Fenyes Vadasz

* **Previous entries in these classes required a placement in an AKC licensed field trial.**

8th Specialty
September 10, 1972
Des Moines, Iowa

41 in competition (14D, 11B)
46 entries
                                                    Judge: Ed Bracey

Winners Dog: **Johnson's Titian Morning Sky   Charles Todd's Rusty ex Zalla of the Field**
Reserve Winners Dog: **Timarkas T Betyar**
Winner's Bitch: **Mihaly's Kisasszony   Ch. Gypsy's Bronze Bomber ex Weedy Creek's Elsie**
Reserve Winners Bitch: **Fld.Ch. Amber's Windy Autumn   Fld.Ch. & Am.Fld. Ch. Jodi of Czuki Barat ex Du.Ch. Brook's Amber Mist**
Veteran Dog: **Ch. Lucky E's Hunt N' Fun U.D.T.**
Veteran Bitch: **Ch. Wetob's Taffeta**
Fld. Bitch: **Ch. Arra's Miss Tasha**
Best of Breed: **Ch. Gold-N-Rust Daredevil U.D.** (4th Sporting Group)   **Ch. Golden Rust's Kernel ex Windswept Futaki**
Best of Winners: **Johnson's Titian Morning Sky**
Best of Opposite Sex: **Ch. Timarka's Tsindee of Amber C.D.** (B)   **Fld.Ch. Jodi of Czuki Barat ex Du.Ch. Brook's Amber Mist**
Brood Bitch: **Ch. Trigger's Charlotte**

4th Futurity
(1972)

Judge: Hollis Wilson

Best in Futurity: **Jodi's Jump-N-Bing Bang Bucz** (M)   **Fld.Ch. Jodi of Czuki Barat ex Ch. Jump-N-Jill.**
Best of Opposite Sex to Best in Futurity: **Ch. Bratt's FK Satin Valentine** (F)
Ch. Janos VW Come Lately ex Du.Ch. Szekeres' Kis Szereto

9th Specialty
September 9, 1973
Tarrytown, New York

88 in competition (22D, 28B)
105 entries
                                                    Judge: L. Downey

357

Winners Dog: Kalon Autumn Brandy   Ch. Gold-N-Rust Country Rogue ex Ch. Cariad's Kalon Szerette

Reserve Winners Dog: Rotkopf's Magyar Kutya   Ch. Mikos Heliker ex Ch. Rotkopf's Regina of Sageacre

Winner's Bitch: Rotkopf's Geymant   Ch. Miklos Heliker ex Ch. Rotkopf's Regina of Sageacre

Reserve Winners Bitch: Kalon's Golden Rust Duchess Olca

Veteran Dog / Veteran Bitch: Ch. Szekeres' Aranyo Hega

Field Dog / Field Bitch: Ch. Gretl Von Tatabanya

Best of Breed: Ch. Gold-N-Rust Daring Gambler (D)   Ch. Gold-N-Rust Daredevil U.D. ex Ch. Glen Cottage Bar Rit Jay Jay

Best of Winners: Kalon Autumn Brandy

Best of Opposite Sex: Ch. JinJa Richards (B)   Ch. Glen Cottage Loki Barat C.D.X. ex Ch. Elsa Richards

Stud Dog: Ch. Gold-N-Rust Country Rogue

Brood Bitch: Ch. Cariad's Kalon Szerette

5th Futurity
(1973)

Judge: Elsworth Howell

Best in Futurity: Ch. Kalon's Konok Kipit (M)   Ch. Gold-N-Rust Country Rogue ex Ch. Cariad's Kalon Szerette

Best of Opposite Sex to Best in Futurity: Rotkopf's Tia D'Russet Leather (F) Ch. Miklos Heliker ex Ch. Rotkopf's Regina of Sageacre

10th Specialty
July 28, 1974
Santa Barbara, California

83 in competition (28D, 32B)   Judge: Mrs. E. W. Tipton

Winners Dog: Sandor Miklos Heliker   Ch. Miklos Heliker ex Ch. Amber Shambles Shamrock

Reserve Winners Dog: Pinar Barat

Winners Bitch: Mako Kisch

Reserve Winners Bitch: Cher of Sandor Barat   Ch. Sandor Barat ex Phoenician Princess

Best of Breed: Ch. Totton's Jo'B Russet Leather (D)   Ch. Napkelte Vadasz ex Burnt Gold Becket of Randan

Best of Winners: Cher of Sandor Barat

Best of Opposite Sex: Dutchess Banbi Boyd (D)   Wisemann's Eion Copper ex Wismann's Joli Penny

6th Futurity
(1974)

Judge: Thomas A. Bradley III

Best in Futurity: Totton's Mikhail of Rotkopf (M)   Ch. Napkelte Vadasz Dalos C.D. ex Ch. Totton's Stephania of Rotkopf

Best of Opposite Sex to Best in Futurity: Totton's Samantha Von Rotkopf (F) Ch. Napkelte Vadasz Dalos C.D. ex Ch. Totton's Stephania of Rotkopf

11th Specialty
1st Combined Specialty & Field Trial
October 24, 1975
Malcolm, Nebraska

56 in competition (18D, 15B) Judge: B. W. Ziessow

Winners Dog: Mehagian's Pistol Pete Ch. Totton's JO'B Russet Leather ex Ch. Lady Warwica Selle
Reserve Winners Dog: Popple Dungeon Tolgfa Du. & Am.Fld.Ch. Pirolin ex Ch. Uropuyka
Winners Bitch: Popple Dungeon Lilliom Du. & Am.Fld.Ch. Sir Lancelot ex Reko's Golden Pepper
Reserve Winners Bitch: Totton's Princess of Rotkopf Ch. Napkelte Vadasz C.D. ex Ch. Totton's Stephania of Rotkopf
Veteran Dog: Ch. Glen Cottage Loki Barat C.D.X.
Veteran Bitch: Du. & Am. Fld. Ch. Brook's Amber Mist
Field Dog: Du.Ch. Sir Amber Sam
Field Bitch: Ch. Gretl Von Tatabanya
Best of Breed: Ch. Johnson's Titian Morning Sky (D) Charles Todd's Rusty ex Zalla of the Field
Best of Winners: Mehagian's Pistol Pete
Best of Opposite Sex: Ch. Jin Ja Richards (F) Ch. Glen Cottage Loki Barat ex Ch. Elsa Richards
Stud Dog: Ch. Glen Cottage Loki Barat C.D.X.

7th Futurity
(1975)
Judge: Mrs. Helen Case

Best in Futurity: Ashby Von Donn (M) Ch. Debreceny Dezso ex Ch. Juliana's Aranaya
Best of Opposite Sex in Futurity: Ch. Kalon's Megan (F) Ch. Gold-N-Rust Country Rogue ex Ch. Cariad's Kalon Szerette

12th Specialty
2nd Combined Specialty & Field Trial
October 8, 1976
Medford, New Jersey

115 in competition (27D, 40B) Judge: J. R. Lawreck

Winners Dog: Renbroks Only One Son Of A Gun Ch. Great Guns Riding High ex Renie's Amber Gypsy C.D.
Reserve Winners Dog: Bakkers Duddy Fonzi Ch. Hussar Barat ex Brandy's Ginger Selle
Winners Bitch: Firebrand's Kivanosi Ch. Caeser ex Ch. Firebrands Cariad Zenzo
Reserve Winners Bitch: Cariad's Galadriel Ch. Tisza's Kish Fiu ex Cariad's Liebestraum Barat C.D.
Veteran Dog: Ch. Glen Cottage Loki Barat C.D.X.
Veteran Bitch: Ch. Cariad's Gaybine C.D.
Field Dog: Valhi's Stick To Your Guns
Field Bitch: Tardosi Ancsa Nagymama

Best of Breed: Ch. Joshua Melto (D)   Ch. Johnson's Titian Charger ex Ch. Taunee's Cariann

Best of Winners: Renbroks Only One Son Of A Gun

Best of Opposite Sex: Ch. Renbroks Ginger Peach (B)   Ch. Great Guns Riding High ex Renie's Amber Gypsy C.D.

Brood Bitch: Renie's Amber Gypsy C.D.

Highest Scoring Dog in Regular Classes (3 in competition)

Novice A: Dorratz Ramriver Beethoven 190

8th Futurity
1976)

Judge: Mrs. Margaret Meminger

Best in Futurity: Ch. Renbrok's Only One Son Of A Gun (M)   Ch. Great Guns Riding High ex Renie's Amber Gypsy C.D.

Best of Opposite Sex to Best in Futurity: Renbrok's Greta Hegyi (F)   Ch. Great Guns Riding High ex Renie's Amber Gypsy C.D.

13th Specialty
3rd Combined Specialty & Field Trial
October 21, 1977
Monterey, California

92 in competition (28D, 27B)   Judge: D. G. Rayne

Winners Dog: Voro Tars Futo Medve   Ch. Rotkopf's Dancing Wheat Seek ex Ch. Mehagian's Rusti

Reserve Winners Dog: Jomars Big Bad John   Ch. Rogue LSR Jacobs ex Ch. Jomars Cinncamon Cindy C.D.

Winner's Bitch: Renbroks Tara Hegyi   Ch. Great Guns Riding High ex Renie's Amber Gypsy C.D.

Reserve Winners Bitch: Waynes Dainty Lady   Rusty Get Your Gun of Lakewood ex Chauncey's Brandi Jean Panni

Field Dog: Masha's B.B. Red Baron

Field Bitch: Ch. Cariad's Taunee Glow   Ch. Glen Cottage Loki Barat ex Ch. Renbrok's Ginger Peach

Best of Breed: Ch. Totton's Mikhail of Rotkopf (D)   Ch. Napkelte Vadasz Dalos C.D. ex Ch. Totton's Stephania of Rotkopf

Stud Dog: Ch. Rotkopf's Dancing Wheat Seek

Brood Bitch: Ch. Rotkopf's Regina of Sageacre

Brace Class: Renbrook's Tara Hegi   Ch. Renbrok's Greta Hegi

Veteran Bitch: Ch. Rotkopf's Regina of Sageacre

Highest Scoring Dog in Regular Classes (4 in competition)

Novice A: Ch. Sageacres Ravishing Ruby 196½

14th Specialty
4th Combined Specialty & Field Trial
November 5, 1978
Amboy, Illinois

95 in competition (21D, 31B)   Judge: J. Fagel

Winners Dog: Cariad's Alydar Loki Santana   Ch. Taunee's Loki Santana C.D. ex Ch. Eszaki Cinka Panna

Reserve Winners Dog: Renbroks Royal Highness of KMA   Ch. Great Guns Riding High ex Renie's Amber Gypsy, C.D.

Winners Bitch: Russet Leather Wild Embers   Ch. Rotkopf's Dancing Wheat Seek ex Ch. Russet Leather's Ricca Luna
Reserve Winners Bitch: Boshar's Budapest Babe   Blitzkrieg ex Jamella
Field Dog: Am. & Can.Ch. Valhi's Stick to Your Guns
Field Bitch: KMA's High's delightful Dolly
Best of Breed: Am. & Can.Ch. Joshua Melto   Ch. Johnson's Titian Charger ex Ch. Taunee's Cariann
Best of Winners: Cariad's Alydar Loki Santana
Best of Opposite Sex: Russet Leather Wild Embers   Ch. Rotkopf's Dancing Wheat Seek ex Ch. Russet Leather's Ricca Luna
Stud Dog: Ch. Soapstone's Sampson
Brood Bitch: Ch. Dian Agi C.D.
Brace Class: Ch. Murphy's Christi Lew   Champion Piper's Tijuana Red
Highest Scoring Dog in Regular Classes (7 in competition)
Open B: Ch. Mehagian's Misty Moonlight C.D.X.
Veteran Dog: Ch. Taunee's Loki Santana
Veteran Bitch: Ch. Jin Ja Richards

15th Specialty
5th Combined Specialty & Field Trial
October 21, 1979
Hightstown, New Jersey

172 in competition (81D, 83B)   Judge: Miklos Farkashazi

Winners Dog: Kalons Bronson   Ch. Joshua Melto ex Ch. Kalon's Megan
Reserve Winners Dog: Renbroks Royal Highness of KMA   Ch. Great Guns Riding High ex Renie's Amber Gypsy C.D.
Winners Bitch: Camarily Rambling Rose   Ch. Rich's Pirosch Aranya, C.D. ex Ch. Sloane's Palinka
Reserve Winners Bitch: Sleepy Hollow Valo Lany   Ch. Sandor's Zach Von Kurtzmark ex Ch. Cher of Sandor Barat
Field Dog: Ch. Boyd's Kerek Richard's
Field Bitch: Du. & Am.Fld.Ch. Mehagian's Peppy Paloma
Best of Breed: Ch. Meltos Csaba Zenesz   Ch. Johnson's Titian Charger ex Ch. Taunee's Cariann
Best of Winners: Kalon's Bronson
Best of Opposite Sex: Ch. Miss Midge of Behi C.D.   Du.Ch. & Am.Fld.Ch. Victor of Holzworth Farm ex Fld.Ch. & Am.Fld.Ch. Behi Csecse Csiny
Stud Dog: Ch. Joshua Melto
Brood Bitch: Renie's Amber Gypsy C.D.
Brace Class: Upwind Meta Kemble / Ch. Upwind Jzette Taber
Highest Scoring Dog in Regular Classes (8 in competition)
Open B: Du.Ch. Cardiad's Kutya Kai Costa, U.D. 195

1st Puppy Sweepstakes
October 21, 1979
Hightstown, New Jersey

34 in competition (17D, 17B)   Judge: Robert McKowan

Best in Sweepstakes: Harann's Tulipann (B)   Ch. Cariad's Trefas Szereto ex Ch. Harann's Kristiana Penn V. Dunna
Best of Opposite Sex to Best In Sweepstakes: Okee's Windy Rowdy Rebel (D) Rowdy Rebel Windy's Knight ex Ch. Miss Missy of Zanger

361

16th Specialty
6th Combined Specialty & Field Trial
October 31, 1980
Sierra Vista, Arizona

110 in competition (44D, 54B)   Judge: Edward Loebe
(Including 12 in obedience classes only)

Winners Dog: Cedar Wood Of Sleepy Hollow   Ch. Hall's Desert Don Juan
C.D.X. ex Pieces of April
Reserve Winners Dog: Oakleaf's Top Priority   Du.Ch. Cline's Olympia Blitz
ex Fox Meadow's Gretchen
Winner's Bitch: Glenogen Mali E'szaki   Ch. E'szaki Biro ex Ch. Topian's Satin
Doll C.D.
Reserve Winners Bitch: Nyiris Dear Abbey Of Charisma   Charisma's Zolton
Carob C.D. ex Ch. Magda Charisma's C.D.
Field Dog: Ch. Baron of Paradise
Field Bitch: Ch. Rotkopf's Suzsannah
Best of Breed: Ch. Sleepy Hollow's Autumn Wind (B)   Ch. Sandor's Zach Von
Kurtzmark C.D. ex Ch. Cher Of Sandor Barat
Best of Winners: Glenogen Mali E'szaki
Best of Opposite Sex: Ch. Rotkopf's Copper Casey (D)   Ch. Jado's Copper
Cannon C.D. ex Ch. Rotkopf's Gyemont
Stud Dog: Ch. Sandor's Zach Von Kurtzmark C.D.
Brood Bitch: Ch. Mehagian's Pici Lany
Brace Class: Ch. Kamet Gunner   Ch. Kamet Cheyenne Rebel
Highest Scoring Dog in Regular Classes (23 in competition)
Du.Ch. & Obed.Trial Ch. Cariad's Kutya Kai Costa 196½

2nd Puppy Sweepstakes
October 31, 1980
Sierra Vista, Arizona

33 in competition (17D, 16B)   Judge: Carl Anderson

Best in Sweepstakes: Glenogen Mali E'Szaki (B)
Best of Opposite Sex to Best in Sweepstakes: Upwind Erazim Barat (M)

17th Specialty
7th Combined Specialty & Field Trial
October 28, 1981
Lincoln, Nebraska

96 in competition (29D, 50B)   Judge: Richard D. Renihan
(Including 17 in obedience classes only)

Winners Dog: Beau Jangles II   Ch. Fieldstone's Tip Top Timmy ex Ch. Redef's
Hellza Poppin
Reserve Winners Dog: My-T-Hi Thunder Storm   Du. & Am.Fld.Ch. Brook's
Willie Whompum ex Ch. Piper's Mystical Gypsy Lady
Winners Bitch: Arnell Splendid Arrangement   Ch. Rotkopf's Lord Sean Royal
ex Ch. Rebel Rouser's Fanci Pants C.D.

362

Reserve Winners Bitch: Monomoy Kelli Piper   Du. & Am.Fld.Ch. Bratt's FK Gippen ex Ch. Piper's Peppermint Patti
Field Dog: Ch. Valhi's Stick To Your Guns
Field Bitch: Fld.Ch. & Am.Fld Ch. Rotkopf's Vand Suzsannah
Best of Breed: Ch. Rotkopf's Super Charger (M)   Ch. Johnson's Titian Charger ex Ch. Rotkopf's Gyement
Best of Winners: Beau Jangles II
Best of Opposite Sex: Ch. Deacon's Popple D Wild Daisy   Ch. Valhi's Stick To Your Guns ex Ch. Popple Dungeon Lillion
Stud Dog: Ch. Valhi's Stick To Your Guns
Brood Bitch: Ch. Boshar's Budapest Babe
Brace Class: Ch. Dian Gyongy   Ch. Dian Agi C.D.
Highest Scoring Dog in Regular Classes (17 in competition)
Coffee's Little Red Moppet 196½

3rd Puppy Sweepstakes
October 28, 1981
Lincoln, Nebraska

30 in competition (11D, 17B)   Judge: Vic Boutwell

Best in Sweepstakes: Ch. Yorsla-N-Alydar Yankee Boy (M)
Best of Opposite Sex to Best in Sweepstakes: Yorsla's Amber Independence

(note numbers in competition subject to change
when compared to official AKC records)

CHAMPIONS OF RECORD IN ORDER LISTED IN
THE AMERICAN KENNEL GAZETTE—PURE BRED DOGS

1961

1 Miclos Schloss Loosdorf (D)
2 Csicskas of Goncoltanya (B) (also Csisckas)
3 Annavolgyi Arany (Foreign) (B)
4 Dutchess of Shirbob, C. D. (B)
5 Paton's Zsomi Selle (D)
6 Golden Girl (B)
7 Peter Von Chinook (D)
8 Souvenir Csabe Lidi
9 Kedves V Hunt, C. D. (B)

1962

10 Ripp (D)
11 Warhorse Cindy Bea (B)
12 Warhorse O-Jay (D)
13 Kinchem (D)
14 Sogen's Typhoon (D)
15 Sandor Von Debretsin (D)
16 Campbell's Lady Winfield (B)
17 Campbell's Lord Clem
18 Campbell's Brass Button, C. D. (B)
19 Hunor (D)
20 Campbell's Copper Penny (B)
21 Nikki's Arco (D)

1963

22 Bona von Holt Derupp (B)
23 Golden Shandor, C. D. X. (D)
24 Wilson's Pal Joey (D)
25 Kisaszony Selle
26 Sergeant Loosdorf (D)

(D) dog   (B) bitch

27 Strawbridge Antal (D)
28 Zibb V Olca Zima (D)
29 Redfield's Duke of Brok (D)
30 Warhorse Sheila (B)
31 Woodlyn's Tanya of Alreen (B)

1964

32 Csic-Ked's Amas Jodie (D)
33 Fruska Kisfaldi (B)
34 Rufus V Theron, C. D. (D)
35 Glen Cottage Max Selle (D)
36 Big D Selle (D)
37 Brok Selle Son of A Gun (D)
38 Gold Star Kandi (B)
39 Autumn's Golden Nocturne (B)
40 Capet Anal (D)
41 Roz of Rozda
42 Warhorse Sammy (D)
43 Csic-Ked's Alca, C. D. (B)
44 Don-Djecki-Jelenski
45 Ken Salan Molly Barat (B)
46 Besa Von Debretsin (B)
47 Madonna's Joaquin (D)
48 Sandy Paprika (D)
49 Szekeres' Kezdet (B)
50 Luko of Shirbob
51 Misty Hills Arpad Aaron
52 Warhorse Miska
53 Barbann of Cartwright (B)
54 Rok of Rozda (D)

1965

55 Palfa's Eric Reh (D)

364

56	Piros of Mile High (D)
57	Mar-Ray's Futaki Igric (D)
58	Anglodale's Mezei Magda (B)
59	Count Jonish Mignotte (D)
60	Dardai Csitri's Cindy (B)
61	Sziki (D)
62	Christie Lee Woodlyn's (B)
63	Colonel Loosdorf (D)
64	Ede De Dus (D)
65	Erzsi De Dus (B)
66	Golden Boy Michael (D)
67	J'Ann of Misty Hills (B)
68	Field Ch. Futaki Darocz (D)
69	Mar-Ray's Jodanar (B)
70	Rozelle of Rozda (B)
71	Csic-Ked's Ardent (D)
72	Diane's Golden Karratz (B)
73	Eve De Dus (B)
74	Golden Queen (B)
75	Gypsy's Bronze Bomber (D)
76	Rittie (B)
77	Eneri Goncoltanya (D)
78	Golden Boy's Flash (D)

1966

79	Marianka, C.D. (B)
80	Misty Hills Lolli Selle Barat (B)
81	Sikitiko of Goncoltanya (D)
82	Zlatna Devojka V Hunt (B)
83	Akil Von Debretsin (D)
84	Bystra Csibesz Povazia (D)
85	Jan Bodri V Barrington, C.D.X. (D)
86	Rocking DN's Gold Piece (D)
87	Szekeres' Kelet Szel (D)
88	Golden Rust's Queen (B)
89	Sogen's Taffy Apple (B)
90	Csopi V Hunt (D)
91	Gold Star's Valdar (D)
92	Sintex Jumey Vinn, C. D. (B)
93	Jolly Gismo of Happy Hollow, C.D. (B)
94	Morog V Hunt, C. D. (D)
95	Puerco Pete Barat (D)
96	Summer Arpad (D)
97	Lady of Centerline (B)
98	Bolen's Geza Bell (B)
99	Boske Von Debretsin, C.D. (B)
100	Caesar (D)
101	Csinos V Hunt, C. D. (B)
102	De La Francesca (B)
103	Ginger Karpat (B)
104	Paetra's Dan (D)

105	Rustic Fun Galore (D)
106	Golden Boy Tito (D)
107	Heide Von Chappel (B)
108	Red Rust of Terian (D)
109	Fenyes Vadasz (D)
110	Magyar's Tundor Karratz (B)
111	Nestler's Arpad (D)
112	Redish Von Loosdorf (D)

1967

113	Glen Cottage Diva (B)
114	How'Lyn's Cherokee Rocket, C.D. (D)
115	Stelmar Cselszi V Hunt (B)
116	Behi's Csinos Csiny (B)
117	Rusty Roman (D)
118	Holloway's Red Victor (D)
119	Silver Cholla Cactus (B)
120	Enon Jack's Vihar (D)
121	Fenyes Leany (B)
122	Sandor Barat (D)
123	Wetobe's Taffeta (B)
124	Debreceny Sosija (B)
125	Glen Cottage Charlie (D)
126	Golden Rust's Kernel (D)
127	Brook's Amber Mist (B)
128	Hlasky Lee of Laurel Ridge (B)
129	Paprika of Magyar (D)
130	Ripp Barat Balaton, C.D. (D)
131	Szekeres' Aranyos Heja (B)
132	Szekeres' Sarga Rigo (D)
133	Anglodale's Mezei Melba (B)
134	Capet Annamoric (B)
135	Debreceny Dezso (D)
136	Lucky-E's Hunt's Fun, C.D. (D)
137	Szekeres Magyal (B)
138	Twin Acres Cassador Selle (D)
139	Bakony Balatoni Katinka (B)
140	Bakony Balatoni Keve (D)
141	Glen Cottage Dark Surprise (D)
142	Pirolin (D)
143	Shasta T. Goncoltanya (B)
144	Tisza Z Debreceny (B)

1968

145	Glen Cottage D'Hadur (D)
146	Grindl of Big Duke (B)
147	Markos Von Debrecen (D)
148	Stelmar Boske V Tolgyes (B)
149	Tartary Lulu (B)
150	Gold-N-Rust Brutus (D)
151	Shady Oaks Tsarina (B)
152	Zsa Zsa Graham (B)

153	Bimitz Bo (D)
154	Magyar's Mimi Zem Biro (B)
155	Sogen's Tysue (B)
156	Kerulet Borka of Laurel Ridge (D)
157	Kiraly X Rokudvar (D)
158	Prince Brandiwyne (D)
159	Buglair Tara of Twin Acres (B)
160	Glen Cottage Bar-Rit Jay Jay (B)
161	Ridgeland's Cigany V Selle (D)
162	Bannik's Regal Hun (D)
163	Hollaway's Sun Victress (B)
164	Pajta's Von Szaguldo Pacsirta (D)
165	Batu Kan The Tartar (D)
166	Csitri Von Mihalyi (B)
167	Debreceny Lila (B)
168	Magyar's Mizzentop Dajka (B)
169	Maxmillan-Ridgewick Clan (D)
170	Shelby Heights Sari (B)
171	Szekeres' Kis Szereto (B)
172	Blue Oak's Ember of Sage Acre (B)
173	Old Weird Harold (D)
174	Rothan's Betyar Gaza (D)
175	Jakab V Hunt (D)
176	Karratz' Amber Edition (B)
177	Piros Rozsa Hercege (D)

1969

178	Glen Cottage Fred Barbarosa (D)
179	Napkelte Vadasz Dalos (D)
180	Bela Brok Vincent (D)
181	Golden Lady II (B)
182	Klasik Fun Galore (B)
183	Mencye's Pipe Dream (B)
184	Miss Nessi (B)
185	Sageacre Piros Mihaszna (B)
186	Sogen's Belle Starr (B)
187	Szekeres' Csillag (B)
188	Triggers Charlotte (B)
189	Koski's Radar Von Sandor (D)
190	Thora's Hau Tascha (B)
191	Nik V Romarlin (D)
192	Glen Cottage Dina, C. D. (B)
193	Gold-N-Rust Daredevil, C.D. (D)
194	Fleckes of Sageacre (D)
195	Golden Rex of LeSueur (D)
196	Bela Selle (D)
197	Jomar's Cinnamom Sam (D)
198	Del Roble Greta (B)
199	Glen Cottage Peppi (D)
200	Jump-N-Jill (B)
201	Aranjos Virag V Magyar (B)
202	Glen Cottage Loki Barat (D)
203	Great Gun's Joska (D)

204	Juliana's Aranya (B)
205	Kocka Cukor of Windsor Forest (B)
206	Slim's Jolie Coquette (B)
207	Timarka's Thorny (D)
208	Zomar's Brute (D)
209	Arpad Jonish Mignotte (D)
210	Duchess Golden Sissy (B)
211	Golden Honey Karratz (B)
212	Good Upland Jet (D)
213	Primo Uno (D)
214	Jov Wasil Debretsin (D)
215	Teuer Rotkopf (D)
216	Timarkas Thumper (D)
217	Fld. Ch. Weedy Creek Lobo (D)
218	Milehi Barat's Copper (D)
219	Timarka's Tsindee of Amber (B)

1970

220	Cigany Csillag, C. D. (B)
221	Hutchins' Csakitumi Hun (B)
222	Aranyos Adeleen (B)
223	Arco's Arco (D)
224	Debreceny Thurba (B)
225	Caitlin of Highland Falls (B)
226	Miska of Mount Rose (D)
227	Carob's Miklos (D)
228	Gaal's Vihar of Twin Acres (B)
229	Sirius of Triple Raven (D)
230	Anastasia Pooh Van Alstyne (B)
231	Buda's Pest of Zanger (D)
232	Rudi's Spunky (D)
233	Sienna Gold Tasha (B)
234	Geza Istvan Jorgi (D)
235	Tanja of Twin Acres (B)
236	Fld. Ch. Bobo Buck Selle (D)
237	Futaki Spice (D)
238	Glen Cottage Alena Diva (B)
239	Janos VW Come Lately (D)
240	Bako's Mistique (B)
241	Behi Heves Hanos (B)
242	Gold-N-Rust Baron (D)
243	Oury's Alfi Staraza (D)
244.	Totton's Prince Magyar Delite (D)
245	Balatoni Sassy Olca (B)
246	Crain's Sigi (D)
247	Glen Cottage Talisman (D)
248	Gold-N-Rust of Go Leor (B)
249	Rino Gad Gala (D)
250	Tartary Zsoka (B)

1971

| 251 | Arco's Zarr V Hunt (D) |
| 252 | Cariad's Kalon Szerette (B) |

253	Csokos Huszar (D)	304	Hockley of Bethwood (B)
254	Duke Nicholas Von Ellasar (D)	305	Justhill's Plain Jane (B)
255	Gaal's Kedves Voros Baron (D)	306	Magyar Arany Kiralynoje (B)
256	Huba De Sepru (D)	307	Magyar's Tizsa (B)
257	Johnson's T. L. Autumn Haze (B)	308	Major Red Rebel (D)
258	Peter Fun Galore (D)	309	O'Brian's King (D)
259	Rittie's Taschi (D)	310	Szekeres' Boldog Rogi (D)
260	Starshine Tisza (B)	311	Zebulon Nagy (D)
261	Tasha Z. Ravenwood Ridge (B)	312	Zorha Zahav Adam (D)
262	Debreceny Elemer (D)	313	Cariad's Derekas Garm (D)
263	Napkeltei Vadasz Hiros (D)	314	Gold-N-Rust Country Rogue (D)
264	Wazek Z Ravenswood (D)	315	Gold-N-Rust Twinkle (B)
265	Debreceny Tazsi (B)	316	High Point's Buckskin (D)
266	Donner's Sun Dance Kid (B)	317	Rothan's Rozsda Kisanya, C.D. (B)
267	Jason's Golden Fleece II (D)	318	Rustin V Zomar Lark (D)
268	Magyar's Tanar of Mizzentop (D)	319	Timarka's Twiggy (B)
269	Mica K Lajos Kossuth (D)		
270	Baron Von Vizsla, C.D. (D)	1972	
271	Csilla Star of Lovey (B)		
272	Debreceny Dijana (D)	320	Arra's Miss Brandi (B)
273	Hockley's Nugget of Bethwood, C.D. (D)	321	Bell-Tel, C.D.X. (B)
		322	Brandie's Golden Jasper (D)
274	Parade's Red Baroness Panni (B)	323	Di Jon's Golden Princess (B)
275	Ridgeland's Red Baron (D)	324	El-Jo's Prince (D)
276	Thora's Hau Talleria (B)	325	Johnny's Rebel (D)
277	Tolgyessy Sararany (B)	326	Marhos Tokaj C Selle (D)
278	Arra's Miss Tasha (B)	327	Cariad's Liebestraum Barat (B)
279	Brandies Pride Tara (B)	328	Gee Whiz Miss Agnes
280	Jodi's Mickey Finn (D)	329	Glen Cottage Chi Chi Barat (D)
281	Marisa's Meg of Maryijo (B)	330	Gold-In-Hills Fitsko (D)
282	Mizzentop's Best Link (D)	331	Jomar's Cinnamon Candy (B)
283	Sally Selle (D)	332	Jim Ja Richard (B)
284	Sogen's Buzzing Buckeroo (D)	333	Sageacre Dezdemona (B)
285	Stelmar Okos V Hunt (D)	334	Fld. Ch. Sir Lancelot (D)
286	Sascha of Kislany (D)	335	Amber Shambles Shamrock (B)
287	Totton's Lisa Es Grossenshush (B)	336	Behi Csintalan (D)
288	Miklos Heliker (D)	337	Call Me Tokay (B)
289	Mizzentop's Alchemist (B)	338	Debreceny Badger (D)
290	Timarka's Lexington Lady (B)	339	Emperor Cinnamon Fire (D)
291	Chuba Czuki Barat (B)	340	Fruska's Gold-In-Hills Magyar (B)
292	Cleary's Irish Woods Fawn (B)	341	Glen C. Cruzana Tiki Barat (B)
293	Ole Olympus Helios (D)	342	Great Guns Riding High (D)
294	Ed's Golden Gypsy of Hanover (D)	343	Juliana's Ziguener of Kazi (D)
295	Gretl Von Tatabanya (B)	344	Juno of Green Oaks C.D. (B)
296	Kis Cignay's Bright Star (D)	345	Lady Zorina of Nine Oaks C.D. (B)
297	Magyar Herr Valent Von Zybura, C.D. (D)	346	Sergeant's Pride (B)
		347	Doktor Fether (D)
298	Timarka's Taffi (B)	348	Gold-N-Rust Clay (D)
299	Broc Bey of Bethwood (D)	349	Totton's Jo-B Russet Leather (D)
300	Caread's Gaybine (B)	350	Count Victor The Red (D)
301	Glen Cottage Adam (D)	351	Elsa Richards (B)
302	Gold Star's Spartan (D)	352	Jay-Jay of Bethwood (B)
303	Hell Cat Heidi (B)	353	Rotkopf's Regina of Sageacre (B)

354. Arra's Mr. Jason (D)
355. Tolgessy La Favorita (B)
356. Vee Selle (B)
357. Arra's Mr. Jake (D)
358. Johnson's Titian Charger (D)
359. Rippi of Webster Woodlands (D)
360. Taunee's Loki Santana (D)
361. Trisha's Copper Lady C.D. (B)
362. Bratt's FK Satin Valentine (B)
363. Herr Ripp Barat Von Zybura (D)
364. Mehagian's Golden Stereo (B)
365. Peter's High Velocity (D)
366. Aranybol Leany (B)
367. Baron Corky of Hari (D)
368. Brandie's Pride Maximus (D)
369. Gold-N-Rust Daring Gambler (D)
370. Lobo's Lucky Lad (D)
371. Kiraly's Barna Karoly (D)
372. Linden's Junai (B)
373. Mehagian's Christy Penn Barat (B)
374. Princes of Czuki Barat (B)
375. Sageacre Voros Kutya V Tazsar (D)
376. Taunee's Cariann (B)
377. Totton's Baron Hiduk (D)
378. Totton's Stephania of Rotkopf (B)
379. Fld. Ch. Amber's Windy Autumn (B)
380. Bowcot Lancelot (D)
381. Gold-N-Rust Jay Dare (B)
382. Jados Copper Queen (B)
383. Lady Little-Bit Smith (B)
384. Dena Tsigany (B)
385. Happy Go Lucky Of Rokudvar (B)
386. Miklos Von Wold (D)
387. Sassy's Keves Lazado (B)
388. Totton's Fenyes Vadasz (B)
389. Wild Russian Vanya (B)

1973

390. Fld. Ch. Chip Odysseus (D)
391. Cool Hand Luke C.D. (D)
392. Jezebel's Juba (B)
393. Kalon's Hunyadi Csilla (B)
394. Rip (D)
395. Carob's Rhea Sztar (B)
396. Firebrand's Joshua (D)
397. Funny Hunny Bun (B)
398. Jumey's Chula U.D. (B)
399. Noblis Fredrikus Von Faro (D)
400. Big Buck (D)
401. Bourbon Pest of Zanger (D)

402. Cinnamon Richards (B)
403. El-Jo's Country Gent (D)
404. Hussar Barat (D)
405. Jesco's Paprikosh Red Rebel (D)
406. Johnson's Titian Morning Sky (D)
407. Juliana's Abrandozo (D)
408. Mary Mac's Rusty Babe C.D. (B)
409. Mehagian's Kis Lany (B)
410. Sugar Creek Tia (B)
411. Zsuzsi IV (B)
412. Merrilane's Mariah (B)
413. Trinka III (B)
414. Marlijo's Papa Nicklos (D)
415. Tavolyi Arany Leany (B)
416. Boots Bey Of Bethwood (B)
417. Kati Shiloh Trooper (D)
418. Sir Lancelot's Atida Amber (B)
419. Tisza' Kish Fiu (D)
420. Cariad's Zenesz Husvet (D)
421. Futaki Tahi (B)
422. Kalon's Konok Kipit (D)
423. Rich's Pirosch Aranya (D)
424. Bar Bey Of Bethwood C.D. (D)
425. Bratt's FK Kataki (B)
426. Joco Z Ravenswood Ridge (D)
427. Majita's Golden Hope (B)
428. Mistral Kalon Cherub (B)
429. Mormac's Guinevere Of Amber (B)
430. Rotkopf Crypto (D)
431. Sogen's Fussy Fellow (D)
432. Visse's Mihaly Draga C.D. (B)
433. Zulton Prince Of Boja (D)
434. Bones Blue Boy (D)
435. Csibesz Rotkopf (D)
436. Lance Of Hampshire (D)
437. Silo De Grandplace (FDSB) (B)
438. Tartary Couscous (B)
     Bar Bey Of Bethwood (D) repeated
439. Baron Janos Rakossy (D)
440. Brahms Golden Exodus (B)
441. Gold-N-Rust-Kos (D)
442. Olga Budapesti (B)
443. Schnapsnamen's Budweiser (D)
444. Sir Lancelot II (D)
445. Tascha Zee (B)
446. Vizsta's Bakony Forest (D)
447. Dezso's Damon Of Mar-Hayven (D)
448. Mistral Kalon Szeraf (B)
449. Weedy Creek Rebel (D)

1974

450. Hollandia's Holgy C.D. (B)

451. Jodi's Jump-N-Bing Bang Bucz (D)
452. Kalon Autumn Brandy (D)
453. Bethwood Jordan Bugg (B)
454. Cativa's Honey Bee Myne (B)
455. Gypsy's Beau Aristo Of Hanover (D)
456. La Caza Nina (B)
457. Mehagian's Yellow Rose O' Texas (B)
458. Mihaly's Kisasszony (B)
459. Miskolci Csibesz Von Lovey's (D)
460. Prince Selle E (D)
461. Rotkopf's Gyemant (B)
462. Rotkopf's Magyar Kutya (D)
463. Rotkopf's Tia D'Russet Leather (B)
464. Merrilane's Windstorm (B)
465. Renbrok's Viscount of Valhi (D)
466. Russet Leather's Ricca Luna (B)
467. Totton's Highland Rocky Road C.D. (D)
468. Stelmar Tuzar V Aranymuve (D)
469. Anastasia Du Merrell C.D. (B)
470. Gold-N-Rust Sascha Of Diamond M (B)
471. Ron's Sir Fredico (D)
472. Sylvester The Great (D)
473. Elenka Vilam (D)
474. Schnapsnamen Apricot Brandy (B)
475. Vinnie Van Go (D)
476. Lady Rustic (B)
477. Pendell Paradise Joie (B)
478. Shakeitoff Duke (D)
479. Vizsta's Jezza V Exodus (B)
480. Cariad's Hunyadi Csipet (B)
481. Cariad's Szeketo Arpad (D)
482. Regal Hun's Bena (D)
483. Timarka's Maggy Mae (B)
484. Dutchess Banbi Boyd (B)
485. Gold-N-Rust Olca (B)
486. Lady Eva Von Wisenbaker (B)
487. Piper's Lord Dudley (D)
488. Field Champion Rebel Rouser Duke (D)
489. Sageacre Vidam Gazember (B)
490. Timarka's Tabu (B)
491. Tizsai Atalanta (B)
492. Von Bruin's Lady Megen (B)
493. Amstar's Draga Tarsch (D)
494. Arra's Trini (D)
495. Arra's Valor Blitz (B)
496. Cariad's Bekesegi Hercegno (B)
497. Carmen Of Zanger (B)

498. Chip Off Rip Of Crested J C.D.X. (D)
499. Flower's Top Of The Morning (D)
500. Gold-N-Rust Chip's Julie Gingee (B)
501. Keresd Meg Erny (B)
502. Panni IV (B)
503. Renbrok's Ginger Peach (B)
504. Sissy's Golden Lady (B)
505. Valhi's Liberty Valance (D)
506. Zinger of Zanger Bowcot (D)
507. Bry-Lynn's Golden Taurus (D)
508. Debreceny Dezsone (B)
509. Debreceny Robbi (D)
510. Edmar's Lil Roustabout (D)
511. Evelyn's Red Pride (D)
512. Gold-N-Rust Josse (B)
513. Merrilane's Dancing Wheat Annie (B)
514. Pendell Gold-N-Rust Crandevil (D)
515. Sandor Miklos Heliker (D)
516. Sloane's Palinka (B)
517. Timarko's Taco (D)
518. Von Bruin's Land Rover (D)
519. Zoltan Huszar (D)
520. Bundle's Red Ruffian (D)
521. Cariad's Edes Palinka (B)
522. Carob's Golden Mist Of Redondo (B)
523. Firebrand's Odin The Red (D)
524. Grayglens Panacea Rotkopf (B)
525. Hollandia's Magas Remelem (D)
526. Jado's Copper Cannon (D)
527. Jado's Rusty King Von Dezso (D)
528. Johnson's Titian Titlist (D)
529. Lady Rustic (B)
530. Marisa Of Lisuanda C.D. (B)
531. Matai's Redwood (D)
532. Pendell Szep Cimbora (D)
533. Renbrok's Toka Torta (B)
534. Rotkopf's Dancing Wheat Seek (D)
535. Slotki Corancha's Blaze (D)

1975

536. Arany Fiju Brutus (D)
537. Cariad's Barat Sir Guy (D)
538. Cativa's Count Andrassi (D)
539. Ginger Of Brookshire (B)
540. Kelanoa Csillag (B)
541. Peg's Spice Cake (B)
542. Piroska Checkmate V Lobo (D)
543. Schnapsnamen Speak-Easy Gin (B)
544. Siena Primavera De Oporto (B)
545. Trisha's Bogart By Loki (D)

546. Amiga De Wolfgang (B)
547. Bayzil Richards (D)
548. Cher of Sandor Barat (B)
549. El-Jo's Country Girl (B)
550. Lobo's Tally Ho Of El-Jo (B)
551. Warhorse Cinnamon Mika (D)
552. Zomar's Sari (B)
553. A Whisper of Russet Leather (B)
554. Bowcot Gold-N-Rust Notable (D)
555. Carob's Ripple Red (D)
556. Renbrok's Autumn Pride (B)
557. Renbrok's Stoikus Joy Boy (D)
558. Sandor's Magyar Miss (B)
559. Uropuyka (B)
560. Vizsta's De Oro Baron (D)
561. Cinnamon Panna Day Kisfaludi (B)
562. Eszaki Biro (D)
563. Johnston's T L What Me Worry (D)
564. Pinar Barat (D)
565. Timmahoe Red (D)
566. Bakers Tasha Santana (B)
567. Barat's Amber Autumn (D)
568. Cariad's Edes Lepke (B)
569. Kenlor's Autumn Mist (D)
570. Lady Warwica Selle (B)
571. Lightfoot Mutz (D)
572. Baron Of Paradise (D)
573. Kelanoa Tibor (D)
574. Mako Kisch (B)
575. Mehagian's La Selle O'Barat (B)
576. Papa Niklos' Roger (D)
577. Soapstone's Sampson (D)
578. Totton's Mikhail Of Rotkopf (D)
579. Futaki Nyir Of Popple Dungeon (D)
580. Hollandia's Lenyes Kezdet C.D. (B)
581. Kalon's Megan (B)
582. Kutya Kesdi Eloral Of Tartary (D)
583. Miss Mingo Terreparte (B)
584. Rogue LSR Jacobs (D)
585. Sandor's Beau Barat (D)
586. Tawnee Penny Flirt'in (B)
587. Tiffany III (B)
588. Brown's Old Man Moses C.D.
T.D.X. T.D. (D)
589. Cariad's Hercegno Natisha C.D. (B)
590. Carob's Sweet Karalyne (B)
591. Gold-N-Rust Lady Jane (B)
592. Magyar's Pride (B)
593. Melto's Csaba Zenesz (D)
594. Merrilane's Techachapi Pass (D)
595. Vadasz Marco Polo (D)
596. Valhi's Curry Rice (D)
597. Bowcot's The Kip (B)

598. Firebrand's Cariad Zenzo (B)
599. Hall's Desert Samantha (B)
600. Hollandia's Hebe Hoba (D)
601. Joshua Melto (D)
602. Murrey (D)
603. Pendell Safranin Glory (B)
604. Piroska Tick Tock Of Renbrock (B)
605. Semper Fi Peleliu (B)
606. Warhorse Bona (D)
607. Brook's Berry Mist (B)
608. Cariad's Egyke Barat (B)
609. El-Jo's Ticker Barat (B)
610. Feather Richards (D)
611. Firebrand's Dontcha Dare (D)
612. Hanama Alexander (D)
613. Jolly Aranyos Vadasz (D)
614. Majita's Golden Honey (B)
615. Timarki's Trini (D)
616. Valhi's Robin Of Renbrok (B)
617. Cariad's Upwind Vardos (B)
618. Ellis Buda From Loveys (D)
619. Jados Copper Sandal Lady (B)
620. Kalon's Kricket (D)
621. Kizvon Kristina Von Zybura (B)
622. Masha's Super Sara (B)
623. Rhubarb Kai (D)
624. Field Champion Sir Amber Sam (D)
625. Totton's Zeus (D)
626. Arra's Miss Ginger Snap (B)
627. Count Esterhazy (D)
628. El-Jo's Ochoa (D)
629. Frau Rez Mez Von Zybura (B)
630. Miss Missy Of Zanger (B)

1976

631. El-Jo's Samantha Newhouse (B)
632. Mavams Zarzan Of Ruedelapaix (D)
633. Brookwood's Roc O' Dez-Tsindee (D)
634. Mehagian's Pistil Pete (D)
635. Mizzentop's Zabelle (B)
636. Popple Dungeon Lilliom (B)
637. Mavam's Bronzar Diana (B)
638. Mehagian's Red Ruff Barat (D)
639. Mehagian's Rusti Barat (D)
640. Napkeltei Bajos Perri (B)
641. Tunde Of Gyor (B)
642. Ashby Von Donn (D)
643. Carob's Carina Of Chestry (B)
644. Rebels Misty Morning Sky (B)
645. Winsloh's Jodi Of Sienna Gold (D)
646. Bihari Flotas Csikcsicsoi (B)

647. Dezso's Miki Musket (B)
648. Jados Copper Rusty (D)
649. Lackeys' Rebel Rogue (D)
650. Sir Stach Of Bervy C.D. (D)
651. Winsloh's Vitez Barat (D)
652. Zomar's Brok Selle Debretsin (D)
653. Brown's Bronze Bonanza C.D. (B)
654. Cariad's Golden Topaz C.D. (B)
655. Dian Agi (B)
656. Frau Barsony Kutya Von Zybura C.D. (B)
657. Kamet Keri (B)
658. Mehagian's Rippi Birdacute (B)
659. The Magician Of Melto (D)
660. Bowcott Hungarian Rhapsody C.D.X. (D)
661. Cariad's Gay Leanyka (B)
662. Firebrand's I Dare You Darling (B)
663. Lymricks Admiral Zumwalt (D)
664. Vulkan Of Verity (D)
665. Boyds Jason Richards (D)
666. Chasity (B)
667. Diamond K's Lusty Of Hanover (D)
668. Halls Desert Don Juan C.D. (D)
669. Merrilane's Haiwee Pass (D)
670. Natasha Loki Paprika Barat (B)
671. Timarka's Terri (D)
672. Winsloh's Amber Winged (D)
673. Arco's Prince Harry (D)
674. Cigany Piros Kutya (B)
675. Dust N Miss' Mini Of Hanover (B)
676. Frau Verseny Leany Von Zybura (B)
677. Kislany (B)
678. Mistral Dawn Barat (B)
679. Phoenician Princess (B)
680. Piper's Tijuana Red (D)
681. Prancing Golden Brandee (D)
682. Sageacres Ravishing Ruby (B)
683. Silent Partner Of L and C C.D. (D)
684. Thunder (D)
685. Bethwood's Balaton Benjy (D)
686. J-C's Sugar Pine Princess (B)
687. Mistral Dresden Doll (B)
688. Mizzentop's Baron Max D Aubin (D)
689. Peeptoad's Spicey Cinnamon (B)
690. Renbrok's Greta Hegyi (B)
691. Sandor Miklo's Ishi Debretsin (D)
692. Vizsta's Kati V Exodus (B)
693. Anton Arany Victorffy C.D. (D)
694. Fld. Ch. & Am. Fld. Ch. Brook's Willie Whompum (D)

695. Cariad's Kutya Kai Costa C.D. (D)
696. Carrie Star Of Pendell T.D. (B)
697. Fieldstone's Hey Duke (D)
698. Godolloi Miska (D)
699. Gold-N-Rust Hope (B)
700. Kief Von Lee (D)
701. Lady Sobaka (B)
702. Lady Winnie Von Bruin (B)
703. Neishka Of Woodhill (B)
704. Pendell Rowdy Rebbel (D)
705. Popple Dungeon Tolgyfa (D)
706. Renbrok's Sand Pebble (B)
707. Spoiled Brat (B)
708. Beke (B)
709. Charisma's Crimson Zachery (D)
710. Cinnabar's Tanya Of Totton (B)
711. Eszaki Cinka Panna (B)
712. Hungarian Magic (B)
713. Jaunzeme's Magda Aranka (B)
714. Kahala Sandra (B)
715. Kataki's Copper Chopper (D)
716. Mehagian Misty Moonlight C.D. (B)
717. Mehagian's Christmas Poppy C.D. (D)
718. Napkeltei Talizman (D)
719. Nuggie Bey Of Bethwood (B)
720. Renbrok's Pride Of Szeretet C.D. (D)
721. Stelmar Emo V Russet Leather (D)
722. Totton's Princess Of Rotkopf (B)
723. Valhi's Stick To Your Guns (D)

1977

724. Kalon Golden Rusty (D)
725. Renbrok's Only One Son Of A Gun (D)
726. Sandor's Zach Von Kurtzmark (D)
727. Barat's Desert Sunshine (D)
728. Dakota Red's Tasha (B)
729. Frau Vana Von Zybura (B)
730. Gold-N-Rust Katinka (B)
731. Hall's Desert Bestar Izz (D)
732. W. D. Regina (B)
734. Amber-Lance Terry (B)
735. Baker's Buddy Fonzi (D)
736. Dorratz Ramriver Beethoven (D)
737. Iselinyas Kirohan Szendrodi (D)
738. Meltos Kedves Kolto (D)
739. Stelmar Csiela V Tolgyes (B)
740. Bowcot Gamester (D)
741. Bugaco's Siena Do Madeira (B)
742. Firebrand's Kivancsi (B)
743. Harann's Kristiana Penn V Duna C.D. (B)
744. Poplar Kaps Sporting Goods (D)

745. Vizsta's Magnum Ryder (D)
746. Lancewick's Pumpkin Pie (B)
747. Loki Santana's Texas Rose (B)
748. Mehagian's Pauncho Von Sandor (D)
749. Merrilane's Tioga Pass (D)
750. Misha De Amiga (D)
751. Tartary Hausa (D)
752. Trifari's Carly By Bogart (B)
753. Cariad's Ripp Loki Santana (D)
754. Heidi Of Highland Falls (B)
755. Jessie II (B)
756. Kamet Komanche (D)
757. Piper's Sunburst Abigale (B)
758. San-Dal's Pumpkin Spice (B)
759. Amstars Russet Leather Xztra (D)
760. Beautar's Nutzi Fagan O Hanover (D)
761. Bonhomme Richards (D)
762. Gold-N-Rust Hollandia's Huzel (D)
763. Kazraws Taryn Of Bervy (B)
764. Mistral Diamond Jim (D)
765. Murphy's Rustic Rebel (D)
766. Rizsa's Me And My Shadow (B)
767. Russet Leather Inyo Kern (D)
768. Schnapsnamen Marta Natasha (B)
769. Cariad's Brandy Luv (B)
770. Cariad's Joska Barat (D)
771. Carmel Sage (D)
772. Eszaki Biro (D)
773. Gamblers Easy Money V Dirigo (D)
774. Kamet Rocket (D)
775. Mehagian's Pic Lany (B)
776. Rochan's Flying Dutchess (B)
777. Sageacre Whispering Wind (B)
778. Tulos Vadasz Kutyaja (B)
779. Abby Hill's Ruben James (D)
780. Apollo (D)
781. Cariad's Trefas Szereto (D)
782. Carobs Tsarina Cresent Bliss (B)
783. Charisma's Royal Carrina (B)
784. Cline's Olympia Blitz (D)
785. Flower's Sunshine Partner (D)
786. Gold-N-Rust Gabrielle (B)
787. Gypsygold's Firebrand Astra (B)
788. Primo III (D)
789. Rotkopf Rebel Rouser Dinah (B)
790. Tartary Juji (D)
791. Cariad's Jesse James (D)
792. Comtessa Of Lancewick (B)
793. Kamet Kiraly De Kapus (D)
794. Mister Valdez Of Barat C.D. (D)

795. Rizsa's Keystone Copper Bob (D)
796. Bing Bang's Liberty Belle (B)
797. Cariad's Lively Rhythm (B)
798. Chauncey's Rusty Bit O'Spice (D)
799. Chestry's Tequila Sunrise (B)
800. Kizvon's Karen Of Valor (B)
801. Kizvon's Kountess Of Melto (B)
802. Muzzle-Loadin' Odin (D)
803. Piroska Son Gypsy Rhodes Lee (D)
804. Puff The Golden Dragon C.D.X. (B)
805. Rizsa's Song Of Ginger Peach (D)
806. Rotkopf's Vand Suzsannah (B)
807. Russet Leather Shawnee Brave (D)
808. Shale Of Verity (D)
809. Soapstone's Annushka (B)
810. Tartary Litka (B)
811. Vizshaar's Adam (D)
812. Zoltan Barat (D)

1978

813. California Babe Of Rotkopf (B)
814. Cariad's Elkenyeztetett (B)
815. Mako Makk (D)
816. Melto's Pippin Hercegno (B)
817. Rochan's Sam T (D)
818. Ruedelapaix Zippizap Zarzan (D)
819. San-Dal's California Pride (D)
820. Cariad's Taunee Glow (B)
821. Charisma's Dancing Lady Luka (B)
822. Chumash Russet Leather Bo-M (D)
823. Fieldstone's Nagy Egy (D)
824. Heelmark Patriots Golden Gem (B)
825. Jerimaih Zig Zag (D)
826. Ka-Dee's Misty Morn Of Bethwood (B)
827. Minka (B)
828. Soapstone's Puzsla Diszno C.D. (D)
829. Soapstone's Pyewacket (D)
830. Voros Tars' Futo Medve (D)
831. Behi Csecse Gyors Lab (B)
832. Gamblers Dice Of Grayglen (Sex not listed)
833. Russet Leather Apple Snyder (B)
834. Brylynn's Kirt Of Somerhill (D)
835. Flower's Sada At Wedgewood (B)
836. Heelmark's Dontcha Tarnish (B)
837. Mako Flora The Red Menace (B)
838. Renbrok's Golden Rock 'N Rye (D)
839. Roka Voros Vadasz (D)
840. Vindecks' Fannie Of Firebird (B)
841. Brance N Carob's Shenandoah (B)
842. Country Roamer – Moose – (D)

843. Luv's Rebel Yell (D)
844. Magyar Of Hungarian Magic (B)
845. Mariposa Mon Amie C.D. (B)
846. Mehagian's Paco V Sandor Barat (D)
847. Ron's Szep Kis Pipacs (B)
848. Rotkopf's Brandy-Wine (B)
849. Watkins Baroness Mitzi (B)
850. Cariad's Csardas Barat (D)
851. Cariad's Half A Sixpence (D)
852. Chestry And Carob's Solo Sun (D)
853. Fairwynde Circle S Cukor (B)
854. Flowers' Forget-Me-Not (B)
855. Freemans Chief Joseph (D)
856. Jados Copper Rose (B)
857. Jomars Big Bad Jon (D)
858. Laross's Duke Kamehameha (D)
859. Magda Charisma's C.D. (B)
860. Mavan's De Bretzsa (D)
861. Piper's Mystical Gypsy Lady (B)
862. Saras Coat Of Russet Leather (B)
863. Topian's Bing Bang Mykie C.D. (D)
864. Foxsea Mama Of Totton (B)
865. Isle Of Sienna Gold Magda (B)
866. Ladies Golden Jake (D)
867. Mavam's Bar-Tokay (B)
868. Mehagian's Ripok Barat (D)
869. Rozsda Kisanya Of Bervy (B)
870. Wayne's Dainty Lady (B)
871. Zachary Of Sleepy Hollow (D)
872. Count Whiski Of Magic Bey (D)
873. Duke's Pest Of Zanger (D)
874. Jolie D'Arcy (B)
875. Jung Frau Richards C.D. (B)
876. Mavam's Bakony Cherib C.D. (B)
877. Piper's Moonstruck Moppet (B)
878. Sunbar's Something Xtra (B)
879. Upwind Kis Trefa (D)
880. Vizshaar's Liberty Belle (B)
881. Zulelka Von Kurtzmark (B)
882. Firebrand's Constant Comment (B)
883. Frau Draga Jeles Von Zybura (B)
884. Magyar Philatelist (D)
885. Mavam's Bartok Jude C.D. (D)
886. Melto's Roziann (B)
887. Murphy's Christi Luv (B)
888. Renbrok's Springfield (B)
889. Sally Of Southampton C.D. (B)
890. Sweet Lady Cecella (B)
891. Arra's Upwind Tzigane C.D. (B)
892. Cariad's Cimar Ron (D)
893. Hacienda's Second Hand Rose (B)
894. Huba Vezer SZ (D)
895. Jan's Choice Hawkhelper (D)

896. Kalon's Fletcher (D)
897. Kazraw's Contender (D)
898. La-Risan Vicount Darth Vader (D)
899. Owen's Valentine Susan (B)
900. Rebel Rousers Fanci Pants (B)
901. Redef's J-Paces Rush (D)
902. Viscount's Royal Viking (D)
903. Boshar's Autumn Zsa Zsa C.D. (B)
904. Brook's Red Alert (D)
905. Cinnabar's Firebrand Ivan (D)
906. Firebrand's Mercurial Magic (D)
907. Terreparte Troy (D)
908. Carob's Sammena (B)
909. Frau Dea Selle Von Zybura (B)
910. Golden Aura's Bustem Up Jesse (D)
911. Kataki's Cho Cho Tchena (B)
912. Kataki's General Stuart (D)
913. Mistral Kashmiri (B)
914. Rotkopf's Lord Sean Royal (D)
915. Russet Leather Gypsy Sandal (B)
916. Sageacre Romanze (B)
917. Upwind Firebrand Elena (B)
918. Fld. Ch. & Am. Fld. Ch. Victor of
Holzworth Farm (D)

1979

919. Ann's Satyn Ambrosia (B)
920. Iluska Sz (B)
921. Jagersthal Baron Von Zybura (D)
922. Leanyka Voros Vadasz (B)
923. Fld. Ch. & Am. Fld. Ch. Mehagian's
Peppy Paloma (B)
924. Piroska Sharpshooter (D)
925. Renbrok's Fiddle Stix (D)
926. Renbrok's Tara Hegi (B)
927. Richey's Pretty Penny (B)
928. Tis Ishl's Pepper Z Fawnridge (B)
929. Topian's Satin Doll (B)
930. Topian's Shooter Luke C.D. (D)
931. Totton's Mariska Of Anglodale (B)
932. Firebrand's Christopher (D)
933. Piroska Buzz-Bomb (D)
934. Zephyr Azen Csoki Nak Csepel (D)
935. Eszaki Gut Z (B)
936. Firebrand's Vitez Csibesz C.D. (D)
937. Hacienda's Magic Of Cinnabar (D)
938. Hyatt's Russet Tiffany (B)
939. J. D. Of Sandy Point (B)
940. Miss Midge of Behi (B)
941. Russet Leather Wild Embers (B)
942. Taunees Cariad Charisma (B)
943. Boyd's Kerek Richards (D)

944. Cariad's Tisza Kenyes (B)
945. Dian Gungedin (D)
946. Gold-N-Rust Herceg Gulyas (D)
947. Kezdet's Forward On Lance (D)
948. Mehagian's Rusty Sandor Barat (D)
949. Pilgrim's Pride (D)
950. Rizsa's Peter Pumpkin (D)
951. Viscount Szelamzee (B)
952. Cariad's Alydar Loki Santana (D)
53. Cariad's Jakab Barat (D)
954. Melto's Anoka Joe (D)
955. Mistral Karousel (B)
956. Reignbo's Lunchalot V. Zephyr (D)
957. Rotkopf's Copper Casey (D)
958. Russet Leather Candlelite (B)
959. Sleepy Hollow's Autumn Wind (B)
960. Sleepy Hollow's Prince Rupert (D)
961. Totton S Sagramore L'Desirous (D)
962. Firebrand's Moonspinner (B)
963. Merrilane's Olancha Pass (B)
964. Terreparte Miss Carmel (B)
965. Piper's Panama Red (D)
966. Vizsta's Magnum Enforcer (D)
967. Aelin Zebulon (D)
968. Eszaki Cinka's Bo (D)
969. Milton Sunshine C.D.X. (D)
970. Natasha Of Sandor Barat (B)
971. Reignbo's Grit C.D. (D)
972. Reignbo's Morgaine La Fee (B)
973. Russet Leather Sinabar Sioux (B)
974. Tek's Wildfire Of Kalon (D)
975. Tis Ishi's Cayenne Debretsin (B)
976. Vizsta Ferenc Miklos Heliker (D)
977. Chestry and Carob's Summer Sun (B)
978. Eszaki Cinka's Con Man (D)
979. Fieldstone's Tip Top Timmy (D)
980. Firebrand's Witchy Woman (B)
981. George Bey Of Bethwood (D)
982. Kahala Queen (B)
983. Mistys Mountain Man (D)
984. Rotkopf's Sensational Robin (B)
985. Rotkopf's Szuros Kati (B)
986. Sage Richards (B)
987. Taunee Golden Rust (B)
988. Upwind Izette Taber (B)
989. Vizsta's Shannara V Exodus (B)
990. Boshar's Budapest Babe (B)
991. Copper Silk Of Sleepy Hollow (B)
992. Csinos Magyar Marta (B)
993. Fairwynde's Gift of Gab (B)
994. Hollandia's Upwind Reese (B)
995. Karacsony Kincs Costa C.D.X. (D)

996. Masha's B.B. Red Baron (D)
997. Paradox Szaladas Medve (D)
998. Popple Dungeon Narcisz (B)
999. Sienna Gold's Token Camelot (B)
1000. Willie N Berry's Calidar (B)
1001. Autumn Gold Shifta (B)
1002. Cinnabar's Nicholas (D)
1003. Glennora Eric Von Wheaton (D)
1004. Hollandia's Hiedelem (D)
1005. Komar's Roby Powell C.D. (D)
1006. Paradox Magas Szalad (B)
1007. Piper's Peppermint Patii (B)
1008. Piper's Rex Stout C.D. (D)
1009. Sunbar's Cooper Canyon (D)
1010. Beggar My Taylor Three (D)
1011. Bowcot Bugler (D)
      Fairwynde's Gift Of Gab
      (second time listed)
1012. Firebrand's Flash (D)
1013. Glenora Got Th' Rhythm (B)
1014. Herr Jagersthal Valo V Zybura C.D. (D)
1015. Jodi's Daphne (B)
1016. Kadee's Mr. Tibbs (D)
1017. Kamet Gunner (D)
1018. Lady Huntumall C.D. T.D. (B)
1019. Longruns Marimba Muzette C.D. (B)
1020. Rotkopf's Spicy Nutmeg (B)

1980

1021. Boldog Henrik (D)
1022. Cariad's Tori Barat (D)
1023. Hacienda's Martina (B)
1024. Reignbo's Lady Of The Lake (B)
1025. Russet Leather Cheyenne (B)
1026. Cariad's Eszaki Pulya (B)
1027. Kamet Cheyenne Rebel (D)
1028. Melto's Java (B)
1029. Pirok Kodi (D)
1030. Sleepy Hollow's Gitana (B)
1031. Soapstone's Marika (B)
1032. The Baron Of Batavia (D)
1033. Totton's Coppercopy V Rotkopf (D)
1034. Waltmars Ruddy Rudy (D)
1035. Aelin Zarda (B)
1936. Cariad's Masterpiece (D)
1037. Firebrand's Remeny Gero (B)
1038. Hacienda's Diplomat (D)
1039. Hacienda's Hugo (D)
1040. Mr. Bojangles II (D)
1041. Nyiri's Mylow Charisma (B)
1042. Princess Remeny Of Piroska (B)

374

1043. Rocks And Shoals Verity (D)
1044. Rustic Valor Of Nevada C.D.X. (D)
1045. Stelmar Gloria V Tolgyes (B)
1046. Upwind Meta Kemble (B)
1047. Yorsia's Cariad Kali (B)
1048. Bucaco's Bandit Jericho (D)
1049. Charisma's Crimson Buck (D)
1050. Grouse Point's Jasper Chip (D)
1051. Kahala Hunter (D)
1052. Mehagian's Cobre Chispas C.D.X. (B)
1053. Okee's Windy Rowdy Rebel C.D. (D)
1054. Piper's Kid Coffee (D)
1055. Russet Leather Indian Xmas (B)
1056. Paradox Raketa Kep (D)
1057. Stelmar Crissi V Tolgyes (B)
1058. Bratt's FK Gippen (D)
1059. Brown's Bronze Obisi (B)
1060. Cariad's Leap Year Pipacs (B)
1061. Cariad's Repeat Performance (D)
1062. Kalon's Kismet (B)
1063. Kirova's Eagle Dancer (D)
1064. Penlee's Terrence (D)
1065. Prince Of Magic Hearth (D)
1066. Settups Vt City Slicker (D)
1067. Sleepy Hollow Dream Weaver (D)
1068. Stelmar Tina V Tolgyes (B)
1069. Diamond M Tatian Gold-N-Rust (B)
1070. Green Oak's Bjoa C.D. (B)
1071. Hacienda's The Imperialist (D)
1072. Mehagian's Miklos Rex C.D. (D)
1073. Willie's Cedar Chip C.D. (D)
1074. Deacon Blue Kisfaludi (D)
1075. Debreceny Sageacre Ria (B)
1076. Kamet Cody (D)
1077. Kisfaludi's Lady Patricia (B)
1078. Upwind's Saucy Honey D'Aubin (B)
1079. Behi's Rhinestone Cowboy (D)
1080. Brance N Carob's Moon River (B)
1081. Bucaco's Rowdy Rudy (D)
1082. Coffee's Tijuana Sandpiper (D)
1083. Harann's Tulipann (B)
1084. Jeber's Copper Reflection (B)
1085. Kamet Quasar (D)
1086. Kizvon's Banjoette Of Barat (B)
1087. Melto's Medicine Man (D)
1088. Miklos Bey Of Bethwood (D)
1089. Misty's Magic Moment (B)
1090. Pasareti Igric (D)
1091. Piper's Naughty Nellie (B)

1092. Reilloc's Draga Leany (B)
1093. Renbrok's Royal Highness Of KMA (D)
1094. Selle's Katy Did (B)
1095. Jagertal Bieder Banner (D)
1096. Kis Moe (D)
1097. Nagy's Tany Piroska Of Ledwood C.D. (B)
1098. Verity' Amber Psyche (B)
1099. Vizsta's Tazz V Exodus (D)
1100. Behi's Jeri Redef (B)
1101. Bucaco's Rusticana Gold (B)
1102. Cove's Rusty Bethwood (D)
1103. Dabescka's Hermosa Brandy (B)
1104. Eszaki Cinka's Bell (B)
1105. Fairwynde's Kincs Lada (B)
1106. Finom's Enuf Is Enuf (D)
1107. Glenogen Eszaki Express (D)
1108. Glenogen Suni Song Eszaki (B)
1109. Hacienda's Natalia (B)
1110. Hirolin's Stolen Promises C.D. (B)
1111. Penlee's Lady Wiggles (B)
1112. Pipers' Asey Mayo (D)
1113. Piroska Jazmin (B)
1114. Renbrok's Rocky V Douglas (D)
1115. Rotkopf's Super Charger (D)
1116. Russet Leather's Summer Wind (D)
1117. Soapstone's Boldie Estvan C.D.X. (D)
1118. Soapstone's Wild Rose (B)
1119. Sweet Gypsy Valentine (B)
1120. Baron Aurelius Cyrus (D)
1121. Bowcot O'Henry (D)
1122. Ceasar's Image Barging Buck (D)
1123. Count Arpad (D)
1124. Gina IV (B)
1125. Jaunzeme's Golden Sand (D)
1126. Kadee's Nick Velvet (D)
1127. MacKo Von Bautches Piper J (D)
1128. Magyar's Prince Cid (D)
1129. Piroska Circus Ringmaster (D)
1130. Piroska Tigger (D)
1131. Sam's Big Red (D)
1132. Settups Vt Kopper Kidd (B)
1133. Taunee Luvs Breeze Along (D)
1134. Topian's Madcap Miranda (B)
1135. Viscount's Adorable Endora (B)
1136. Viscount's Vonzo Vadasz (D)
1137. Vizsta's Jolla (B)
1138. Vizsta's Myya V Exodus (B)

1981

1139. Arrugo's Ruga (B)

375

1140. Bucaco's Sweet Sebastian (D)
1141. Debreceny Nate (D)
1142. Fass's Crazy Corey (B)
1143. Firebrand's Sunny Rebecca (B)
1144. Melto's Sweet Annie Bracken (B)
1145. Miklos-Lazlo Of Old Saybook CDX TD (D)
1146. Royal Count Jacob (D)
1147. Tinmar's Foxy Lady (B)
1148. Upwind Grams Brat Brandi (B)
1149. Fieldstone's Golden Jubilee (B)
1150. Glenogen Mali Esazki (B)
1151. Sleepy Hollow's Valo Lany (B)
1152. Alfie Of Sleepy Hollow (D)
1153. Foxsea Jolly King Neptune (D)
1154. Kadee's Ruger Redhawk (D)
1155. Legend Of Sleepy Hollow CD (B)
1156. Mehagian's Sultan Pepper (D)
1157. Pete's Pride (D)
1158. Redef's Hellza Poppin (B)
1159. Ruedelapaix Luvbird Zarzan (B)
1160. Shilo Kisfaludi Bo-M (B)
1161. Vizsta's Tessa Tzarina (B)
1162. Von Donns Abigail (B)
1163. Deejay's Vedo (D)
1164. Little Heidi Heartbreaker (B)
1165. Rivendell Cracklin' Rosie (B)
1166. Rockabye Dior (D)
1167. Russetleather Robles Shaman (D)
1168. Camarily Rambling Rose C.D. (B)
1169. Fawnridge Ishi's Yahi (D)
1170. Hacienda's Crimson Victory (B)
1171. Isle Of Sienna Gold Joshua (D)
1172. Lucchesi's Golden Tequila (B)
1173. Pirok Keramia (B)
1174. Pyburn's Rusty (D)
1175. Rivendell Wild Turkey (D)
1176. Russet Leather Geronimo (D)
1177. Warlord Kahn Fire (D)
1178. Csilla Ii Von Lovey's Star (B)
1179. Jason Kedves Vadasz CD (D)
1180. Kadee's Kopper Keda CD (B)
1181. Laross' Pele De'Esse Da'Mour (B)
1182. Mavam's De Luv CD (D)
1183. Nyiris Dear Abbey Of Charisma (B)
1184. Russet Leather Navajo Scout (D)
1185. Yorsla's Karie Ann (B)
1186. Dian Gyongy (B)
1187. Hacienda's Tia Maria (B)
1188. Ki's Rez Csibesz Lany (B)
1189. Kurtzmark Brok (D)
1190. Oakleaf's Top Priority (D)

1191. Rozsda's Vadasz Kutya (D)
1192. Sarika Voros Vadasz (B)
1193. Schnapsnamen Freddie (B)
1194. Settups Vt Country Gal (B)
1195. Deacon's Popple D Wild Daisy (B)
1196. Dirigo Gemstones Gambl'N Spree (D)
1197. Firebrand's Ziggy Stardust (B)
1198. Foxsea Tsunami (B)
1199. Glen's Country Rhythm (D)
1200. Jin's Clove Richards (B)
1201. Richard's Mr Bogart (D)
1202. Russet Leather Misha Mata (B)
1203. Scare A Moochee Of Behi (D)
1204. Verity's Mud Larkin' (D)
1205. Yorsla's Hay Look Me Over (B)
1206. Boelte's Bronze Beauty (B)
1207. Copper Cannon's Red Cloud (D)
1208. Greffin's Ha'Penny (B)
1209. Hirolin's Summer Pecan (B)
1210. Mehagian's Voros Vedur CD (D)
1211. My-T-Hi Luck Of The Draw (B)
1212. Polar Kaps Copper Rhodes (D)
1213. Russetleather Warpaint (D)
1214. Bear Creek's Bartok (D)
1215. Behi Csecse Kovacs (D)
1216. Cariad's Gypsy Sprite (B)
1217. Cariad's Szives Orion (D)
1218. Fieldstone's Tip Top Chester (D)
1219. Finom's Kahala Rusty (D)
1220. Golden Joshua Of Zar (D)
1221. Grouse Point's Wildfire (D)
1222. Kadee's Sparkle Plenty (B)
1223. Kalon's Cardinal Micah (D)
1224. Kalon's Finom-Inal Karby (D)
1225. Melto Szent Istvan Koronaja (D)
1226. Nagy's Laszlo Of Ledwood CD (D)
1227. Oakleaf's Fawn (B)
1228. Sageacre Debreceny Jana (B)
1229. San-Dal Lady Titia (B)
1230. Sarika Voros Vadasz (B)
1231. Sunbar's Dee Dee (B)
1232. Upwind Erazim Barat (D)
1233. Abby Hill's Tia (D)
1234. Arnell's Cool Hand Luke (D)
1235. Bear Creek's Redwood Casey CDX (B)
1236. Brance N Carob's Solo's Son (D)
1237. Firebrand's Blaise (B)
1238. Glen's Pop Rhythm (D)
1239. Hacienda's Rhythm (B)
1240. Hacienda's Kiss Me Kate (B)
1241. Pirolin's Soda Pop (D)

Index

385

VCA Open All Age Stakes 343
VCA Open Derby Stakes 339-40
VCA Open Gun Dog Stakes 341-42
VCA Open Limited All Age Stakes 342-43
VCA Open Limited Gun Dog Stakes 342
VCA Open Puppy Stakes 338-39
VCA Specialty Shows 354-63
Vegvari Betyar 23
Verecke 14
Vertessy, Colonel 17
Versatile Uplander 36, 275
veterinarian 86, 90, 92, 96
Victor of Holzworth Farm 123, 126, 131, 217
Vienna Chronicle 25, 27-8
virus, airborne 286
Visse, Sandra & Richard 117
Visse's Mihaly Draga 117
Vizsla Booster 310
Vizsla Club of America 11, 32-4, 37, 67, 79, 286, 296-7
Vizsla Club of Canada 304
Vizsla Club of Holland 316
Vizsla Club of Western Canada 304
"Vizsla News" 297
"Vizsla News and Views" 304
Vizsla, replacement 243, 276, 279
Vizsla Society of Canada 304
Vizsla Society of Ontario 308
"Vizsla Varia" 316
"Vizsla Voice" 304
Vizsla, wirehaired 36, 43, 49, 247-8, 275
Vizsla rash 91-2
Vizslas, other countries 303
Vizsta's Inga Krishna 139
Vizsta's Jezza V Exodus 125, 139
Vizsta's Magnum Ryder 125, 139
Vizsta's Shannara V Exodus 139
Vizsta's Tazz V Exodus 139
voice inflection 69
Vola, Carol 137
Von Willebrand's disease 292

Wag Inn's Kedish 120, 129
Walt Disney Studios 75
Walton, Elizabeth S. 133
Wanjon, Beverly Sartor 136
Warholm, Harvey 31
warts 294
water 33, 75, 88
water entry 253-5, 259

water retriever 247, 249
water retrieving 146, 246
water stake, all age 256
water stake, amateur 256
water stake, derby 256
water stake, puppy 255
water trial judging sheet 258
water trial stakes 252-3
water trials 252-3, 255-7
W. D. Regina 213
weaning 283
Weedy Creek Dutches 207, 231
Weedy Creek Lobo 217, 229, 235, 245
Weedy Creek Merya 229
Weedy Creek Skol 229, 231
weight 13, 42, 45, 74, 86
Weimaraner 12, 20, 22, 233, 293, 314
Weiss, Susan & Stanley 211
Westminster Kennel Club 122, 128, 142, 316
whelping 280
whelping box 150, 277, 280
whiskers, trimming 90, 102, 118
whistle 194, 230
whoa 220
Windy Duke's Rex 213
Wingerter, Harold 217, 229
Winnipeg (Canada) 304
Wion, William E. 119, 134
wire crate 81-2, 210
wirehaired German pointer 43
wirehaired Hungarian pointer 43
Witti 22
white 22
white coat 152
Wolfe, Dr. & Mrs. Maynard 115
Wonderful World of Dogs 159
World War II 24, 26, 264
Worth, Lynn 114, 122, 135
Wright, Phil A., Dr. 304-5

x-ray 31, 93, 239, 275, 286

Yamamoto, George 29
Yugoslavia 22, 24, 312

Zay 18
Zezza, Carlo & Elizabeth 120, 126, 129, 133
zinc 94
Zindi 273
Zsoka of Sashegy 23

390